Published by the Federal Minister
for Labour and Social Affairs, 53 Bonn

1972
Printed by Buch- und Offsetdruckerei E. Seidl, 53 Bonn-Beuel 1, Postfach 510 848

Survey of # Social Security

in the Federal Republic of Germany

by

Dieter Schewe
Ministerialrat

Karlhugo Nordhorn
Regierungsrat

Klaus Schenke
Regierungsrat

Translation by
Mr. Frank Kenny, M. B. E.

Position as at: June 1970

Social Security is our Concern

The Ministers' Foreword

The system of social security in the Federal Republic of Germany displays a great diversity of regulations and institutions. It is intended — as announced in the Governments's Policy Statement of October 28, 1969 — to make this system more easy to appraise and more easily intelligible. In order to keep the public informed on new socio-political aspects and aims, I have already submitted the Social Report and the Social Budget. Understanding for the further development of social policy, and for new problems arising, is dependent on the extent to which every citizen is informed on the current state of the law, and on the realities of social security. It is the object of this survey to disseminate such understanding. The contents and extent of this, its eighth edition, have been considerably enlarged. And so it is designed to help the reader to an understanding of our highly diversified yet effective system of social services, from its origins, with its conditions, and on its intentions.

It is an ever recurring experience that full advantage is not being taken of all the aids provided for in the laws on social services. But every member of our society must be given the opportunity of knowing exactly what his social rights are. It is probable that a not inconsiderable number of still existing cases of social need could be met if all the claims on, and the possibilities available for, the receipt of the social benefits described in this work were fully realised and utilised.

Social demands still outstanding when all existing claims have been met are a matter for the legislator, and for the politician. It is they who are called upon to implement the claims to social justice. It is not the desire or the intention of the Federal Government merely to maintain the present position in this field, and to intervene only when social problems have become acute, but to anticipate new objectives on its own initiative, for example, a flexible age of retirement. No-one preparing to discuss such objectives with real understanding will be able to dispense with a knowledge of the current system of social services. The present work is intended to make a contribution to the dissemination of such knowledge.

Walter Arendt
Federal Minister of Labour and Social Order

The Survey covers the Major Fields

of Social Insurance, in particular
  Industrial Injuries Insurance
  Health Insurance
  Pensions Insurance, including
  Retirement Pensions for Self-employed Persons
of Civil Service Pensions
of Unemployment Insurance and Labour Promotion
of Family Security
of War Pensions and Related Services
of The Equalisation of Burdens
of Social Aid

Special Sections deal with
  Promotion of Vocational Training and Education
  Rent Allowances
  Aid to Refugees
  International Social Security
  Social Courts Jurisdiction
  Self-Government in Social Insurance
  Advice and Information Offices.

The "Survey of Social Security in Germany" covers with social insurance, unemployment insurance, war pensions and related services, social jurisdiction, and self-government in social insurance, the sphere of responsibility of the Federal Ministry of Labour and Social Order, whereas Children's Allowances legislation are the responsibility of the Federal Ministry for Youth, Families, and Health, Civil Service Pensions that of the Federal Ministry of the Interior, the Equalisation of Burdens that of the Federal Ministry of Finance and the Federal Equalisation of Burdens Department, and rent allowances that of the Ministry for Town Planning and Housing.

The purpose of the Survey is to provide persons interested in this field with an introduction into the regulations governing social security in Germany. It cannot give a fully detailed account of the manifold legislative provisions involved; it cannot be a substitute for the texts of the laws themselves, nor can it give authoritative decisions in individual cases — that is the business of the administrations of the social security schemes, and of the courts. The statistical reports are taken in the main from the publishers own figures; they have relevance to the position in each field in the Federal Republic of Germany at any one stated time. So far as figures for certain years prior to 1965 are concerned, now omitted, the reader is referred to previous editions.

Contents

Contents

8

Contents

Contents

Contents

Contents

Abbreviations

AK	=	Pensions Fund
Ang	=	Non-manual Worker
AnV	=	Pensions Insurance of Non-manual Workers
Arb	=	Manual Worker
ArV	=	Pensions Insurance of Manual Workers
BG	=	Industrial Injuries Insurance Institute
BU	=	Reduced Employability in Customary Occupation
BKK	=	Works Health Insurance Fund
BGBl	=	Federal Law Journal
DDR	=	German Democratic Republic
DM	=	German Mark
DGB	=	German Trade Union Federation
EU	=	Unemployability
HwV	=	Insurance of Self-Employed Artisans
IKK	=	Trade Association Health Insurance Fund
KnRV	=	Miners' Special Scheme Pensions Insurance
KK	=	Health Insurance Fund
KV	=	Health Insurance
LAA	=	Regional Employment Office
LKK	=	Land Insurance Fund
LAK	=	Agricultural Pensions Fund
LVA	=	Land Insurance Institute
LVamt	=	Land Pensions Office
LSG	=	Land Social Court
MdE	=	Reduced Employability
OAK	=	Local Health Insurance Fund
SG	=	Social Court
SV	=	Social Insurance
UV	=	Industrial Injuries Insurance

Structural Principles of Present Day Social Security

Introduction by Ministerialdirektor Prof. Dr. Kurt J a n t z
Secretary General for Social Reform

I.

Social Security in Germany in its present form is the outcome of eighty years of history. In the course of its development it has undergone manifold and radical changes. These have been simultaneously in part an expression of the manifold changes which the structure of the economy and of society have themselves undergone. Technical, economic and social causes and effects, all of which are closely interwoven, have played a considerable role in effecting these changes. The emergence of ever new economic potentialities and sociological changes exercises a permanent mutual influence, the one on the other, and they are mutually dependent on one another. Structural changes occur in the most varied fields Town and country have come closer together. Rural working and living conditions are coming more closely to resemble urban conditions. The importance of family life for the individual member of the family, the position of the individual member within the family group, have been transformed in a manner which has exercised a decisive influence on social legislation. The numbers of workers have increased very considerably. Labour and productivity have acquired increasing social and economic significance in comparison with land and capital. In the case of selfemployed persons, in particular of the free professions, problems in connection with certain situations in life have arisen during the last few decades, the possibility of whose solution by social security measures has only gradually been realised. The development of an industrial society, with its repercussions on production and consumption, has reached one of its peaks at the present time.

Technical progress has led not only to fundamental changes in living and working conditions, in particular those of the broad masses of the population. It also entails the possibility of increased productivity, the effects of which are of vital importance, not only for economic policy but also for social policy. Increasing productivity resulting from technical progress and the consequential increase in the production of commodities make possible, and indeed — here is a further problem — demand increasing consumption of the goods produced Increased consumption expresses itself in a rising standard of living And this gives rise, as a part of the problem, to the question as to the extent to which, in addition to those still in employment, those people could and should share in the benefits who either temporarily or finally are no longer able to be employed in productive processes, for reasons for which they are not themselves responsible, or who no longer need to go on working on grounds for which legal provision is made.

The confidence of the individual in the community in which he was born, and in which he has to work, in whose overall activities he plays his part, must be strengthened by the knowledge that, in particular in that important and final period towards the end of his life, he is not cut off from his relations with the community as a whole, nor from its social and economic development, but that he is able to enjoy his share in its progress. The solution of this problem was one of the main points at issue in Pensions Reform.

In close connection with the idea of maintaining a solidarity relationship between those still in employment and those who, through no fault of their own, are not in employment, is the further aim of keeping insured persons, so long as possible, and to the greatest extent possible, fit and well as full members of their community up to the time they reach the age of retirement. This purpose is served by preventive and rehabilitation measures in all fields of social security. They are an indispensible instrument of modern social policy. Medical, occupational, and social rehabilitation are constantly being improved. The same is true of preventive measures. The whole of the measures here described are an expression of the determination to strengthen the efficiency of the whole community by strengthening that of the individuals within it.

Whereas social insurance, at the period of its inception, was linked to the contract of service, and was confined to providing safeguards for employed employees, or at best for smaller self-employed persons whose financial and social situation was comparable to that of wage and salary earners, and, in the case of accident insurance, to employers who were exposed to the same hazards in the works as their employees, social security has moved far beyond these bounds in recent years. This again is a result of the increasing significance of labour and the product of labour in comparison with other forms of security (land and capital). Special forms of security have been developed for agriculture, for self-employed craftsmen, and for the free professions, taking account in each case of the particular requirements and wishes of the different occupational groups. These forms of cover are, in the main, confined to provision for retirement and for survivors, but also, in part, make provision for unemployability and reduced standard of occupation.

The preceding remarks emphasise the importance of labour and the product of labour. The security of the financial and social means of livelihood of the individual through his labour, and the maintenance during involuntary interruptions of his working capacity, and at the end of his working life, of the social status he has reached, are two sides of the same medal. And at this point it is necessary to avoid a misunderstanding: To place too great a stress on labour as the expression of human personality, as has been done too often, bears within itself the characteristic of one-sidedness. If, in the early phases of the industrial era, the worker was constantly subjected to the strain of overwork, he is now, as a result of increasing mechanisation, in danger of boredom. Increasing importance therefore attaches to the endeavours being made to enable as many members as possible of all classes to have their share in other forms of social values. Amongst these — and that can be indicated only briefly in this survey of social security — are the efforts to promote the formation of capital in the hands of the workers, which efforts are finding their expression in legislation in many different forms.

In the field of social security, social policy must also take account of the changes here described in technical, economic, and social conditions. The legislature can properly fulfill its task only if it, too, bases itself on the new situation. This is not merely a matter of Amending Laws, but of Laws which give expression to a system of Social Reform designed to create a new Social Order. It must be a characteristic of this new Social Order that it no longer regards the nation as a whole as being split into opposing classes of poor and rich, but that it considers the social problems of all classes of the people, though without aiming at uniform model solutions.

II.

The main emphasis of social security lies in social insurance. In it are implemented the principal requirements of our Constitution, the principle of the democratic and social state under the rule of law: inviolable and inalienable human rights, the free development of personality (Art. 20 (I), Art. 2 (I) of the Basic Law). It is the endeavour of the whole legislation governing social insurance to give the greatest possible effect to the principles of individuality and solidarity, as laid down in the Constitution. They resemble the focal point of an ellipse which circumscribes the field of social insurance. The intrinsic value of the person and his integration in the community, freedom and security, personal responsibility and solidarity, are not antitheses, but formative principles, each permeating the other.

In reaching this point social insurance has moved beyond the bounds of its original purpose, which was merely to provide help in the case of extreme need. It is no longer confined, either in its nature or its amount merely to the relief of distress, but is designed to safeguard the social status of the insured person and his survivors.

In Pensions Insurance the amount payable, varying with the individual, is based on the number of insurance years and the amount of earnings on which contributions have been paid. This involves a rejection of a system of flat rate contributions. The pension is thus calculated to a greater degree on the value of the work performed for the national economy. This method of relating pensions to earnings also ensures that the higher value of labour in general, which is reflected in rising wages, is also reflected in the amount of the pension. Further, during the time the pension is payable, increases in wages and salaries are reflected in the increases based on the annual Adjustement Laws. Pensions thus rise with wages to a greater extent than price increases. Pensioners and wage and salary earners enjoy in principle socio-political equality though at quantitatively varying levels of benefits.

It appeared advisable to apply the same principle to the adjustment of industrial injuries pensions, more particularly since such pensions have always been assessed in the first place on the basis of actual wages and salaries, in principle on the annual earnings of the year preceding the accident, that is to say, on a more favourable basis than in the case of pensions insurance. In addition to the abstract compensation in the form of accident pension for the losses sustained, come the losses suffered by the injured person arising from the fact that he no longer has the benefit of rising wage levels.

In the case, also, of persons who have been driven from their homes as a result of the war, pensions are now assessed according to a new principle — the principle of integration — in such a manner as though they had acquired their entitlement within the social structure of the Federal Republic, and, further, in such a manner that they retain their accrued rights under pensions insurance.

The object of retaining the acquired status in society, a status conforming to the abilities of those concerned, that is, of doing more than merely relieving distress, is served by preventive and rehabilitation measures. In order to achieve this objective the conditions, nature, and extent of measures for the maintenance, improvement, and restitution of employability have also been substantially improved under Pensions Insurance by the Reform Laws. In lieu of the limited objective of providing medical treatment in order to avoid the need to award a pension, the administrations of Pensions Insurance have undertaken a new task, in cooperation with other relevant Social Insurance Funds: to maintain the employability, the will to work, of the insured person when it is endangered, to improve it if it is diminished, and, if possible, to restore it completely. Measures of medical, occupational, and social rehabilitation are devoted to this end. Similar measures, even though conditioned by the differing objectives arising from the specific nature of Industrial Injuries Insurance, are undertaken by the Accident Funds for the restoration of employability, for assistance at work and in the occupation (Occupational Aid), and to alleviate the effects of the injury. The spread of the idea that rehabilitation and prevention should be further developed as one of the up-to-date tasks of a system of social security also finds expression in the discussions on the statutory obligation of Health Insurance to provide relief.

In the matter of benefits in case of sickness, social insurance legislative and labour legislative provisions complement each other. Based on the long standing obligation of employers to pay salaried staff their full salaries for the first six weeks of unfitness for work, all workers have had a similar claim with effect from January 1, 1970 — i.e., for at least six weeks.

If unfitness is of longer duration, benefits become payable under Health Insurance. Sick benefit is payable almost to the same amount as net earnings until the illness is cured, or until Pensions Insurance assumes the responsibility. The result of this system is that exhaustion of benefit has been almost completely eliminated, and an uninterrupted transfer from Health Insurance to Pensions Insurance benefits is assured. In the same manner as the payment of sich pay, hospital treatment is, in principle, granted for an unlimited period. The members of the insured persons's family also covered by his insurance are legally entitled to the same benefits in kind as the insured person himself. Further, all pensioners enjoy the full protection of statutory Health Insurance, without being required to pay contributions. Thus benefits provided ensure that the insured person and his family do not suffer any loss of social status, as is also true in the case of the recipients of unemployment benefit.

III.

The system of social security established in the Federal Republic of Germany has proved successful in its principles, as well as in a whole range of individual provisions. Constant investigations, and reports of the most varied nature, serve the purpose of keeping a check on results achieved, and of making preparations for further improvements. Pensions Adjustments Reports, Social Reports, Social Budgets, to name only a few of the main examples, with their manifold forecasts, provide constant assistance in the formation of a progressive social policy designed to strengthen the ties between the individual and the community. Social benefits in the Federal Republic of Germany, moulded on the principles of individuality and solidarity, are designed to preserve a free social order, an aim which social security is also intended to serve.

Social security is substantially based on the principle that the workers who are producing the national product, that is to say from the product of their labour and by abstention from consumption resulting from the payment of contributions, enable those not able to work, through no fault of their own, to live from the national product. They do so in the expectation guaranteed by the legislator, that they themselves, in times when they are unable to work (e.g. in sickness or old age), will be entitled to the same benefits at the hands of those in employment, benefits corresponding to their own productive labour and abstention from consumption: security based on their own labours during their working life, security based on the labours of others during involuntary breaks during their working life, or at the end of their working life. In this manner the relation between the individual and the community, from a socio-political viewpoint, acquires its special characteristic features, through labour and the product of labour. Man as a social being is here seen as a member of the working societas, his own labours and the product thereof being measured against the labours of all and the product of all, the society in which he lives being regarded as a society of workers.

At the same time, within the system of social insurance, at least to a certain extent, a balance is achieved between the weaker and the stronger, between the healthy and the sick, between young and old, between the childless and families with children — a partial re-distribution of the burdens arising. The concept of solidarity is applicable not only to the relation between workers and non-workers; it also permeates the relation as between workers themselves. This problem leads out beyond the narrower confines of social security. In particular there arise problems as to how far fiscal measures designed to ensure greater social equity require further revision.

A further extension of capital formation in the hands of the workers is intended to consolidate the position of the individual within the community. He is to be given an opportunity, over and above the indispensable solidarity security, to acquire a portion of financial security for himself during his working life.

The community of the workers is an economic community. Social policy and economic policy are two fields of community policy, which, each proceeding from its own starting point, each pursuing its own specific aims, mutually permeate each other. The blending of these two spheres of policy have the effect that their juxtaposition is abandoned in favour of integration. Economic policy itself is pursuing socio-political aims, and social policy is also serving the aims of economic policy. The fact that the concepts and aims of both spheres affirm the elimination, so far as possible, of tensions in both spheres, which are not always avoidable, will finally lead to a fruitful synthesis between them.

A social policy of this nature serves a humanitarian purpose. It has been customary in the past to assess the cultural achievements of a nation principally on the basis of its scientific and artistic works. In addition to this intelligible aesthetic component there is now a social component — the relief of distress and misery, improvement of living standards and of joy in living, the development of individuality, equal chances in life for all men.

Review of the Origins of Social Security

German social insurance originated as the first comprehensive body of legislation in the world intended for the security of the workers. It was inaugurated by the Imperial Decree of 17.11.1881, and founded on the Law on the Health Insurance of the Workers (1883), the Law on Industrial Injuries Insurance (1884), and the Law on Disablement and Old Age Pensions Insurance (1889). These three laws were codified in a uniform body of legislation in 1911, the still valid Imperial Insurance Code. In 1911, the Law on the Insurance of Non-Manual Workers was also enacted.

After the First World War there followed the Law on the Miners' Insurance Special Scheme (Knappschaftsgesetz) (1923, Revised 1926), which codified the widely disbursed provisions of various Land Laws governing this, the oldest sector of German Social Security, and the Law on Labour Placing and Unemployment Insurance (1927). Benefits under Pensions Insurance were considerably improved in the years between 1922 and 1928.

Following reductions consequent on the Emergency Regulations issued during the years 1930 to 1932, a number of subsequent amending laws and regulations led to not inconsiderable changes in the structure of the German social insurance system, in particular the so-called Reconstruction Law (Aufbaugesetz) and its implementing regulations (from 1934 onwards). In addition, there came various regulations consequent on the second world war, some of which are still in force. In 1938 the Self-employed Artisans Pension Law was enacted. Again following on restrictions imposed by the Occupation Powers in the years 1945 to 1947, the Social Insurance Adjustment Law was enacted in 1949, launching a whole series of Benefits Improvement Laws. During the same period the organisation and jurisdiction of social insurance was consolidated, and in part revised. Following on a protracted period of preparation and intensive public discussion, the reform of *Pensions Insurance* reached its apex in 1957 in the three Laws on the Reform of Pensions Insurance. Since that time pensions have been adjusted to economic developments in 12 successive years. The Reformed Law on Non-Contributors and Foreign Pensions (1960) (Fremdrenten and Auslandsrenten-Neuregelungsgesetz) has integrated expellees into the new pensions system.

In 1965 a large number of improvements governing the assessment of pensions were introduced. In 1967 the Finance Amending Law abolished the insurance ceiling for non-manual workers' pensions insurance. As a consequence of the economic recession of 1966/67, and of the measures taken to combat it, the financial bases of pensions' insurance were consolidated, and in 1969 the Miners Insurance Special Scheme Pensions were codified in the Federal Miners Special Scheme (Bundesknappschaft). The Agricultural Old Age Benefits Scheme (1957, amended and considerably extended and improved in 1969), the Self-employed Artisans Insurance (1960), and the Federal and Land legislation for free professions (e.g. doctors), all provide evidence of the extension of social security in old age to self-employed persons.

In *Health Insurance* — apart from several amendments to the insurable ceiling — the first reforms affected the Health Insurance of Pensioners and the law as affecting Health Insurance doctors. The Law on the Improvement of the Financial Security of Workers in the Case of Sickness (1957, amended 1961) provided such workers with higher cash benefits, plus a supplement from the employer. Since the beginning of 1970 manual workers are on an equal footing with non-manual workers in this respect; the employer is required to continue to pay wages for the first six weeks of sickness. At the same time a certain refund became payable to insured persons not reporting sick, whilst the price of prescribed medicines was increased. In 1967 the Health Insurance of Pensioners was extended, though at the same time a deduction of 2 % of the Pension to cover Health Insurance was enacted, but again abolished in 1970. Maternity Benefits were again increased in 1965/1967. The reform of Industrial Injuries Insurance was concluded in 1963. In line with the changes in the labour market, *Unemployment Insurance* has again been frequently amended. In the period following the second world war the original very high contribution rate of 6,5 % of insurable earnings has gradually been reduced to 1,3 %. In 1956 a comprehensive Amending Law brought the relevant legislation to a certain conclusion. In 1959 the first steps were taken to promote all-the-year-round employment in the building industry. In 1966 and 1967 benefits were, above all, geared to economic developments. In 1969 the legislation not only changed the name of the existing institute to that of the „Federal Institute for Labour", but also conferred new functions on it in the framework of employment policy. In the preceding years the Federal Institute had already been entrusted with the promotion of further training.

The most recent branch of social security in the Federal Republic of Germany is the legislation governing *Children's Allowances*, which began in 1954 with the award of Allowances to families with at least 3 children, was extended in 1961 to families with two children, and which reached its final phase in the Federal Children's Allowance Law of 1964. Since that time Children's Allowances have been financed by the Federal Budget — this led during the 1967 recession to the cancellation of allowances, first approved in 1965, designed to facilitate attendance in schools of further education, payable by the Federal Institute for Labour. Additional to the Children's Allowances Law came, in 1969, the introduction on the basis of Federal legislation of training grants.

At the end of the second world war the legislation of the Federal Republic of Germany found itself faced by the task of mitigating the consequences of the war and of spreading over the resultant burdens in a more equitable manner. This has been accomplished in the main by virtue of *War Pensions and Related Services* and the legislation on the Equalisation of Burdens. The care of the victims of the two world wars, that is to say the war invalids, the war widows and orphans, was already the subject of legislation in 1950. The relevant Federal Law of 1950 has been frequently amended, and provision for war victims considerably improved. Legislation was revised in 1960, 1964 and 1966. On the basis of the War Victims Report of the Federal Government, war pensions were not only increased by 16 % in 1970, but provision was made for them to be revised annually in line with rising wages and salaries. Provision for Expellees and Refugees, which began in 1949 with the Immediate Aid Law, was continued by the *Equalisation of Burdens* Law (1952) and has since been improved by 22 Amending Laws. Legislation on the Equalisation of Burdens, which, conceived in the spirit of social justice, endeavours to compensate for the loss of the home, and for other losses resultant on the war, is probably unique throughout the world. It was considerably expanded in its scope by the inclusion of former residents in Eastern Germany, who have benefited by the Equalisation of Burdens Law and by the improvements of its provisions. In the field of *Public Assistance* the most important legislative provisions went back to 1924. The Federal Social Aid Law of 1961 has transformed this legislation into an up-to-date form of individual aid, and has, for the first time, codified it in a comprehensive body of legislation. It has since been frequently amended, the last occasion being in 1969.

The first Federal Parliament — the *Bundestag* — (1949—1953) transformed the conditions consequent on the war and its aftermath into a more normal state of affairs. The second Bundestag (1953—1957), by virtue of its fundamental reform of Pensions Insurance, made great progress in the direction of the goal of social security. During this period (1949—1957) Anton Storch was the Federal Minister of Labour. The third Bundestag (1957—1961) and the fourth Bundestag (1961—65) gradually enacted a whole body of legislation (Industrial Injuries Insurance, Children's Allowances, Social Aid); the Federal Minister of Labour was Theodor Blank (1957—1965). The 5th Bundestag (1965—1969, Federal Minister of Labour Hans Katzer), during whose last two years of office the two major parties formed a Coalition, managed in this short period to bring the twenty years of social development to a certain finality with the enactment of the following laws: Continued Payment of Wages to Manual Workers during Sickness, Consolidating Law on Pensions Insurance and Pensions Adjustments, the Labour Promotion Law, and the Vocational Training Promotion Law. The content of, and the course taken by, these laws was decisively influenced by Prof. Dr. Schellenberg, for many years chairman of the Social Policy Committee of the German Federal Parliament. During the last two decades, social security, whose foundations reach back into the last century, has been adapted to the changed social and economic conditions of the present day. The new Federal Minister of Labour, Walter Arendt, has already given the new (6th) Bundestag notice of new social aims.

Introduction of a new flexible age limit in Pensions Insurance, together with an enquiry into a gradual reduction of the present fixed pensionable ages — Assessment of Pensions on a points system — old age pensions for self-employed persons and other social groups — further development of Health Insurance, including adjustment of the insurable ceiling for non-manual workers — increase of Children's Allowances — Extension and Adjustment of Family Aid and Vocational Training Promotion — Preparation of a Social Legislation Code (Sozialgesetzbuch).

Legislation on social security has at all times been accompanied by intensive public and scientific discussion. At this point we can mention only the plans originated by the Federal Government, and of these only the most important reports submitted on its instructions, and by the Consultative Committees appointed by it.

When, in 1952, the proposal made by the Social Democratic Parliamentary Party to appoint a „Social Studies Committee" had failed to gain acceptance, the Federal Minister of Labour appointed, in 1953, pursuant to a parliamentary resolution, an *Advisory Committee for the Reform of Social Services,* with several sub-committees. This Committee outlined the framework for the discussion of the legislation which commenced in 1956/57, including the social aid sector. The report prepared for this Committee by Prof. Dr. Bogs in 1954 exercised a palpable influence on the reform of Pensions Insurance, and on the annual adjustment of pensions to wages movements. At about the same time the Statistical Federal Office submitted the conclusions of the so-called L-Statistics, dealing with the payment of more than one pension to one and the same person. In the spring of 1955 Minister Storch published his "Basic Ideas on the Overall Reform on Social Services". In 1955, at the request of Federal Chancellor Adenauer, four professors submitted the so-called Rothenfelser Memorandum, containing too far-reaching proposals for amendments. Decisions on the reform of Pensions Insurance were at that time reached within the Federal Government, as prepared by the first Social Cabinet; all subsequent governments have appointed relevant ad hoc committees. Since 1957 the annual adjustment of pension scales has been based on the report of a legally appointed *Social Advisory Council* under the chairmanship, for many years, of Prof. Dr. Meinhold; the reports of this Committee contributed fundamentally to the periodical adjustment of pensions to increasing wage and salary rates. In the years subsequent to 1958, the so-called "Social Packet", including continued payment of wages to manual workers during (the first six weeks of) sickness, part payment of costs by insured persons themselves during sickness, payment of Children's Allowances from Federal Funds, occupied the continual attention of the government and the legislator, though only the Children's Allowances have been dealt with on this basis. In order to provide a new starting point for legislation on social security the Federal Government, under Chancellor Erhard, appointed five scientists in 1954 to prepare a Social Experts' Report, the purpose of which was to present current social legislation and its social and economic repercussions in a clear and unmistakable form. In the upshot this Committee, under the chairmanship of Prof. Dr. Bogs, confirmed in its report that current developments in this field were largely following the right course. Further developments in social insurance in the years 1966/67 were strongly influenced by the measures taken to overcome the economic recession of 1966/67 and its aftermath, and to relieve the Federal Budget of some of its financial burdens. In 1969 Federal Minister of Labour Katzer submitted the first *Social Budget* a — non-committal — forecast of the costs of public social services, as a counterpart to the Interim-term Finance Planning of the Federal Budget. Based on Chancellor Brandt's statement of governmental policy, Federal Minister of Labour Arendt appointed two Expert Commissions in 1970, one for the preparation of the Social Legislation Code, one for the further development of Health Insurance reform. These committees have already begun their labours. In addition to the usual annual report on pensions adjustments, there is to appear this year, for the first time, a comprehensive Social Report.

Overall picture of present day Social Security

The overall picture of social security in the Federal Republic of Germany is a manifold one. It is only the comprehensive account of all social benefits as provided in the Social Budget that presents a picture of its development and importance, which must both be seen against the background of the development of the population and the economic strength of the Federal Republic. The figures and other details first acquire life when it is possible to visualise the use to which the expenditure is put.

The Social budget

The Social Budget was developed in 1968 from the forgoing figures of net expenditure on public social benefits (since 1950). In contrast to these figures it estimates the development of social benefits in advance, on each occasion for four years ahead, and includes, not only the limitations applied by the International Labour Office, but also other costs of social security, namely the costs of public health services, the pensions and children's allowances in the public services, but, in addition, since 1970, rent allowances, supplementary pensions in the public services, maintenance allowances for soldiers, and certain compensation benefits.

Since 1969/70 the Social Budget has been presented from two aspects: In the first place, expenditure is broken down by institutions, above all by branches of insurance, secondly according to its functions, that is to say the obejects of the benefits (risks, cause of loss or injury), e.g. on the grounds of sickness, age, unemployment; in this connection its application has been further extended to include the private disbursements of employers, and tax rebates. A further extension is to be anticipated in the coming years.

The purpose of the Social Budget is to provide medium term orientation on the amounts, structure, and development of the costs of social security, and to be of assistance in reaching decisions, to the benefit of recipients of social benefits, on the distribution of income. In the case of the first Social Budget, 1968, the primary intention was to ascertain the amount of the costs devolving on tax payers and contributors, and justifying the actual social benefit quota by calling attention to the fact that social benefits not only help consumption, but that they also conduce to promote the growth of the economy. It came to the conclusion that, between 1950 and 1968, despite the increasing burdens borne by the workers, above all in the form of taxation and higher contributions, the real living standard of the workers had risen, on an average, by one and one third. The Scond Social Budget 1969/70 anticipates that social benefits will increase in the period 1970—1973 somewhat more rapidly than the Gross National Product (GNP). This estimate takes into account wage and salary increases per capita of + 12 % in 1970. and of + 5,8 % from 1971 onwards.

The Quota of Social Benefits

The quota of social benefits in relation to the GNP is designated the Social Benefits Quota. The following survey provides details:

The Social Budget (in millard DM)

Year	Net Expenditure	Income	Social Benefits Quota[1]
1963	62,6	65,9	16,6
1964	69,1	73,0	16,7
1965	77,9	81,6	17,2
1966	85,8	89,2	17,8
1967	94,0	92,8	19,4
1968	100,4	99,1	19,0
1969	108,5	108,3	18,3
1970	115,8	119,7	17,9
1971	125,0	128,6	18,2
1972	134,5	138,2	18,5
1973	145,9	150,7	18,9

1) Quota of net expenditure in relation to GNP.

For the period prior to 1963, the calculation of the social benefits quota can be based on the net expenditure for public social benefits, as set out on the following survey. On the other hand, the following further public expenditure is included in the Social Budged: in particular, pensions, children's allowances, and supplementary pensions in the public services, youth aid, rent allowances, public health services, and other compensation benefits.

The quota of social benefits has increased during the course of the past decades. Following the second world war there was, however, little change until the major pensions insurance reform of 1957, as a result of which it rose by almost a quarter, to commence falling again from 1959 onwards.

Social Budget (institutional) in Mill. DM

Year	Pensions Insurance of manual workers	non-manual	Miners Special Scheme Pensions Insurance	Total Pensions Insurance	Farmers' Pensions	Health Insurance and Maternity	Accident Insurance	Unemployment Insurance Promotions of Employment	Total Social Insurance	Childrens' Allowances	Social Aid
1950	2 385	945	568	3 898	–	2 521	585	1 871	8 875	–	962
1955	4 487	2 067	1 194	7 748	–	4 685	1 027	1 811	15 271	463	1 288
1960	10 532	5 294	2 433	18 259	182	9 621	1 733	1 070	30 865	916	1 620
1965	16 347	8 983	3 648	28 978	487	15 926	3 120	1 395	49 906	2 820	2 495
1966	18 030	10 049	4 009	32 088	657	18 556	3 452	1 365	56 118	2 981	2 736
1967	20 264	11 325	4 428	36 017	700	19 444	3 604	2 787	62 552	2 694	2 990
1968	22 215	12 501	4 796	39 512	723	21 516	3 809	2 731	68 291	2 635	3 116
1969	24 804	13 685	5 169	43 658	837	23 600	4 013	2 566	74 674	2 732	3 300
1970	26 801	15 030	5 499	47 330	887	23 447	3 696	2 771	78 131	2 995	3 710
1971	28 720	16 313	5 697	50 730	910	25 729	3 955	3 170	84 494	3 402	4 090
1972	30 940	17 794	6 002	54 736	931	28 268	4 305	3 342	91 582	3 523	4 400
1973	33 904	19 732	6 477	60 193	951	31 111	4 516	3 524	100 215	3 655	4 750

Social Budget (institutional) in percentage

Year	manual workers	non-manual	Miners	Total Pensions	Farmers'	Health	Accident	Unemployment	Total Social Insurance	Childrens' Allowances	Social Aid
1950	2,4	1,0	0,6	4,0	–	2,6	0,6	1,9	9,1	–	1,0
1955	2,5	1,1	0,7	4,3	–	2,6	0,6	1,0	8,5	0,3	0,7
1960	3,5	1,7	0,8	6,0	0,0	3,2	0,6	0,4	10,2	0,2	0,5
1965	3,6	2,0	0,8	6,4	0,1	3,5	0,7	0,3	11,0	0,6	0,6
1966	3,8	2,1	0,8	6,7	0,1	3,9	0,7	0,3	11,7	0,6	0,6
1967	4,2	2,3	0,9	7,4	0,1	4,0	0,7	0,6	12,8	0,6	0,6
1968	4,2	2,4	0,9	7,5	0,1	4,1	0,7	0,5	12,9	0,5	0,6
1969	4,2	2,3	0,9	7,4	0,1	4,0	0,7	0,4	12,6	0,5	0,6
1970	4,1	2,3	0,8	7,2	0,1	3,6	0,6	0,5	12,0	0,5	0,6
1971	4,2	2,4	0,8	7,4	0,1	3,8	0,6	0,5	12,4	0,5	0,6
1972	4,2	2,4	0,8	7,4	0,1	3,9	0,6	0,5	12,5	0,5	0,7
1973	4,4	2,5	0,8	7,7	0,1	4,0	0,6	0,5	12,9	0,5	0,6

Survey of Net Expenditure[1] for Public Social Services 1927 – 1938

Year	Total		Pensions insurance		Health insurance Protection of mother hood		Industrial injuries insurance		Unemployment insurance unemployment		War Pensions and related services		Welfare	
	Mill RM	% VE	Mill RM	% VE	Mio RM	% VE	Mio RM	% VE	Mio RM	% VE	Mio RM	% VE	Mio RM	% VE
1927	7 360	10,4	1 276	1,8	1 739	2,5	337	0,5	918	1,3	1 616	2,3	1 474	2,1
1930	10 525	15,0	1 941	2,8	2 010	2,9	429	0,6	2 144	3,1	1 702	2,4	2 299	3,3
1933	8 565	18,4	1 651	3,6	1 180	2,5	307	0,7	1 436	3,1	1 231	2,7	2 760	5,9
1936	7 541	11,4	1 877	2,9	1 524	2,3	349	0,5	840	1,3	1 130	1,7	1 821	2,8
1938	7 265	8,9	2 024	2,5	1 787	2,2	394	0,5	441	0,5	1 081	1,3	1 538	1,9

1) Net Expenditure: Gross expenditure less payment to other institutions. The percentages have reference to the national income within the then limits.

Between 1963 and 1968 social benefits, within the extended limits of the Social Budget, have increased by 60.4 % as compared with an increase in the Gross National Product of 40.3 %. The steepest rise in the social benefits quota, in the years 1965–1967, resulting, apart from improved benefits, in the main from the considerable effects of the recession of 1967, in which a stagnation of the GNP coincided with increased expenditure caused by the state of the market, in particular in the case of unemployment insurance. The highest social benefits quota so far was reached in 1967. The forecasts of the GNP indicate that this quota will not again be reached until 1973.

The Social Budget (institutional) in Mill. DM

Aids for Youth	Rent Allowances	Public Health Services	Total of other Social Services	Pensions	Childrens Allowances	Supplementary Pensions in the Public Services	Totals	War Pensions and Related Services	Equalisation of Burdens	Other compensation Payments	Total Compensation Payments	Total Social Budget
27	–	123	1 112	2 479	441	·	2 920	2 087	718	·	2 805	15 712
51	–	218	2 020	5 094	760	·	5 854	3 206	980	·	4 186	27 331
54	–	342	2 932	6 859	1 031	·	7 890	3 678	1 345	·	5 023	46 710
793	175	667	6 950	10 410	1 634	486	12 530	5 801	1 990	655	8 529	77 915
897	445	710	7 769	11 153	1 651	518	13 322	5 905	1 955	729	8 589	85 798
959	480	733	7 856	12 018	1 665	570	14 253	6 762	1 803	771	9 336	93 997
1 030	567	785	8 133	12 500	1 681	772	14 953	6 616	1 812	630	9 058	100 435
1 130	640	834	8 636	13 870	1 700	714	16 284	6 586	1 742	650	8 978	108 572
1 240	1 090	883	9 918	15 500	1 720	777	17 997	7 456	1 676	658	9 790	115 836
1 360	1 590	932	11 374	16 730	1 740	830	19 300	7 768	1 470	642	9 880	125 048
1 490	1 750	981	12 144	18 050	1 760	892	20 702	8 133	1 373	575	10 081	134 509
1 630	1 950	1 030	13 015	19 480	1 780	974	22 234	8 641	1 276	558	10 475	145 939

Social Budget (institutional) in percentage

0,0	–	0,1	1,1	2,5	0,5	·	3,0	2,1	0,7	·	2,8	16,0
0,0	–	0,1	1,1	2,8	0,4	·	3,2	1,8	0,5	·	2,3	15,2
0,0	–	0,1	1,0	2,3	0,3	·	2,6	1,2	0,4	·	1,6	15,5
0,2	0,0	0,1	1,5	2,3	0,4	0,1	2,8	1,3	0,4	0,2	1,9	17,2
0,2	0,1	0,1	1,6	2,3	0,3	0,1	2,7	1,2	0,4	0,2	1,8	17,8
0,2	0,1	0,1	1,6	2,5	0,3	0,1	2,9	1,4	0,4	0,1	1,9	19,4
0,2	0,1	0,1	1,5	2,4	0,3	0,1	2,8	1,3	0,3	0,1	1,7	19,0
0,2	0,1	0,1	1,5	2,3	0,3	0,1	2,7	1,1	0,3	0,1	1,5	18,3
0,2	0,1	0,1	1,5	2,4	0,3	0,1	2,8	1,1	0,3	0,1	1,5	17,9
0,2	0,2	0,1	1,6	2,4	0,3	0,1	2,8	1,1	0,2	0,1	1,4	18,2
0,2	0,2	0,1	1,7	2,5	0,2	0,1	2,8	1,1	0,2	0,1	1,4	18,5
0,2	0,3	0,1	1,7	2,5	0,2	0,1	2,8	1,1	0,2	0,1	1,4	18,9

The Functional Social Budget

The purpose of the Social Budget is to sectionalise social benefits in accordance with their objectives, in order to show where the main stress lies. This break down permits the presentation of social benefits as provided by the different sectors seperately, for sickness, disablement, and death, arising from differing causes (Political events, industrial injuries, other causes), for the benefit of differing groups of persons (insured persons, family members), in the form of cash benefits and benefits in kind. Benefits provided by employers, and indirectly by the State, are additionally included in the Social Budget. The Functional Social Budget shows that the major portion of benefits is devoted to pensions and care in old age. Of 97 milliard DM expended in 1968, 28 milliard DM, or 27.3 %, was devoted to this purpose; by 1973 the quota will have risen to 31.7 %. Provision for survivors, at 16.7 %, occupied the second place in 1968; although this quota is rising, it will have been overhauled by expenditure on health measures by 1973.

Expenditure in the remaining social benefits field is declining relatively between 1963 and 1973, though it is rising absolutely. Pensions in respect of old age and disablement are declining, above all because of the changing age composition. Family benefits will decline relatively, since the number of children will increase only slightly up to 1973. The reduction of payments in respect of sickness is, however, only a statistical factor, since the continued payment of wages by employers during sickness from 1970 onwards is not shown in this sector of the Social Budget. Costs arising from the aftermath of the war are also on the decline.

The Social Budget broken down according to Functions

		Mrd. DM			%		
		1963	1968	1973	1963	1968	1973
Grants of income to old persons, less family allowances		16,4	28,3	44,5	27,3	29,3	31,7
Income for survivors	in so far as political events or industrial injury or disease are the cause	10,0	16,2	24,8	16,7	16,7	17,7
Health measures for the sick		8,3	15,6	26,1	13,8	16,1	18,6
Income for the Disabled, less family allowances		4,9	6,5	8,6	8,1	6,7	6,1
Grants of income solely on account of the size of the family		3,2	5,2	6,8	5,4	5,4	4,9
Other items		17,3	24,9	29,4	28,7	25,8	21,0
Total		60,1	96,7	140,2	100	100	100

Structure of Social Services

Within the system of public social service the main emphasis lies on social insurance; expenditure in this field accounts for almost seven tenths of all services.

Social insurance provides the most important security against the exigencies of life (sickness, industrial injuries and diseases, reduced standard of employment, unemployability, old age, death, maternity, unemployment). Comparable benefits in the public services (pensions, children's allowances, supplementary superannuation) account for about 15 %, compensation payments (war pensions and related services, equalisation of burdens, current restitution payments, etc.) for about 9 %. All remaining social services together show the same percentage.

The different forms of development in social services have led during the last two decades to shifts in the composition of the overall picture. Whereas the costs arising out of the aftermath of the war, war pensions and related services, and equalisation of burdens, are decreasing with the years since the end of the war, social pensions' insurance and social health insurance have gained in importance. During the last two decades the quota of pensions insurance has risen from one quarter to two fifths. Health insurance accounted for a good fifth of total expenditure by 1969. This quota has declined statistically in 1970, since expenditure on sick pay is, to a large extent, no longer shown as expenditure by the statutory Sick Funds since the introdiction on a legal basis of continued payment of wages by employers to sick workers for the first six seeks of sickness.

Developments in the field of pensions and health insurance now dominate the overall picture of social security. Of the total expenditure on social benefits a good quarter is provided each by workers and employers, and two fifths by the Federal and Land Governments and by Local Authorities. In 1970 the Federal Government will expend about 26 milliard DM on social services in the widest sense of the word — i.e. 28 % of all expenditure. This contribution from the Federal Budget to social services declined from the record height of almost 39 % in 1953 to 24 % in 1963, since when it has again risen slightly. Nevertheless, the increase has still remained far behind the increase in the total Federal Budget during the period named.

Reasons for the growth of social services

In the long run the extent and growth of social services derive from the development of an industrial society, and in particular from the increase in the number of workers. These factors are reflected in changes in legislation and of economic conditions (e.g. reduction in unemployment and in the number of agricultural workers). In addition, the development of social services finds its explanation to a large part in the age structure of the population, in compensation for the consequences of the war, and in changes in family structure.

AGE Composition

At the end of 1969 there were approximately 61.2 mill. people living in the Federal Republic of Germany, 29.2 mill men and 32 mill. women, The age structure is by no means uniform. The number of older persons has increased considerably during the last 20 years, not only absolutely, but also in relation to the numbers of working age.

In 1939 7.3 % of the population were aged 65 and over, in 1950 the figure was already 9.3 %, by the end of 1968 12.9 %, and the percentage will increase to 14.5 % by 1980; from then on it will gradually fall again to the current figure; the quota of persons of

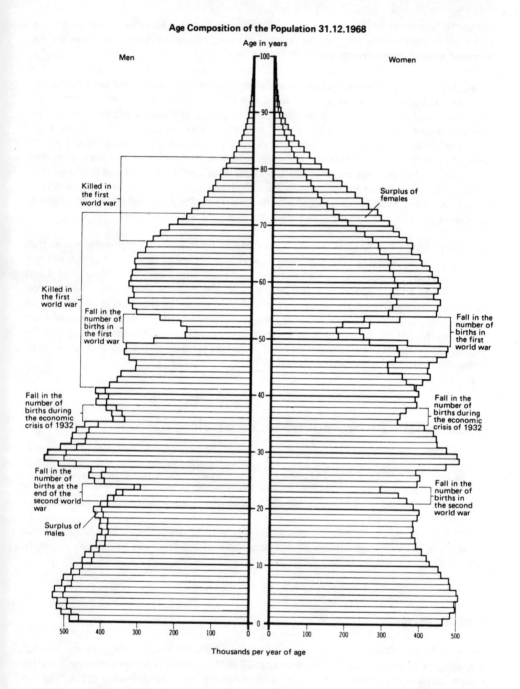

Age Composition of the Population 31.12.1968

Age in years

Men

Women

Killed in the first world war

Surplus of females

Killed in the first world war

Fall in the number of births in the first world war

Fall in the number of births in the first world war

Fall in the number of births during the economic crisis of 1932

Fall in the number of births during the economic crisis of 1932

Fall in the number of births at the end of the second world war

Fall in the number of births in the second world war

Surplus of males

Thousands per year of age

working age (15 to 65) will decline from about 70 % to 64 %. This is due to the declining number of births during this century, the decline in mortality, and the migrations consequent on the second world war. Expectation of life has also increased considerably. It was round about 36 years 100 years ago, to day it is about 68 years in the case of men, and 74 years in the case of women (compared with 38 years).

For social security purposes this means in particular that the number of retirement and disablement pensions is increasing, even though not to an equal extent, and that, at any one time, an ever greater amount of the national product must be devoted to pensions. The incidence of sickness in the population, which, as experience shows, increases with age, will presumably be affected by the change in the age structure.

Consequences of the War

The age pyramid of the population has been shaped by the fate of the German people in the past, and by the great losses suffered. The war losses, and the reduced birth rate, were most pronounced during three periods. Owing to the reduced birth rate during the first world war, there were considerable discrepencies between the number of men and women in the case of those between 50 and 55 in 1970.

For instance, the number of women aged 55 was, for this reason, only about half the number aged 60, namely those who were born before the first world war. Another gap, though not so broad and deep, resulted from the reduced birth rate during the world economic crisis around 1930. Finally, another gap was created by the drop in the birth rate at the end of the second world war. In nearly all fields of social security, though naturally primarily in the field of war pensions and related services, and equalisation of burdens, expenditure on services for war injured and war widows continues to play a considerable role.

Change of Family Structure

The claims for social services have also changed in their nature: the number of new families founded has increased, the size of families has declined. At the turn of the century four and more persons were living in 64 % of all households, to-day the figure is 27 %. Consequently, at that time, only 7 % ran their households alone, in 1939 10 %, by 1950 the figure had increased to 19 %, to reach a quarter of all the 22 mill. households in 1968. At present 28 % are living in two person households, and in three person households 20 % of the total population. The effect of this change in the structure of families is that even less persons can rely on help in kind from their relatives than formerly, and are consequently dependent to a much greater extent on cash allowances from public sources.

The number of social benefits

In the matter of social benefits the various administrations make almost 250 mill. payments annually — pensions, sick pay, and similar payments — that is about 21 mill. payments monthly.

The quota of the population with a claim to social benefits is in each instance shown in the separate sectors for the relevant type of social benefit. Pensions and current allowances were payable in 1969 in a total of 18 mill. cases. In 1962 the number was about 15 mill., in 1965 about 16 mill. cases.

According to the microcensus of 1968 some 6.6 mill. persons were in receipt of only one pension, or a similar payment, whilst 11.4 mill. pensions were payable in respect of 2.4 mill. persons in receipt of two or more pensions. Approximately 70 % of all pensioners are at least 65 years old; a further 23 % are aged between 50 and 65. In addition to drawing a pension, nearly a quarter of all pensioners were still working, most of them recipients of war pensions or accidents pensions.

Social services are rendered for the most varied reasons and for differing purposes. Nevertheless, in view of the multiplicity of such services available, and the composition of the groups of persons to whom they are payable, it cannot be avoided that one and the same cause sometimes leads to the payment of more than one benefit. If payments of two or more benefits are made to a single person they are usually not alone so high that they would suffice to meet the whole cost of living, as, for example the basic war pension. In many instances it is only a double pension that suffices for this purpose, for instance, a widow's pension plus a pension payable in respect of her own insured occupation. The effects of the payment of more than one pension to a single person should not, therefore, be overestimated, either in respect of an individual case, or of possible economies in expenditure. By means of adjustments between the various types of social benefits it is estimated that, at present a 4 % saving in cash expenditure is being effected, mainly in the cases of the equalisation of burdens, rent allowances, and social aid.

International comparisons

The very considerable extent of the social services provided in Germany is shown by comparisons with other countries. Of all the countries in the European Community the Federal Republic of Germany has, since 1958, provided the highest standard of social services, measured by its gross national product. In the last few years, however, the quotas have displayed more equal proportions, for the reason, amongst others, that the relatively high quota in respect of expenditure arising out of the consequences of the war is gradually receding in the Federal Republic.

The higher percentage as compared with the Social Budget results from the additional inclusion of private continued payment of salaries to non-manual workers in the case of illness, and of a part of benefits payable in respect of the protection of motherhood.

Social Expenditure in % of the Gross National Product

Country	1962	1965
Germany	17.0	18.1
France	15.6	17.3
Italy	14.8	18.0
Holland	13.8	16.9
Belgium	15.5	16.3
Luxembourg	15.7	17.1

In the years 1962 to 1965 social expenditure has risen in the Federal Republic by 35 %, in Belgium by 38 %, in Luxembourg by 40 %, in France by 48 %, in Italy by 64 %, and in Holland by 75 %. These rates of increase include adjustment to rising wage and price levels.

An investigation conducted by the International Labour Office into the costs of Social Security for 1963, which does not include, amongst other items, youth aid, reparations, rent allowances, maintenance allowances payable during military service, additional pensions in the public services, and some compensation payments, shows that the quota of the Federal Republic, at 15.3 %, occupied the second place amongst the 55 countries investigated.

The quotas of other countries were as follows:

Australia	8.0	Iceland	7.2	Holland	12.7
Belgium	13.8	Israel	4.9	Norway	10.6
Denmark	11.9	Italy	12.8	Austria	15.9
England	11.2	Japan		Poland	
Hungary	9.5	USA	6.2		

In the case of the East bloc countries the "net commodities product" was utilized in lieu of the GNP. This does not include, apart from other differences in method — governmental and a part of private services, so that it is, in comparison, lower than the GNP, and the reported expenditure on social services based on it appears to be relatively higher than in the other countries.

Supplementary promotion of Social Security

In this survey public social services only can be described. They are supplemented by various other measures undertaken by the State in other fields. The State promotes private provision for the future in many forms.

The Social Aspects of Taxation

In the case of wages and income tax, consideration is given to the financial position of the tax payer. Progression in wages and income tax first commences with an annual income of 11.000 DM for married persons, and 8.000 DM for single persons. These taxes are graded according to family status and the number of children. In order to give due consideration to the special character of the deduction of wages tax from income in comparison with the taxation of income from industry, rents, capital, and self-employment, a tax free amount for workers was introduced in wages tax. In the case of old and sick persons, as well as of handicapped persons, special rebates or deductions are allowable. Payments of insurance contributions, including those to private insurances, are also deductible. Rebates are allowable for self expenditure on vocational training and further training, for payments to pensions funds, and for extraordinary expenditure. Pensions from social insurance are taxable only as to their net yield, as a consequence of which tax is payable only in relatively rare cases. In the case of wealth tax, too, rebates are allowable on the grounds of family status and age. Seriously injured persons are not required to pay car tax.

The burden of taxation falling on a worker in receipt of average earnings (1969 = 992 DM per month), is wages tax at an average 10.2 % of earnings, plus church tax at 0.09 %; in consideration of family status, single persons pay 13.8 % plus 1.2 %; married persons with, for example, 3 children pay only 3.3 % plus 0.03 % of earnings as wages and church tax.

Further, governmental subsidies to a very considerable extent are payable to recipients of social benefits, the effects of which are evident particularly in housing.

Additional Fringe Benefits

By means of tax rebates the State facilitates the granting of private enterprise social benefits. If the continued payment of salaries to non-manual workers in the case of sickness, and, commencing 1970, of wages to manual workers, is left out of account, it will be seen that the bulk of industrial social benefits consists of superannuation payments in the event of disablement and in old age, or payments to survivors. Supplementary pensions in public law are described below in detail; they are also included in the following statements.

It is estimated that about two thirds of all workers in private industry are covered by superannuation schemes. In 1968 expenditure on supplementary benefits included 1.1 milliard DM for superannuation payments, and 0.5 milliard DM for survivors, together about 1.6 milliard DM. About one half each of this sum came from private enterprise employers and from the public services. Expenditure for works superannuation increased between 1957 and 1965 from about 2.4 milliard DM to 3.8 milliard DM; there is probably an amount of 55 milliard DM still available in the works funds; of this sum about 11 milliard is in the public services, which, on the other hand are paying about one half of current payments. The numbers of workers covered, and expenditure, increase as a general rule with the size of the undertaking.

Works superannuation schemes have assumed varied forms, namely works obligations to pay superannuation (about 30.000), works pensions funds providing legal entitlement (about 260), relief funds without legal entitlement (about 8—10.000), direct insurances with industrial insurance companies, and voluntary payment of higher contributions to pensions insurance. At supra-undertaking level there are so-called Guide Line Associations in the iron and steel producing industry, levy funds, group pensions funds, group relief funds and group insurance associations.

To a certain extent the Federal Government has taken over the relevant obligations of firms which have ceased to exist as a result of the war; payments are made by the Federal Insurance Office.

The Social Report 1970 calls attention to the fact that there are certain weaknesses in the system of works superannuation (loss of entitlement on change of job and dismissal, in the event of the bankruptcy of the firm, reckoning of payment from pensions insurance against superannuation entitlement, failure to adjust superannuation to increasing wages and salaries levels). Measures are to be taken to avoid the lapse of entitlement in the future.

Apart from superannuation schemes, other fringe benefits are provided by the enterprises; especially in the public services, grants are made in the case of sickness, supplementary children's allowances are payable to non-manual workers, and social supplements to manual workers. In private industry, too, works and service housing is provided, alternatively rent and house building supplements are payable. Many firms maintain convalescent homes for their workers, and Kindergartens — day nurseries — for the children of the workers. All these benefits are complementary to statutory schemes.

Support for Voluntary Organisations

In very many ways the State promotes and supports the work performed by voluntary organisations in the field of welfare, in particular that of the six top organisation and their specialist departments. (Workers Welfare, Charitable Association, German Red Cross, Diaconie Association, Jewish Cultural Community, Joint Welfare Association).

The voluntary welfare organisations give advice and assistance in the fields of training and education, health, welfare, and integration. For these purposes they maintain advice bureaux, day attendance centres and homes, and make themselves responsible for a variety of social assistance measures. The State supports all these activities by financial contributions from public funds. The Federal Government, the Federal Lands, and local authorities grant subsidies, contribute to the material and personnel expenses of the voluntary organisations, and grant long term loans. In view of their activities in the interests of the common weal, the organisations enjoy tax concessions; for instance, the fact that contributions to these organisations are tax free is of indirect assistance to them in the financing of their activities. Over and above such tax concessions, the State co-operates in the promotion of their benevolent activities by means of legislative and administrative measures, for instance it has endeavoured to help in overcoming the shortage of personnel by legislation (e.g. the Law on the Promotion of the Voluntary Social Year); it has also helped by imposing fines which are made payable to the voluntary organisations, and has sanctioned public collections in their favour.

Promotion of Capital Formation in the Hands of the Workers

The distribution of wealth in the Federal Republic of Germany is unequal. In 1960 1.7 % of private households owned about 35 % of the wealth held by all households, and 70 % of all productively utilised wealth.

Governmental measures are aimed at promoting the formation of capital in the hands of broader sectors of the population, in order to counter the further unilateral accumulation of wealth in the hands of the few, and to improve the financial security of individuals. Since, in cases where incomes are low, or children numerous, very little tax is payable, and very little rebate can be allowed on wages or income tax, the State grants special premiums on savings, particularly on savings for house building or the purchase of shares. In addition, payments for these purposes by the employer are free of tax and insurance contributions to an amount of 312 DM per annum. Whereas in 1961 only 50.000 workers availed themselves of the provisions of the first Capital Formation Law (Vermögensbildungsgesetz), by 1969 some 5 mill. had taken advantage of the improved conditions offered by the Second Capital Formation Law. In 1969 a total of 1.2 milliard DM was invested, an average of 270 DM per person.

The Third Capital Formation Law, enacted in the summer of 1970, increases the tax and social contributions free amount to 624 DM, and introduces, with effect from 1. 1. 1971, in lieu of the tax and contributions free amount, allowances to an amount of 30 % (in the case of more than 2 children 40 %) of the amount saved. It is anticipated that the number of savers taking advantage of this concession will have doubled by 1973.

Governmental funds at low rates of interest, or free of interest, are made available for the building of owner-occupier dwellings, and supplementary family loans are granted. Governmental holdings in some major industrial concerns have been liquidated, in some cases sold at reduced prices. The socio-political value of supplementary security provided by the possession of assets is — in the words of the Social Report — by no means diminished by the fact that it would be Utopian to assume that completely adequate social security for broad sectors of the population could be attained solely by means of such capital formation. The intention is to augment capital formation in the hands of the workers, in particular by means of profit sharing schemes.

Promotion of Youth

The major portion of public social services is devoted to old, sick, and disabled persons, and to widows and orphans. As a consequence of the division of governmental authority between the Federal Government, the Federal Lands and the Local Authorities it is, naturally, not so readily appreciated that public authorities have set up a very extensive system of training and education for juveniles — apart altogether from children's allowances, children's supplements, and training grants. Compulsory school attendance starts at the age of 6, and, generally speaking, continues for nine years of primary school education. The introduction of a tenth year, in differing forms of school, is under consideration. In the form of a pedagogic further development of the educational system, a division of the primary school into a Basic and Main School is under consideration. Secondary and Higher Schools serve the cause of further education. In 1967 some 7.9 million pupils were in attendance in 35.200 public and private schools of general education. Of these, 6 million were in attendance in primary and special schools, 709.000 in secondary schools, and 1.193.000 in higher schools. There were 320.000 full time teachers, and some 50.000 part- time teachers. In addition, there are numerous technical colleges, universities, and schools of advanced education. In the winter of 1968 there were 288.000 fully matriculated students in the 48 high schools of science.

Apart from free attendance in the primary schools, and in most Federal Lands, in the secondary and higher schools, the following are provided to a very considerable extent: exemption from school fees, free study materials, scholarships of all kinds, free dental care, free school meals, reduced fares and fare concessions for students and pupils, and many other forms of aid. In the urban and rural districts there are Juvenile Offices; in many instances special Youth Officers are installed, governmental and communal expenditure on Youth Welfare amounted in 1969 to 1.1 milliard DM. The Federal Government, in its annual Federal Youth Plans, has provided considerable sums for the promotion of Youth. A report on the situation of youth, and on the endeavours in the field of aid to youth, is submitted every 4 years to the Federal Parliament and the Federal Council.

The Federal Government, the Lands, Local Authorities, and School Aid Associations, expended on the education system: 1955 — 3.5 milliard DM, 1964 — 9.4 milliard DM,

1969 — about 15 milliard DM. For the universities and the schools of advanced technical education, about 2.8 milliard DM was provided in 1969. A considerable increase in this expenditure is anticipated (1980 — about 100 milliard DM). In June 1970 the Federal Government submitted its report on education policy, giving an account of the most important developments in the school and high school spere since 1945, and of its education policy objectives.

Overall economic and social background of Social Services

Production and distribution of economic wealth

Future disbursements on social services will be more easily financed by all gainfully employed persons if the economy continues to expand at the present rate. The gross national product (GNP) is expected to exceed 675 milliard DM in 1970, and so to have increased nominally six and a half-fold in the last 20 years, real five-fold (about 525 milliard DM). The rate of growth of the GNP amounted in 1965 to 9.4 %, in 1966 to 6.6 %, in 1967 to 0.8 %, in 1968 to 8.9 %, in 1969 to 11.6 %, and will amount in 1970 to 12.4 %.

Year	GNP at market price		National Income		National Income per employed person	
	in millrd. DM	1950 = 100	in millrd. DM	1950 = 100	in DM/year	1950 = 100
1950	97,9	100	75,2	100	3759	100
1955	180,4	184	139,5	186	6109	163
1960	302,3	309	229,8	306	8982	247
1965	460,4	492	343,6	455	13083	348
1966	490,7	502	364,5	485	13924	373
1967	494,6	506	361,6	481	14266	379
1968	538,5	561	415,3	552	15766	411
1969	601,0	616	457,3	608	17148	456
1970	675,7	692	519,1	690	.	.
1971	687,0	702	.	.		
1972	729,0	745	.	.		
1973	774,0	791	.	.		

The following table provides information on the distribution of the product of the economy, as well as the share falling to pensions from social insurance and other public institutions (social aid, equalisation of burdens) and to Civil Service pensions. The table also permits a comparison between social services and other sources of income.

Income, Consumption and Savings of Private Households in milliard DM.

	1950	1955	1960	1965	1968	1969
Gross Wages and Salaries	39,8	73,9	124,2	202,7	232,3	260,6
-- Taxes and S.I.* Contributions	5,0	10,5	19,6	34,6	45,3	54,5
= Net Wages and Salaries	34,8	63,4	104,6	168,7	187,0	206,6
+ Transfer of Income	(11,7)	(20,2)	(36,7)	(57,6)	(72,7)	(78,0)
Pensions from S.I. and other public sources	9,6	16,2	30,8	48,3	61,5	65,6
Civil Service Pensions (net)	2,1	4,0	5,9	9,3	11,2	12,3
= Mass Income	46,4	83,6	141,3	225,8	259,7	287,5
+ Private Drawings of Self-employed	18,9	29,7	44,0	65,3	78,4	89,4
- Disposable Income of Private Households	65,4	113,3	185,4	291,1	338,1	373,9
- Private Consumption	63,4	106,2	170,0	255,7	297,3	328,2
= Private Savings less Transfer of Assets	2,0	7,1	15,4	35,4	40,8	45,6
Savings Quota in %	3,2	6,3	8,3	12,2	12,1	12,2

1968 and 1969 provisional figures

*S.I. = Social Insurance

Structure of Employment — Labour Force

For the year 1969 the gainfully employed population (including soldiers) is estimated at 26.8 mill., namely 17.2 mill. men and 9.2 mill. women, i.e. about 60 % of the male population and about 30 % of the female population.

The quota, as a whole, but particularly in the case of the younger age groups, has declined since 1955, for the reason, amongst others, that the younger age groups are continuing longer in education and training. Of men over 65 rather more than one fifth are still employed. Employment amongst women aged 25 to 55 is on the increase. In 1965 more than four fifths of the gainfully employed population, (excluding soldiers) were in paid employment as employees or public officials, namely 21.3 mill. persons, or 81 %. Self-employed persons numbered 2.9 mill. or 11.2 %. The number of employed family members was about 2 million, or 7.8 %. Their number has been reduced by one half since 1950. In contrast, the quota of employees in employment, and of public officials, has increased since 1950 from 69 % to 81 %.

Amongst those in paid employment, the non-manual workers group is continuously on the increase. In 1950 the comparable figures of manual and non-manual workers were 1.000 to 324, in 1969 1.000 to 596. Of the total number of 20 mill. in paid employment in 1969, 12.53 mill. were manual workers and 7.47 mill. non-manual workers. This regrouping process has a permanent effect on the social security system.

Of all gainfully employed persons in 1968 there were:
2.6 mill. in agriculture and forestry,
12.5 mill. in industrial production,
4.7 mill. in commerce, transport and communications,
6.5 mill. in other branches of the economy.

The numbers in agriculture and forestry have declined by about one half since 1950, and will continue to decrease. The further development of social security for farmers and retired farmers is, therefore, of especial importance.

Movements in Population and Occupation

Year	Total Population in 1.000s	Employed in 1.000s	Population in %	Unemployed in 1.000s	in % of employed population
1950	47 850	21 960	45,9	1584	7,2
1955	50 186	24 165	48,2	935	3,9
1960	55 785	26 247	47,0	271	1,0
1965	59 297	27 153	45,8	147	0,5
1966	59 793	27 082	45,3	161	0,7
1967	59 949	26 292	43,8	459	2,1
1968	60 463	26 342	43,6	323	1,5
1969	61 195	26 822	43,8	179	0,9

In addition to an increase in productivity, the economic product of the Federal Republic has been achieved by increased employment. The number of employed employees rose between 1950 and 1969 from 14 mill. (excluding Berlin) to 21.3 mill., i.e. by more than 50 %. By the middle of 1965 the number of unemployed had fallen to 70.000; it then rose to more than 600.000 in the years 1966/67, to fall again by the middle of 1970 to 95.000. Full employment reached its highest level in 1970, when almost 900.000 unfilled vacancies were registered. In order to cope with the high demands for labour, some 1.8

mill. foreign workers were employed in the Federal territory in 1970. For the purpose of recruiting this labour, the Federal Government has concluded agreements with the supplying countries. Of the 1.8 mill. foreign workers

about 370.000 came from Italy
about 389.000 came from Yugoslavia
about 328.000 came from Turkey,
about 229.000 came from Greece
about 166.000 came from Spain
about 40.000 came from Portugal

A great number of these foreign workers remain in the Federal Republic for many years, many of them with their marriage partners. In 1968 there were about 400.000 children of foreign workers in the Federal Republic, of whom more than one third were attending school.

In the event of unemployment in the Federal Republic of Germany, precautions taken are aimed from the outset at the maintenance of full employment, and, consequently, at the avoidance of unemployment. Since full employment has been reached, there is at present little recourse to unemployment benefit and unemployment assistance. Of particular importance for labour market policy in recent years have been the support measures undertaken for areas with a high unemployment quota (e.g. the districts contiguous to the eastern zonal boundaries), and measures for the promotion of all-the-year-round employment in the building industry (productive winter building operations).

The placing of workers in occupations with a demand for labour is the responsibility of the Federal Institute for Labour, which is also responsible for unemployment insurance, and which acts as agent for unemployment assistance. It is also responsible for careers' guidance, and particularly for the placing of apprentices, above all for juveniles entering employment for the first time. In the course of labour placing, special attention is devoted to the requirements of particular groups, of long term unemployed, and of seriously injured persons. It is estimated that 4 mill. persons are suffering from some form of physical hanicap. The Seiously Injured Persons Law facilitates the preferential integration of seriously injured persons into employment. It imposes a duty on firms to employ a defined number of such persons, and permits dismissal only with official sanction.

In order to facilitate the rapid and complete integration of handicapped persons, the Federal Government drew up in April 1970 an Action Programme for the Promotion of the Rehabilitation of Handicapped Persons. The number of such persons in the Federal Republic of Germany is estimated at 4 million. Improved rehabilitation schemes are to make it possible for them to take their part in the life of the community. For this purpose it is particularly necessary to ensure improved co-ordination of rehabilitation, the extension of a system of linked clinics and training centres, and an improvement of rehabilitation procedure in individual cases. The training and retraining of handicapped persons is designed to transcend the bounds of hitherto customary occupations. Further, the labour market and the possibilities of employment open to them must be kept under constant review. The co-ordination of research and documentation, uniform rehabilitation statistics, the overcoming of building and technical obstacles, improved publicity, in particular with the object of breaking down prejudice against handicapped persons, and the implementation of measures designed to enable them to take part in everyday life outside their work and occupation, are further tasks which must be accomplished in order to help them medically, educationally, occupationally and socially.

Conditions of employment

The State has issued many varied regulations governing conditions of employment. The protection of labour serves the purpose of the avoidance of industrial accidents and industrial diseases. Legal regulations and prohibitions govern the employment of women and juveniles. The job of a seriously injured worker enjoys legal protection. Regulations govern maximum permissible hours of work. The regulation of terms and conditions of employment is a matter for the trade unions and the employers' associations.

The Vocational Education Law of 1969 laid the foundations for a modern and dynamic form of occupational education; It serves the implementation of the right of everyman, as guaranteed in the Basic Law, to an equal start and equal chances in the matter of occupational education. For the whole field — vocational training, further training, and retraining — a uniform Federal basis has been established; all fields are regarded as being links in a chain of a uniform and lifelong training and educational process, closely related and harmonised. The Vocational Education Law affirms the dual system of training in office and workshop and in Vocational Schools, and adapts it to the up-to-date requirements of society and of the economy.

In the years between 1960 and 1965, and in 1969/70, wages and salaries rose more rapidly than in any previous period — in so far as the records of wages movements can be accepted with any degree of reliability. Wage levels and wages movements are shown in the sector "Pensions Insurance". The wages quota (the quota of gross incomes from paid employment in relation to the national income) increased from 58.6 % in 1950, over 60.8 % in 1960, to 64.9 % in 1968. If, however, the increase in the number of workers is taken into account (per capita quota), the wages quota has not increased.

Disposable incomes are distributed in a highly varied manner amongst different sections of the employed population. According to the microcensus of 1968, 40.6 % of the selfemployed, 30.4 % of public officials, and 13.1 % of white collar workers, were in receipt of a net income of more than 1.200 DM per month, but only 0.5 % of manual workers. Conversely 49 % of manual workers had less than 600 DM per month, but only 17.7 % of the self-employed, 8.8 % of public officials, and 37.6 % of white collar workers.

The standard of living of the workers has also improved considerably, even if the higher prices are taken into account. For average working class households they rose from 79

Brutto Income Groups — According to their Position in their Occupation — 1968[1]

in %

Thereof with net monthly income of .... to under .... DM	Self-employed	Public officials Judges	non-manual workers	manual workers	total
under 150	1,8	–	5,5	6,3	5,3
150 – 300	3,7	1,0	7,2	9,0	7,5
300 – 600	12,2	7,5	24,9	33,7	27,6
600 – 800	16,0	19,3	23,1	37,2	29,9
800 – 1200	25,7	41,7	26,2	13,3	20,2
1200 – 1800	18,5	23,7	9,5	0,5	6,3
1800 and more	22,1	6,7	3,6	–	3,4

1) Less employed persons who have not made a statement of their income, as well as self-employed persons in agriculture and employed family members.

points in 1950, to 100 points in 1962, and to 120.6 points in 1969. The increase in real wages, after deduction of the costs of living from nominal wages, is also considerable. The index of real wages had more than doubled between 1950 and 1965, and by 1969 stood at 240 (1950 = 100).

The situation of the workers has also improved since 1950 in respect of their conditions of employment. For example, average agreed weekly hours in industry and in the public services decreased between 1959 and 1969 by 3.5 hours for manual workers and 2.9 hours for non-manual workers to 41 hours. Annual holidays, under the influence of the Federal Holidays Law, have considerably increased. The introduction of paid additional holidays for educational purposes is under consideration.

Health services

The overall picture of public social services must be seen against the background of their public efficacy. Services which are regarded as a matter of course in the Federal Republic, and are seldom mentioned, are elsewhere hailed as great achievements. For example, in the same manner as the public transport system (streets, railways, Federal Post, and communications) is a necessary condition for the functioning of the economy, it is also a necessary condition for the award and utilisation of social benefits that the moneys disbursed can be used for the payment of goods and services.

In the case of sickness, and for the preservation of public health, there are available in the Federal Republic of Germany doctors and hospitals, and a very extensive system of public health services. At the end of 1968 there were 91.000 doctors, 31.000 dental surgeons, nearly 20.000 pharmaceutical chemists and 180.000 nursing personnel. The density of medical practitioners is one of the highest in the world, — one doctor to 665 of the population, one dental surgeon to 1936 of the population. The registration and the activities of medical practitioners, dental surgeons, chemists, midwives, nursing sisters, and similar persons, is regulated by law. In more than 3.600 hospitals and institutions 619.000 beds are available. The hospitals are maintained in part by public authorities (local authorities, the Federal Lands, social insurance Funds), in part by private bodies (denominational and voluntary aid organisations, private sanatoria). For the modernisation and rationalisation of the second types, the Federal Government has provided interest free loans. In 1968 almost 9 mill. people were treated in hospitals for some 218 mill. days; the average period per patient spent in hospital displays a sinking tendency: 1968 — 25.9 days, 1960 — 28.7 days.

The public health system has been systematically developed. In all urban and rural districts there are Public Health Offices — public health control authorities, the school health service, maternity advice bureaux, care of consumptives, measures for combatting drug addiction, and many other relevant services. Public inoculations and immunisations are aimed at the prevention or the spread of infectious diseases. The Public Health Offices, and many other public and private bodies, are devoting a great deal of attention to highly prevalent ailments (cancer, rheumatism, circulatory ailments). In the framework of public health services, mass examinations are conducted, particularly for the detection of tuberculosis of the lungs. For the detection and treatment of venereal diseases there has been special legislative provision since 1927 (the latest version in 1953). The Federal Epidemics Law contains, inter alia, regulations for the control of environmental conditions (pure water, disposal of sewage, extermination of vermin provision is also made for compensation for injuries resulting from inoculations, and for carriers banned from following their normal occupation. There are also Blood Donor Centres, receiving financial aid from the government. For blind persons, for the deaf and hard of hearing, for persons with speech faults, for physically handicapped and mentally disordered persons, for children with deformities, a great many special public and private schools and institutes have been established.

In the 502 Public Health Offices in the Federal Republic are employed: 4.800 medical practitioners, 2.500 school dentists, 4.100 social workers, 705 medical technical assistants.

The production and distribution of food, the manufacture of medicines, the cleanliness of air and water, are legally regulated and controlled. Within the Federal Government the Ministry for Youth, Family, and Health is responsible for all questions of public health, protection against ionisation rays, protection of the public against misleading statements about medicines and food. A great deal of authority in the framework of health legislation is exercised by the Federal Health Branch in Berlin, which has the support of a Federal Health Council. A Federal Committee for Popular Guidance is concerned with the promotion of a healthy way of life, and the avoidance of illness.

Questions of pure air, noise abatement, the quality and hygiene of water and sewage, are the responsibility of the Federal Ministry of the Interior.

Groups in need of special aid

Certain large groups of people are dependent on aid, not only from the State, but also from other groups within society. These include in particular the following groups: In the Federal Republic of Germany there were in 1968 some 4 million = 6.9 % of the population — persons who were physically, mentally and psychically handicapped. On the basis of a supplementary questionaire to the microcensus of 1968 the Statistical Federal Office ascertained the number as 4.1 million, of whom 2.8 million were males, and 1.3 mill. females. That is to say, that of 100 men, ten reported that they were handicapped as a result of a longstanding illness or infirmity, of 100 women, on the other hand, only four; of men over 50 years of age about one quarter were counted amongst the handicapped persons. The most frequent causes in the case of men were: war injuries — 39 %, illness — 19 %, — not counting industrial diseases and infantile paralysis — industrial injuries — 12.5 %. In the case of women nearly half the cases of physical or mental handicap were due to illness. More than 1.3 million persons, 37 % of the men and 26 % of the women, were handicapped by reason of the loss, crippling, or other serious ailments of the limbs, four fifths of the handicaps of the men, and about one half of the ailments and infirmities of the women, are officially recognised. About 500.000 persons are without any fixed address, and are inadequately accomodated. Of these more than one half are children.

During the last few years there were an average of 50 to 60.000 persons in penal institutes; 38 % of them were recidivists.

Price increases are felt much more acutely in the household of recipients of social benefits, especially pensioners households, than in those of wage earners. Their cost of living has been rising particularly steeply for a long time, e.g. in 1969 by 3.4 %, 1970 by 3.9 %. Since 1962 the cost of living for pensioners households has risen from 100 to 124, and to about 127 in 1970.

Many private and public bodies devote themselves to the care of the older generation. Aid for the aged is being stepped up by towns and communities. Increasing numbers of old peoples' homes are being opened. Home building for older persons is being promoted by the provision of public loans.

The system of private insurance

In an industrial society the urge to make provisions for the exigencies of life in the form of cash benefits is constantly growing, that is to say, not in the form of benefits in kind, e.g., maintenance within the family group. Generally speaking, this need cannot be fully satisfied through public social security. In so far as the gaps are not closed by super-annuation schemes, either at undertaking or supra-undertaking level, additional personal provision in the form of private insurance is necessary. In the degree to which wages and salaries are higher than is necessary to cover the actual cost of living, it is that much easier to pay the premiums. This explains the increase in the number of policies, and of the sums insured, with private insurance companies taken out during the last two decades, despite the preceding currency reform and the devaluation of previous entitlements.

At the end of 1969, there were under the supervision of the Federal Supervisory Office for Insurance and House Building Savings Schemes: 100 Life Insurance Companies, 186 Pensions Funds, 111 Death Benefit Funds, and 96 Health Insurance Companies. Contributions to these three sectors amounted to 12 milliard DM, benefits to 6 milliard DM.

At the end of 1969 52.5 million policies were in force in Life Insurance, with an insured sum of 210 milliard DM. Since 1957 it is, in particular, pensions insurances that have been on the increase; their quota has risen from 0.2 to 1.0 %. Premium income in Life Insurance amounted to 9.1 milliard DM, benefits to 2.7 milliard DM. The raising of the compulsory insurance ceiling for non-manual workers in 1957 and 1965, and the abolition of this ceiling on 1.1.68, was accompanied by the opportunity to contract out of statutory insurance by taking out a private policy. In 1957 almost 64.700, in 1965 82.000, and in 1968 220.000 white collar workers availed themselves of this opportunity.

In private Health Insurance there were about 6,2 million policies in force in 1969 (insurance against costs arising during sickness); premiums amounted to 2.3 milliard DM, benefits to 1.6 milliard DM.

Assets in Life Insurance amounted to 48. milliard DM, in Pensions Funds to 8 milliard DM, in Death Benefit Funds to 250 million DM, and in Health Insurance to 2 milliard DM.

The Social Report

The Social Report was the name given until 1969 to the report submitted annually by the Federal Government from 1950 to 1969 on the basis of the Pensions Insurance Amendments Laws in connection with pensions adjustments (in future: Pensions Adjustments Law). In April 1970, with the Social Report announced in the governmental statement of policy, a comprehensive survey of the development tendencies, and the objects of social policy, was presented for the first time by the Federal Government. The Social Report depicts the basic trends of change and tensions present in an expanding economy, inter alia between individual affluence and inadequate social provision, between a functionally efficient social insurance system and the hazards to which individual groups are exposed, between the environmental problems, on the one hand of urban agglomerations, on the other hand of rural districts, between desirable full employment and the scarcity of labour for social services, between great increases in income for some, whilst other groups lag behind. In the field of social security, the Report bases itself on the trend to expansion in social insurance, and insists that the system of social insurance should be made more readily intelligible, above all by the introduction of automatic data processing in pensions insurance, and of a social legislation code. The Social Report 1970 — Section A announces the following intentions of the Federal Government:

- raising of the insurability ceiling in Health Insurance for non-manual workers, and its adjustment to salary movements;
- inclusion of self-employed farmers in Health Insurance;
- improvement of social insurance for married women, in the first place in the case of divorce;
- accident insurance for school children and students;
- relaxation of the fixed age of retirement in pensions insurance, and the introduction of a flexible age of retirement;
- functional and mobility adapted amendments in works superannuation schemes;
- improvement of Land Surrender Pensions for independent farmers (draft law already tabled);
- pensions to be payable to orphans, even when married;
- improvement of benefits in Social Health Insurance;
- Federal subsidies for hospital financing;
- improvements in the field of rehabilitation;
- improvement in socio-political measures for the benefit of the older generation (Old Age Assistance);
- unification of the system of Equalisation of Family Burdens — increase of children's allowances in 1970;
- extension of the promotion of vocational training.

All these projects are at present in the course of preparation. An expert committee is already at work on the preparation of the Social Legislation Code, and the further development of Health Insurance. Important socio-political and other plans are to come up for discussion in the „Socio-Political Discussion Group" of the Federal Ministry of Labour.

Section B of the Social Report contains the Social Budget 1969/70. The Chapter "Overall Picture of Modern Social Security" goes into the details of the Social Budget.

Summary of Old Age, Disablement, and Survivors' Security

Old age, disablement, and survivors' security includes

the Pensions Insurance of Manual Workers
the Pensions Insurance of Non-Manual Workers   for Employees
the Miners' Special Scheme Pensions Insurance

the Pensions Insurance of Self-employed Craftsmen
the Pensions Security for Farmers   for self-employed persons
the Pensions Insurance for Free Professions
the Civil Service Pensions

The costs of these services will amount in 1970 to about 65 milliard DM (including Civil Service Pensions); that is to say, more than half the costs of all social services.

The pensions insurance of employees

It is estimated that almost nine tenths of all old and disabled persons, and of widows and orphans, are mainly dependent for their livelihood on benefits from the pensions insurance of employees; the number continues to increase. This situation arises from the fact that four fifths of the gainfully employed population are employees, that the age groups in the population are changing, and that cash benefits, particularly as a result of the annual adjustment of pensions to rising earnings, have reached a comparatively high level. Since the introduction of pensions insurance 79 years ago, its scope, and the increase of contributions and benefits, have advanced without any long periods of interruption. During the 21 years since 1949, pensions insurance has, by virtue of the gradual increase of contributions and benefits, and of the Pensions Insurance Reform Law of 1957, come to the forefront. In its almost 80 years of history, pensions insurance has at no time enjoyed so continuous and favourable a development as during these 21 years. Even the recession of 1966/67 did not bring any change in the intermediate term development. Pensions during this period increased far more rapidly than prices, and, during the first 10 years, more rapidly than wages. During the period 1957 to 1970, average gross earnings and average pensions have risen by more than 150 percent.

"The Pensions Mound"

The future of pensions insurance will be largely determined by the increase in the number of old persons, and consequently on the number of pensions payable. These factors must, of course, be seen in relation to the number of insured persons at any one time, which again depends on the birthrate, the quota of employed persons, and, amongst other things, the migration of workers. The unfavourable relation of pensions payable to the number of insured persons in this decade has been given the name of "The Pensions Mound". The ascent of this "Pensions Mound" became plainly visible after the second world war. From the starting point in 1958 (see table) about four fifths of the ascent have been accomplished. The peak will be reached in the years 1976—1980. From that time onwards commences a descent, and, in 1985, the position will again be below that in 1970. The disparity between the development of manual workers' pensions insurance and non-manual workers pensions insurance, as well as the Miners' Special Scheme Insurance, is due in greater measure to the changes in the numbers of insured persons arising from structural changes in employment than to the number of pensions payable.

Probable development of the Pensions/Insured Persons Relation in Manual Workers Insurance (M.W.I.) and Non-Manual Workers Insurance (N.M.W.I.) from 1958 to 1985 — in extracts.

Year	ArV MW			AnV NMW			ArV+AnV MW + NMW		
	Insured Persons in 1000s	Pensions	Percent	Ins. pers. in 1000s	pensions	perc.	Ins. pers. in 1000s	MW + NMW Ins.	per cent
1958	·	·	·	·	·	·	16816	5834	34,7
1960	·	·	·	·	·	·	17522	6555	37,4
1965	·	·	·	·	·	·	18469	7569	41,0
1967	11581	6136	53,0	6469	1928	29,8	18050	8064	44,7
1968	11601	6304	54,3	6759	2010	29,7	18360	8314	45,3
1969	11712	6428	54,9	6888	2085	30,3	18600	8513	45,8
1970	11694	6547	56,0	6994	2155	30,8	18688	8702	46,6
1971	11676	6653	57,0	7102	2224	31,3	18778	8877	47,3
1975	11574	6951	60,1	7496	2457	32,7	19070	9407	49,3
1980	11514	6922	60,1	8074	2616	32,4	19588	9538	48,7
1985	11457	6622	57,8	8671	2659	30,7	20128	9281	46,1

The number of insured persons and of pensions payable are based on calculations pursuant to the 3rd Amending Law of 1969.

Financial Forecasts

Income, expenditure, and reserves are annually estimated and registered for the following 15 years. These forecasts are influenced in the main by movements in earnings, the numbers of insured persons, the numbers of pensions payable, and the amount of contributions. The enormous increase in income and expenditure must be adjudged within the framework of overall economic developments, and particularly of the increase of earnings. The increase of expenditure is due, apart from the increase in earnings, above all to the increase in the number of pensions, the annual adjustment of pensions to rising earnings, and the consequent increased contribution rates. Contributions have risen with effect from 1970, to 17 % of insurable earnings, and will rise in 1973 to 18 %. These rates will suffice, on present showing, to support the financial burden of the Pensions Mound, even if reserves do not continue to grow simultaneously.

The Pensions Insurance of Employees is spread over amongst three schemes, manual workers insurance, non-manual workers insurance, and Miners' Special Scheme insurance. The groups of persons affected are variable, but the legislative provision is uniform. In the Miners' Special Scheme, higher benefits are payable under conditions specifically applicable to mining, though these are assessed in principle according to the same pensions formulae.

Development, Income and Expenditure — estimated with effect from 1969. Increase in earnings from 1971 5.8 % contribution rate from 1970, 17 %; from 1973, 18 %; in the Miners Special Scheme 23.5 %

Year	noome in mill. DM		Expenditure in mill. DM		for helath care measures
	total	from contributions	total	Pensions	

Pensions Insurance of Manual Workers

Year	total	from contributions	total	Pensions	for helath care measures
1950	2863	2212	2551	2154	133
1955	6318	4324	4866	4027	289
1960	13032	8904	12164	9366	677
1965	20521	14584	19024	14428	1347
1968	24460	17220	26306	20174	1181
1969	27893	20300	29608	22750	1470
1970	31403	24414	31729	24728	1467[1]
1971	33204	25820	33922	26570	1540
1975	46476	33826	46230	36928	1905
1980	61075	44227	60692	48750	2490
1985	77542	58279	77025	61851	3282

Pensions Insurance of Non-Manual Workers

Year	total	from contributions	total	Pensions	for helath care measures
1950	1123	1001	998	864	49
1955	2878	2049	2192	1917	87
1960	6278	4580	5719	4893	184
1965	10206	7926	9761	8137	444
1968	13831	11403	13553	11431	446
1969	15771	13100	15231	12870	515
1970	17781	15409	16401	14150	570
1971	19220	16561	17790	15375	613
1975	27684	23603	28253	22398	825
1980	38929	34588	40021	31848	1209
1985	56030	50672	51722	43701	1772

Pensions Insurance of Manual and Non-manual Workers together

Year	total	from contributions	total	Pensions	for helath care measures
1950	3986	3213	3549	3018	182
1955	9196	6373	7058	5944	376
1960	19310	13484	17883	14259	861
1965	30727	22510	28785	22565	1791
1968	38291	28623	39859	31605	1627
1969	43664	33400	44839	35620	1985
1970	49184	39823	48130	38878	2037
1971	52424	42381	51712	41945	2153
1975	74160	57429	74483	59326	2730
1980	100004	78815	100713	80598	3699
1985	133572	108951	128747	105552	5054

Miners' Special Scheme Insurance Pensions

Year	total	from contributions	total	Pensions	for helath care measures
1950	616	465	605	546	7
1955	1368	769	1274	1145	21
1960	2726	1025	2688	2386	43
1965	4045	1205	4047	3510	56
1968	5411	973	5411	3705	45
1969	4860	1004	4860	4104	58
1970	5110	1010	5110	4259	68
1971	5416	1090	5416	4486	68
1975	7195	1162	7195	5909	85
1980	9377	1255	9377	7547	113
1985	11228	1313	11228	8621	150

The reduction is due to the introduction of Continued Payment of wages to manual workers during sickness. In compting totals, eht amounts due to refunds in Transferable Insurance, and for pensions payable to independent craftsmen, must be deducted.

Old age and survivors' pensions of self-employed persons

For self-employed persons in the Federal Republic of Germany there are three special forms of statutory insurance, in addition to the continued voluntary insurance of employees, namely Old Age Pensions for Farmers, Self-Employed Artisans' Insurance, and Free Professions Insurance.

In 1968 there were 2.9 million self-employed persons, of these some 850.000 were engaged in agriculture and forestry, 750.000 as independent craftsmen, some 250.000 in the free professions, and there were about 6 million other self-employed persons. For the larger professional and vocational groups there already exists, therefore, a form of compulsory insurance. It must also be remembered that provision for old age and for survivors in the case of self-employed persons is characterised by the fact that provision from private soucres (the possibility of continuing in employment, support by children, private means, life insurance) plays a greater role than in the case of wage and salary earners, and is often combined with statutory pensions insurance.

Statutory pensions and survivors' insurance in the case of self-insured persons is so varied in nature that it is possible only to describe the provisions for different groups separately. Farmers and employed members of their families receive a pension as a supplement to the income still coming to them from the farm (Altenteil) after retirement. Provision for self employed craftsmen is made by a special form of compulsory insurance within the framework of the manual workers scheme. More than half of the free professions are covered by compulsory insurance pursuant to Federal or Land laws. Whereas only certain small groups in business are compulsorily insurable, it is probably in wholesale and retail trade, and in other independent businesses, that the larger proportion of those persons are to be found who continue as voluntary contributors to statutory insurance. The number of self-employed persons voluntarily paying contributions to pensions insurance is included in the total of voluntary contributors; see the sector "Groups of Persons" in the following chapter.

Common to all current forms of statutory insurance is the factor that they take full account of the needs and wishes of the individual groups affected, so that here, too, a special form of statutory insurance meets the needs of self-employed persons. In contrast to the social security of employees, that of the self-employed is, with some exceptions, limited to basic provision. There is no limitation to the insurable ceiling, nor of to the right of continued voluntary insurance based on income levels.

It must be remembered that farmers, self-employed craftsmen and voluntary contributors, receive, with certain limitations, a governmental subsidy to their pensions. In the case of the free professions this is at the moment not the case — except for voluntary contributors to non-manual workers insurance. In order to mitigate the consequences of the war, the War Pensions and Related Services and the Equalisation of Burdens Laws, which do not otherwise distinguish between employed and self-emloyed persons, assume responsibility for the retirement pensions of self-employed persons, with due consideration to their special circumstances (see "Equalisation of Burdens" and "War Pensions and Related Services"). The security of self-employed persons in their old age, and that of their survivors, is thus largely ensured, even though in varied forms. For self-employed persons, above all in trade and industry, who so far have no form of insurance cover, the introduction of old age pensions is under consideration.

Manual workers pensions insurance
Non-manual workers pensions insurance
Miners' special scheme pensions insurance

Introduction

Since the introduction of pensions insurance almost 80 years ago (1891), its development and extension, and the increase of contributions and benefits, have been a continuous process, without any long breaks. The Inaugural Law on Disablement and Old Age Pensions of 1889 was followed in 1905 by the so-called Amending Legislation, and in 1911 by the Consolidation of the Imperial Insurance Code, and by the Non-Manual Workers Insurance Law. Since that time pensions have also been payable to widows and orphans. The first world war and its aftermath brought a great many changes.

In 1916 the 65 years limit for pensions was introduced, without consideration to disablement. In 1923 current Land legislation governing miners' insurance was consolidated in the Imperial Miners' Special Scheme Law (Reichsknappschaftsgesetz). Between 1924 and 1928 a whole series of improvements were effected. The short period during which benefits were reduced, namely between 1929 and 1934, was followed by minor improvements between 1937 and 1942. As a consequence of the Deduction from Earnings Ordinance of 1942 (in lieu of affixing stamps), benefits became payable on an insurable earnings related basis.

Following an interval occasioned by the end of the war there commenced in 1949 a new period of improved benefits and higher pensions. During this period the legislator enacted annually a general increase in pensions, with the exception of the two years 1950 and 1952, in addition to a great many improvements of the conditions under which pensions are payable. Of outstanding importance were the Social Insurance Adjustment Law of 1949, and the Reform of Pensions Insurance of 1957.

Pensions were increased annually — with the exception of the year 1958 — in such a manner that the difference between newly awarded pensions and existing pensions did not become any larger than that which arose from the failure to adjust pensions in 1958. The 13the Pensions Adjustment, increasing pensions by 5.5 % with effect from 1. 1. 71, has now been enacted.

In 1960 the integration of expelles and refugees into pensions insurance was implemented. The original compensation principle, pursuant to which the pensions administrations in the Federal Republic were obliged to meet claims against pensions administrations outside the Federal Republic, was replaced by the integration principle. Expellees and refugees were treated as though their insurance life had been spent in the Federal Republic of Germany. The financial basis was provided by the levy procedure of 1957, modified and amended in 1969.

In addition to minor admendments designed to bring changes in pension insurance into line with changes in other fields of legislation, a first attempt was made in 1965 to draw conclusions from the experiences gained in the previous 8 years in the matter of pensions assessments. The first Pensions Insurance Amendment Law came into force, which effected alterations in certain details of pensions assessment. In 1964 the Insurance Adjustment Law regulating relations between the manual and non-manual workers pensions insurance schemes was revised. A very decisive influence, above all on the financial situation, was exercised by the Finance Adjustment Act of 1967, which, as a consequence of the financial recession of 1966/67, led to a partial suspension of Federal subsidies up to the year 1971, but which, on the other hand, abolished the insurance ceiling in non-manual workers insurance. The Third Pensions Insurance Amendment Law of 1969 may be regarded as a finalisation of the financial measures inaugurated in 1967. It fixed contribution rates for the period up to 1985 with the object of surmounting the "Pensions Mound", levelling out the divergent financial assets position of the different schemes, and of including the non-manual workers pensions insurance scheme in the responsibility for the financial security of the manual workers schemes.

With effect from 1. 1. 1970, the contribution pensioners were required to pay to Health Insurance has been cancelled. This contribution became payable with effect from 1. 1. 1968 to the amount of 2 % of the pension. The date of the preparations for the 13th Pensions Adjustment Law has been brought forward. The Federal Government has recently submitted to Parliament a report on the shortcomings of pensions insurance, and has made proposals for pensions to be payable to divorced wives. A draft law is already before Parliament, the purpose of which is to improve compensation in the field of social insurance for the victims of National Socialist persecution.

The pensions insurance schemes of manual and non-manual workers, and of the Miners' Special Scheme, will be here presented jointly; attention will be called to any divergencies which exist.

The functions of pensions insurance

The functions of the manual and non-manual workers' pension insurance, and of the Miners' Special Scheme, are to ensure the maintenance, improvement, or restoration of the employability of the insured persons, but above all to provide pensions for insured persons and their survivors. Pensions insurance also undertakes as an obligation the payment, or refund, of pensioners' contributions to Health Insurance. Expenditure on pensions accounts for nearly 85 % of all relevant expenditure, and thus tops the list, followed by the Health Insurance of pensioners at 8 %, again higher than the costs of rehabilitation for insured persons at 4 %.

Scope

Pensions insurance is a compulsory form of insurance related to the nature of employment, and does not require the consent of the insured person. Certain exemptions are possible (non-insurability and specific exemption); both forms may be annuled retrospectively by retrospective payment of contributions. Apart from compulsory insurance there is also an entitlement to continuation in insurance, which can be exercised in the form of voluntary contributions or voluntary payment of higher contributions.

The number of persons insured for pensions amounted in 1968 to about 26 million. In manual workers insurance, including self-employed craftsmen, some 12.2 million were compulsorily insured, in non-manual workers insurance 7.0 million. The number of volontarily insured persons in manual workers' insurance can be estimated at 3,8 mill., in non-manual workers' insurance at 2,3 mill., a total of 6,1 million. According to the microcensus of 1968 some 765.000 persons had paid voluntary contributions in the preceding twelve months (April 1967 to March 1968), whereas 5,4 million were in the group of insured persons who had qualified for a pension but had no longer paid contributions (latent insured persons). The number of persons voluntarily paying contributions has continuously decreased during the last few years, for example between 1966 and 1968 by about 18 %. In the Miners' Special Scheme Pensions Insurance there were at the end of 1969 about 353.000 insured persons; the highest number insured under this scheme stood, in 1958, almost twice as high.

The number of persons insured under manual and non-manual workers insurance cannot be ascertained with exactitude. This will not be possible until insurance code numbers have been allocated, since such numbers are essential for the operation of electronic data processing installations. It is intended to allocate a code number to every insured person during the next few years. At the end of 1969 about 4,5 mill. insurance code numbers had already been allocated, and the corresponding accounts had been opened for the insured persons.

At the moment the principle proof of membership held by the insured person is his Insurance Card, light yellow in colour in the case of manual workers, and light green in the case of non-manual workers, numbered consecutively.

In these cards, to which the stamps are affixed, are entered the amount of earnings in respect of which the employer has paid contributions. When the cards are filled with entries or stamps they are exchanged in municipial offices, insurance offices, or health insurance offices, and are collected by the pensions insurance administrations; the insured person receives a corresponding certificate. It is estimated that about 600 million insurance cards are presently stored in the archives of the Land Insurance Institutes and the Federal Institute for Non-Manual Workers in the Federal Republic of Germany. About 26 million insurance cards are in the possession of insured persons; 7 million are exchanged annually.

Compulsory Insurance

All employees working for remuneration are compulsorily insurable, as are apprentices and others engaged in vocational training, even if they receive no pay. In general, persons employed in manual occupations are insurable under the Manual Workers Pensions Insurance Schemes, and the non-manual workers in the Non-Manual Workers Pensions Insurance Scheme, whereas under the Miners' Special Scheme Pensions Insurance those persons are insured who are employed in mining undertakings i.e. in enterprises in which coal, other minerals and similar substances, are produced by mining processes. Compulsory insurance — or exemption therefrom — under the Miners' Special Scheme or the Non-Manual Workers' Scheme has preference over that of the Manual Workers Scheme.

All persons employed for remuneration are compulsorily insurable for pensions insurance, without regard to the amount of their income. The insurance ceiling in the case of non-manual workers and certain senior managerial grades in mining, which was formerly fixed at 21.600 DM annually, was abolished with effect from 1. 1. 1968. Spouses employed by their marriage partners are insurable unless they had applied for exemption before 31. 12. 1969.

In addition the following are insurable, either under the manual or non-manual workers' schemes, according to the nature of their employment: Germans employed abroad in an official Federal Mission, or by a member of such a Mission, and members of religious communities, deaconesses, Red Cross sisters, and members of similar communities during their period of training, or if, in addition to board and lodging, they are in receipt of a monthly payment in excess of one tenth of the general basis of computation (1970 — 180 DM).

Under certain conditions the crew of a ship sailing under a foreign flag is also insurable, if the owner so stipulates.

Anyone performing compulsory military service is insurable, contributions being payable by the State. In the case of public employees compulsory military service does not, as a rule, entail a break in service.

Germans employed abroad for limited periods remain insurable if the employing firm or body so requests.

Further categories amongst self-employed and similar persons insurable under manual workers insurance are: Peddlers, home workers, inshore fishermen and coastwise seamen, teachers, tutors, musicians, children's, babies' and maternity and sick nurses (male and female); variety artists and midwives, as self-employed persons, are insurable under the non-manual workers schemes, as are, with effect from 1. 1. 1970, sea-going pilots.

Legal Exemption from Insurability

Certain occupations are legally exempted from insurability. These include subsidiary occupations followed only temporarily, occasionally, or in return for a small remuneration, if they are limited to three months, or a total of 75 days, annually, or if the remuneration in one month does not exceed one eighth of the amount of the insurable earnings ceiling (1970 = 225 DM), or one fifth of the total income. Anyone following an occupation intended not solely as vocational training, who receives in return only board and lodging (exception: a voluntary social year), or who, as a student, receives wages during the period of his study, is exempt from insurability, as is any person in receipt of remuneration in the framework of statutory vocational re-training.

Certain other groups are exempt if it appears that their security in old age is otherwise assured. In addition to persons already in receipt of retirement pensions, these include in the main established officials, and other employees entitled to similar pensions to those of established officials, or who are in the employment of the Federal Government, the Lands, the Associations of Municipalities, Local Authorities, the Administrations of Social Insurance, the Federal Institute for Labour, the German Federal Bank, and the religious communities recognised as corporations in public law, judges and clergymen. A condition for exemption is that, the persons affected are entitled to lifelong provision for themselves and their survivors on the basis of Civil Service or Ecclesiastical legal regulations. Temporary police officers and temporary and regular soldiers of the Federal Armed Forces are also exempt.

Exemption from Insurability on Application

On application recipients of a pension pursuant to Civil Service regulations or practice, or similar ecclesiastical regulations, may be exempted from insurability on condition that lifelong provision is guaranteed for them and their survivors. Application for exemption may also be made by persons who, by reason of direct or indirect legal compulsion, are members of an insurance institute in public law existing within their profession (e.g. doctors, solicitors).

Corporations and associations in public law, and associations of the administrations of social insurance, whose employees are not legally exempted from insurability, may apply for exemption for them if they provide assurances that provision will be made for them and their survivors according to Civil Service regulations or practice, or corresponding ecclesiastical regulations, and such assurances are accepted als satisfactory. Owners of German seagoing vessels may exempt stateless or foreign members of the crews of their vessels if they have been signed on in a foreign port during the voyage, and if this is not contrary to bilateral or international social insurance agreements. Religious communities, deaconesses associations, the German Red Cross, and similar communities, may be granted exemption for their members if they guarantee lifelong provision for them in the form customary in the community.

Under the Miners' Special Scheme aliens employed temporarily within the framework of a bilateral agreement, or of an international agreement, may be exempted on application, in so far as such exemption is not contrary to a bilateral social insurance agreement or an international social agreement.

Retrospective Insurability

The essence of retrospective insurability is that contributions may be paid retrospectively in respect of a previous employment which, by reason of entitlement to lifelong provision and to a pension, was exempted employment. In this manner, and within the framework of pensions insurance, the consequences ensuing from the termination of employment and the loss of entitlement are made good. Retrospective insurance is conditional on certain insurance regulations: it is possible in the case of established officials and regular soldiers, members of religious communities, and certain groups of persons victims of the second world war and its aftermath. Pursuant to the Third Amending Law of 1. 1. 1970, sea-going pilots became retrospectively insurable, and have thus gained full social security as members of the Non-Manual Workers Insurance Institute. Retrospective insurance is effected in such a manner that, in respect of each person affected, the employing body retrospectively pays the contributions to the Insurance Fund, without any financial contribution from the insured person. By means of this fictive retrospective insurance, the Fund is reimbursed for its outlay on pensions.

Continued Voluntary Contribution

In the case of manual and non-manual workers' pensions insurance, persons who are not compulsorily insurable, but who, within a period of ten years, have paid contributions for at least 60 calendar months in respect of insurable employment, may continue voluntarily in insurance, except in the case of the Miners' Special Scheme. This applies only to formerly insurable employees still employed in mining who have worked for at least 60 calendar months at the coal face, or in comparable employment, or who have paid contributions to the scheme for at least 180 months. The regulation 10-year period may be extended in respect of periods for which the insured person was unable to pay contributions. On reaching pensionable age for Retirement, or Miners' Special Scheme pension, continued insurance is permissible only if the insured person does not draw the pension. If contributions are paid voluntarily after the point at which a pesnion becomes payable, such contributions are taken into account only when the next pesnion becomes payable. Anyone who had paid voluntary contributions up to 31. 12. 1956 may continue in insurance unconditionally.

Retrospective Payment of Voluntary Contributions

Generally speaking such contributions, if they are to be legally valid, may be paid only within two years following the year in respect of which they are paid. There are various exceptions to this rule, above all those whereby the insured person may pay contributions in respect of past periods to an amount fixed by himself. The pattern for this rule was provided by the Pensions. Insurance Reform of 1957, which made provision for retrospective payment of contributions by expellees and refugees, whereby they can continue in insurance, even though the general rules for voluntary further insurance are not applicable, if, prior to their expulsion, flight, or evacuation, they were self-employed persons, and if, within a period of three years following those events, they had entered into an insurable occupation. They may even pay contributions retrospectively for the period between 1. 1. 1924 and their 65th brithday. In the case of an insured person who did not enter into insurable employment before reaching the age of 50, and who, up to the age of 65, had been fully insured, and/ or can prove excused periods, and if the qualifying period of 180 months has not been satisfied, the missing months are admitted as an insurance period. Anyone who, in the period between 1. 1. 1956 and 31. 12. 1966 was employed for wages, and who was excused or exempted from insurance only because he or she was employed by his or her spouse, was permitted under certain conditions to pay contributions retrospectively for that period.

Non-manual workers who, because of the insurance ceiling valid until the end of 1967, were not insurable, or who became uninsurable, may now retrospectively pay contributions up to 31. 12. 1970 to cover the period 31. 12. 1955 to 31. 12. 1967. In addition they enjoy another concession. Persons who have claimed a refund of contributions on the grounds that they were not entitled to continue voluntarily in insurance, may again pay in the contributions refunded for the period subsequent to 31. 12. 1965. Their insurance position is then the same as though no refund has been made.

Female insured persons who, on the basis of the former regulations governing such refunds, had claimed a refund of contributions on marriage may now again pay such contributions back to 1. 1. 1924. A condition is that the insured person is still insurably employed, and that, since the refund of the contributions, she has again paid compulsory contributions for two years. Retrospective payment of contributions is limited to the period for which the contributions had been paid. A draft law of the Federal Government provides that victims of Nazi persecution may in certain cases pay contributions retrospectively. The decision rests with the legislator. A corresponding regulation is provided for farmers if they have surrendered their holdings in the course of structural improvements, and are now insurably employed.

Higher Contributions

The payment of higher contributions in the manual and non-manual workers pensions insurance is a form of voluntary insurance, in which the contributions and benefits are calculated on an actuarial insurance basis as in private insurance. For one and the same contribution a smaller pension amount is awarded with increasing age. A condition of this payment of higher contributions is that basic insurance (compulsory or voluntary insurance) is payable. The insured person can pay additional contributions to his compulsory or voluntary insurance, under the Miners' Special Scheme, however, only into the manual or non-manual workers schemes. So far, the payment of higher contributions was possible only by means of affixing stamps with the superscription "HV". It is now possible to pay by cheque or money order. Higher contributions are payable at the levels prior to 1. 1. 1957, which were additional to compulsory contributions, or contributions paid voluntarily in substitution periods. Benefits from higher contributions are awarded, even though the qualifying periods for the individual pension types have not been satisfied. They are not subject to the reduction regulations applicable to survivors; they are disregarded in the application of suspension regulations and pensions adjustments.

Contributions for increased insurance and their monthly increments 1970

Age of the insured person in the year in which higher contributions were paid	100 17	300 51	500 85	700 119	900 153	1200 204	1800 306
up to the age of 30 (20 %)	0,28	0,85	1,42	1,98	2,55	3,40	5,10
from the age of 31 to 35 (18 %)	0,26	0,77	1,28	1,79	2,30	3,06	4,59
from the age of 36 to 40 (16 %)	0,23	0,68	1,13	1,59	2,04	2,72	4,08
from the age of 41 to 45 (14 %)	0,20	0,60	0,99	1,39	1,79	2,38	3,57
from the age of 46 to 50 (12 %)	0,17	0,51	0,85	1,19	1,53	2,04	3,06
from the age of 51 to 55 (11 %)	0,16	0,47	0,78	1,09	1,40	1,87	2,81
from the 56th year onwards (10 %)	0,14	0,43	0,71	0,99	1,28	1,70	2,55

Benefits under accident insurance

Standard benefits include measures for the maintenance, improvement, or restoration of employability, pensions, commutation of widows' and widowers' pensions, refund of contributions in cases in which qualifying periods have not been satisfied, contributions for the Health Insurance of pensioners, or refund of relevant expenditure. Additional benefits may consist of preventive health measures, financial aid (house building) accommodation in homes (old peoples' homes, children's homes).

Measures for the maintenance, improvement, or restoration of employability

Measures for the maintenance, improvement, or restoration of employability, now generally known under the title of rehabilitation, are based on the concept that measures for the promotion of health and occupation are more rational and advantageous, both for the insured person and the economy as a whole, than the payment of a pension. Such measures have therefore been considerably expanded since 1957, and have now reached a high standard. For curative tratment the Funds maintain 170 institutions with more than 30.000 beds. Health measures are concerned in the main with the following ailments: Complaints of the respiratory organs, debilitation, women's ailments, heart and circulation complaints, nervous complaints, rheumatic complaints, metabolism complaints, TBC.

Number of Health Measures Carried out

Year	Tuberculosis	Other ailments	Total	1965 = 100	Quota of TB in % measures[1]	Occupational Promotion Measures
Pensions Insurance of Manual Workers						
1955	80 220	117 872	198 092	100	40,5	–
1960	69 879	337 301	407 180	206	17,2	
1965	61 171	377 672	438 843	222	13,9	19 657
1968	48 111	356 441	404 552	204	11,9	21 642
1969[2]	42 000	320 000	362 000	.	.	20 000
Pensions Insurance of Non-manual Workers						
1955	25 369	44 362	69 731	100	36,4	–
1960	16 148	137 070	153 218	220	10,5	.
1965	19 772	196 048	217 820	312	9,1	811
1968	14 423	203 364	217 787	312	6,6	2 127
1969[2]	15 000	250 000	265 000	.	.	2 400
Miners Special Scheme Pensions Insurance						
1955	5 294	13 829	19 123	100	27,7	–
1960	3 435	23 093	26 528	139	12,9	.
1965	2 306	21 954	24 260	127	9,5	2 333
1968	1 568	15 561	17 129	90	9,2	2 595
1969[2]	1 200	10 000	11 200	.	.	495

1) excluding vocational promotion
2) estimated

If the employability of an insured person, in certain cases also that of pensioners, a widow or a widower — is endangered or impaired owing to illness or infirmity, and if there are reasonable grounds for assuming that employability can be maintained, considerably improved, or restored, measures for such improvement or restoration may be taken, though only with the consent of the insured person. These include curative treatment, occupational furtherance, and social welfare. *Curative treatment* includes all necessary medical treatment in particular in sanatoria and spas, as well as in special establishments.

Occupational furtherance includes measures for the restoration or improvement of employability in the customary occupation, training for some other occupation which the insured person may reasonably be expected to accept in view of his customary occupation, and help in obtaining and retaining employment.

Social Welfare consists of the payment of transitional payments during the period of medical treatment or occupational furtherance, as well as follow-up treatment and aid. The amount of transitional payments is fixed by a decision of the competent Insurance Fund, with due consideration to the number of family members mainly or wholly maintained by the insured person before treatment or training. Transitional payments amount to a minimum of 50 %, and maximum of 80 %, of the average earnings on which contributions habe been paid in the previous 12 months. If board and lodging are provided, transitional payments may be reduced to one third. Transitional payments are not payable in cases in which wages continue to be payable, or income is available from some other occupation, or a Pension from a social insurance is payable. For the duration of the necessary measures, entitlement to a pesnion rests, unless the pension was already payable, in which event the amount is deducted from transitional payments.

The prevention and treatment of tuberculosis, a measure which the Pensions Funds had accepted voluntarily for decades, was made obligatory on them more than 10 years ago. Insured persons, pensioners, their spouses and children, have a legal claim to curative treatment, occupational furtherance and follow-up care, including transitional payments, if they have active t.b. requiring treatment. The type and degree of benefit is fixed by the Insurance Funds at their own conscientious discretion. Entitlement varies in part as between insured persons, pensioners, spouses and children.

Types of pension

Insured persons are awarded pensions (Miners' Special Scheme Pensions) by reason of reduced employability in the custormary occupation, by reason of unemployability, or a miners pension or retirement pension. Survivors receive a widow's pension, a widower's pension, a pension for the former (divorced) spouse of a deceased insured person, or pensions for full and half orphans.

Almost a million new pensions become payable annually, of which 74 % are payable to insured persons, 21 % to widows, and roughly 5 % to orphans. Whereas the quota of pensions payable in respect of occupational unemployability and total unemployability amounted in 1960 to 34.7 %, and of retirement pensions to 63.5 %, the position in 1969 showed a retirement pensions quota of 73.3 %. The high birth rates of the beginning of this century are now appearing as pensioners; this process will continue until the middle of this decade. The quota of disablement pensions has decreased to 26.8 %

Conditions for the payment of pensions

Pensions become payable when due (on disablement, retirement, death), and when the qualifying period is satisfied.

Manual, Non-manual, and Miners Special Scheme Pensions Insurance

Average amount of pensions in RM/DM per month at the beginning of the year

Year	Insured Persons			Widows Pension			Orphans Pension		
	ArV[1]	AnV[2]	KnV[3]	ArV[1]	AnV[2]	KnV[3]	ArV[1]	AnV[2]	KnV[3]
1926	25,00	.	.	14,30	.	.	10,00	.	.
1930	36,50	.	.	22,10	.	.	15,00	.	.
1938	31,60	69,00	.	19,00	.	.	11,00	.	.
1950	60,50	92,90	.	36,20	48,10	.	23,50	28,50	.
1955	89,70	137,30	175,50	57,50	73,30	96,50	32,30	38,20	38,40
1958	144,00	228,60	210,20	100,30	142,40	105,80	50,60	54,60	38,30

Type of Pension	1960	1965	1969	1970
Pensions Insurance of Manual Workers				
Total number payable	152,00	198,80	294,80	313,20
BU[4]	106,40	121,20	169,70	179,10
EU[5]	128,30	170,80	245,40	257,30
Retirement Pensions at 65	168,20	223,00	331,60	352,60
Retirement Pensions to Unemployed at 60	190,70	284,70	465,80	502,10
Retirement Pensions to Women at 60	129,60	162,30	230,00	241,90
Widows' Pensions — total	110,30	152,40	233,40	249,20
Orphans Pensions — total	54,50	72,90	107,80	114,90
Pensions Insurance of Non-manual Workers (less Independent Craftsmen Insurance)				
Total number payable	244,50	331,70	493,20	534,20
BU[4]	144,00	155,10	213,00	226,70
EU[5]	184,30	243,70	347,30	369,40
Retirement Pensions at 65	273,90	371,10	553,60	605,90
Retirement Pensions to Unemployed at 60	274,70	409,50	641,90	689,90
Retirement Pensions to Women at 60	249,10	326,30	447,90	474,90
Widows' Pensions — total	157,00	216,70	335,20	370,00
Orphans' Pensions — total	59,40	80,50	119,70	127,70
Miners Special Scheme Pensions Insurance				
Total number payable (excluding Kn.-Sold)	305,60	444,50	684,21	.
Miners Pensions				
(reduced employability) in mining	150,70	144,30	209,90	
at the age of 50	179,60	216,50	309,90	
Miners' Special Scheme Pensions				
BU[4]	293,50	398,00	555,50	
EU[5]	334,50	437,80	626,10	
Miners Special Scheme Retirement Pensions				
at 65	387,20	512,00	750,80	
at 60, having left Mining	475,60	619,80	909,70	
at 60, unemployed	335,70	572,50	831,00	
at 60, Women	278,50	313,90	429,90	
Knappschaftssold	–	57,00	39,30	
Widows' Pensions — total	199,50	268,00	399,20	
Orphans' Pensions — total	63,10	81,70	122,00	
Kn.-Ausgleichsleistung	–	578,50	757,10	

1) Manual Workers Insurance
2) Non-manual Workers Insurance
3) Miners Special Scheme Insurance
4) Reduced earning capacity in Customary occupation
5) Unemployability

Pensions payable under the Manual and Non-manual Pensions Insurance
in 1.000s at the beginning of the year

Year	Pensions payable	Insurance Pensions BU[1]	EU[2]	Unem- ployment	year Women	65th year	total	Widows Pension	Orphans Pension
Pensions Insurance of Manual Workers									
1950	3 037	–	–	–	–	–	1 799	679	558
1955	4 512	–	–	–	–	–	2 524	1 111	877
1960	5 336	202	900	12	37	1 893	3 044	1 795	497
1965	5 802	383	766	32	134	2 202	3 517	1 989	296
1968	6 365	365	809	36	226	2 503	3 940	2 113	312
1969	6 540	360	833	52	263	2 569	4 077	2 148	314
1970	6 738	354	856	65	304	2 654	4 233	2 186	319
Pensions Unsurance of Non-manual Workers									
1950	870	–	–	–	–	–	414	309	147
1955	1 477	–	–	–	–	–	715	511	251
1960	1 850	53	238	8	17	655	971	661	218
1965	2 089	88	191	17	74	797	1 167	788	134
1968	2 301	88	188	19	120	904	1 319	862	121
1969	2 368	89	192	23	139	925	1 368	882	118
1970	2 447	90	197	28	161	950	1 425	904	118

Pensions payable under the Miners Special Scheme Pensions Insurance
in 1.000s at the beginning of the year

Year	Pensions payable	Miners Pensions	Miners Scheme BU[1]	Special Pensions EU[2]	Miners Retire- ment Pensions Age 60	Age 65	Knapp- schafts- sold	Total	Widows Pension	Orphans Pension	Knapp- ausgleichs- leistung
1950	550	–	–	–	–	–	30	261	180	79	–
1955	644	–	–	–	–	–	32	327	214	71	–
1960	672	100	8	92	12	145	14	383	243	46	–
1965	718	65	35	75	53	169	3	400	281	37	3
1968	736	44	33	68	51	193	4	388	296	37	14
1969	743	41	32	63	50	202	2	389	304	35	14

1) Pensions on account of decreased working capacity in customary occupation
2) Pensions on account of unemployability

Disablement

The incidence of premature disablement in various employment situations reveals a connection between the state of the labour market, that is to say of the fluctuations between unemployment and full employment, and of disablement. The occurrence of unemployment and of disablement runs, by and large, parallel, even if, in the case of certain groups of persons (women) and of particular labour market situations, deviations occur. Under the term disablement are to be understood reduced standard of employment in the customary occupation (Berufsunfähigkeit), unemployability (Erwerbsfähigkeit), or, under the Miners' Special Scheme, reduced working capacity in the mining industry.

Redced Standard of employment in the custormary occupation is present in the case of an insured person whose earning capacity, as a result of illness or of some other infirmity, or deterioration of his physical or mental health, has been reduced to less than half of that of a physically and mentally healthy person with similar training and equal knowledge and skill. The extent of the employment which he can reasonably be expected to

Amounts of Pensions Payable under Statutory Pensions Insurance
— with effect from 1.1.1968 — in DM per month

Amount	BU	EU	AR 65	AR 60	Total Pensions Men	Women	Total	Women's Quota %	in %
Statutory Pensions Insurance of Manual Workers									
under 100	128552	165403	127210	13512	40651	395172	435823	11,7	90,7
100 up to under 200	112464	246492	900359	93452	265452	1087315	1352767	36.2	80,4
200 up to under 300	50099	106998	369330	83546	330533	279440	609973	16,3	45,8
300 up to under 400	36302	89369	277006	36518	355109	84086	439195	11,8	19,1
400 up to under 500	10327	73843	270581	12221	350408	16564	366972	9,8	4,5
500 up to under 600	2278	43870	251664	7232	302328	2716	305044	8,2	0,9
600 up to under 700	538	14293	166373	3199	183912	491	184403	4,9	0,3
700 up to under 800	215	2647	33315	598	36618	157	36775	1,0	0,4
800 up to under 900	79	534	3586	118	4277	40	4317	0,1	0,9
900 up to under 1000	30	87	969	49	1125	10	1135	0,0	0,9
1000 and more	10	38	238	10	296	–	296	0,0	–
Total	340894	743574	2400631	251601	1870709	1865991	3736700	100.0	49.9
Statutory Pensions Insurance of Non-Manual Workers									
under 100	21161	15903	13707	1866	4976	47661	52637	4.5	90.5
100 up to under 200	27082	41843	77941	14010	28030	132846	160876	13.8	82.6
200 up to under 300	14230	32438	126932	21741	55989	139352	195341	16.7	71.3
300 up to under 400	8144	22402	86062	21207	62813	75002	137815	11.8	54.4
400 up to under 500	5319	17001	76941	20642	68689	51214	119903	10.3	42.7
500 up to under 600	2475	14719	77455	19146	76890	36905	113795	9.7	32.4
600 up to under 700	525	11687	87637	14622	90008	24463	114471	9.8	21.4
700 up to under 800	78	7452	86098	9469	87666	15431	103097	8.8	15.0
800 up to under 900	38	3090	67601	5252	67703	8278	75981	6.5	10.9
900 up to under 1000	10	1175	49825	3043	49712	4341	54053	4.6	8.0
1000 and more	–	300	39357	692	38243	2106	40349	3.5	5.2
Total	79062	168010	789556	131690	630719	537599	1168318	100.0	46.0

Miners' Special Scheme Pensions Insurance

Amount	Miners' Pension	BU	EU	AR 65	AR 60	Total	Women's Quota
under 100	7303	319	726	59	35	8442	2.3
100 up to under 200	14549	972	3382	1197	452	20552	5.7
200 up to under 300	12816	2079	3412	4872	796	23975	6.6
300 up to under 400	4927	4509	4746	9775	936	24893	6.9
400 up to under 500	1350	6286	9048	17424	2458	36566	10.1
500 up to under 600	357	6708	12147	35728	6070	51010	14,0
600 up to under 700	111	5544	11524	31556	10814	59549	16.4
700 up to under 800	38	2778	8741	31140	14465	57162	15.8
800 up to under 900	7	864	4953	22469	14241	42534	11,7
900 up to under 1000	3	266	2003	7437	8517	18226	5,0
1000 and more	1	205	1899	11040	6706	19851	5.5
Total	41462	30530	62581	162697	65490	362760	100,0

Total figures deviate from actual pensions payable, since special pensions are not included.
BU   = Reduced standard of employment
EU   = Unemployability
AR 65= Manual Workers pensions became payable at the age of 65
AR 60= Manual Workers pensions became payable at the age of 60

perform in view of his physical strength and ability, and with due consideration to the duration and extent of his vocational training, as well as of his previous occupation and the strains it has imposed on him, is taken into account. He may reasonably be expected to follow an occupation for which he can successfully be trained or retrained by means of measures for the mantenance, improvement or restoration of his earning capacity. Pursuant to a ruling of the Federal Labour Court, the insured person may only be required to take a job which is not only theoretically reasonable, but of which an adequate number is actually available, even though there are no immediate vacancies; it must not be allowed to happen that the labour market is closed to an insured person in

Age Groups of Pensioners under Statutory Pensions Insurance

Age Group	Insured Pensioners BU	EU	AR 65	AR60	Total	%	Widowed Total	Pensioners %
Statutory Pensions Insurance of Manual Workers								
under 30	1 856	4 342	–	–	6 198	0,2	6 004	0,3
30 up to under 40	7 666	22 267	–	–	29 933	0,8	26 881	1,3
40 up to under 50	20 143	69 832	–	–	89 975	2,3	139 707	6,6
50 up to under 60	93 139	212 287	–	–	305 426	7,7	506 773	24,0
60 up to under 65	153 809	328 858	–	134 102	616 769	15,6	326 237	15,4
65 up to under 70	52 621	98 242	1 042 834	94 447	1 288 144	32,7	334 785	15,8
70 up to under 80	35 038	69 481	1 136 184	33 985	1 273 688	32,3	550 188	26,1
80 up to under 90	436	4 881	305 063	10	310 390	7,9	205 014	9,7
90 and older	–	113	19 319	–	19 432	0,5	17 267	0,8
Total	364 708	809 303	2 503 400	262 544	3 939 955	100,0	2 112 856	100,0
Statutory Pensions Insurance of Non-Manual Workers (excluding Self-employed Artisans Insurance).								
under 30	488	1 217	–	–	1 705	0,1	847	0,1
30 up to under 40	1 772	4 679	–	–	6 451	0,5	4 815	0,6
40 up to under 50	6 906	22 939	–	–	29 845	2,5	23 936	3,1
50 up to under 60	21 850	50 544	–	–	72 394	6,0	135 615	17,6
60 up to under 65	31 280	62 698	–	66 288	160 266	13,3	107 291	13,9
65 up to under 70	10 976	17 509	349 277	50 184	427 946	35,5	128 483	16,6
70 up to under 80	8 805	17 150	375 668	17 557	419 180	34,7	221 103	28,6
80 up to under 90	234	1 202	84 599	10	86 045	7,1	123 983	16,0
90 and older	20	10	3 811	–	3 841	0,3	26 801	3,5
Total	82 331	177 948	813 355	134 039	1 207 673	100,0	772 874	100,0

Miners' Special Scheme Pensions Insurance

Age Group	Insured Pensioners Miners	BU	EU	AR 65	AR 60	Total	%	Widowed Total	Pensioners %
under 30	385	151	137	–	–	701	0,2	522	0,2
30 up to under 40	5 807	1 322	1 243	–	–	8 372	2,2	3 607	1,2
40 up to under 50	11 854	4 431	4 106	–	–	20 391	5,3	13 760	4,7
50 up to under 60	21 428	16 881	20 660	–	–	58 969	15,2	48 689	16,4
60 up to under 65	3 862	8 931	31 762	–	38 294	82 849	21,3	46 523	15,7
65 up to under 70	408	1 002	6 733	66 221	26 180	100 544	25,9	57 342	19,4
70 up to under 80	57	205	84 011	84 011	4 481	91 332	23,5	92 094	31,1
80 up to under 90	5	3	397	23 468	2	23 875	6,1	31 225	10,6
90 and older	–	–	20	1 299	1	1 320	0,3	2 180	0,7
Total	43 834	32 926	67 636	174 999	68 958	388 353	100,0	295 942	100,0

BU = Reduced standard of employment
EU = Unemployability
AR 65 = Manual Workers pensions became payable at the age of 65
AR 60 = Manual Workers pensions became payable at the age of 60

respect of suitable employment. An insured person must be prepared in principle to accept employment anywhere in the Federal territory; if, however, he is capable only of working half shifts, he may be required as a general rule to accept employment only at his own place of residence, or within daily travelling distance. An insured person incapable of employment in his customary occupation is entitled to a pension (or Miners' Special Scheme pension).

Classified as *unemployable* are those insured persons who, by reason of sickness or other infirmity, or weakness of their physical or mental health, are for an unforeseeable period incapable of following a gainful occupation with any degree of regularity, or of earning more than a negligible anount. Unemployability is thus shown to result in a much more serious reduction of earning capacity than a reduced standard of employment in the custormary occupation. Pursuant to the ruling of the Federal Labour Court, similar principles apply in this respect as in the case of reduced employability in the customary occupation. A pension (Miners' Special Scheme pension) on account of unemployability is not payable at the same time as a pension on account of reduced earning capacity in the customary employment. The insured person who is incapable of emloyment is awarded a pension on account of unemployability.

Classified under the heading of "Reduced employability in a mining occupation"are those insured persons who by reason of illness or other infirmity, or weakness of their physical and mental health, are incapable of following their customary occupation in mining, and who are incapable of following some alternative mining employment being performed by other persons in mining undertakings with the same training, knowledge, and skills. Such persons are awarded a Miners' Pension. On the award of a Miners' Special Scheme pension or a Miners' Retirement Pension, the payment of the Miners' Pension ceases.

Provisional pensions on account of reduced employability in the customary occupation, or on account of unemployability, may be payable if there are reasonable grounds for assuming that the condition may be improved within a foreseeable period. The payment of such pensions is normally limited to a period of two years, but this period may be repeatedly extended, to a maximum of four years.

Age Limits

Retirement Pensions (Miners' Special Scheme retirement pensions) are payable when the insured person has reached the age of 65. On application the pension may also become payable when the insured person reaches the age of 60, and has been unemployed for a full year. Temporary, or merely occasional employment, is disregarded in deciding the question of unemployment.

Retirement Pensions (Miners' Special Scheme retirement pensions) are payable on application to insured persons no longer following a gainful occupation if they have reached the age of 60, and have, during the preceding 20 years, mainly followed an occupation insurable for pensions insurance. *Miners' Special Scheme Retirement Pesnions* are also payable on reaching the age of 60 in cases in which the insured person has regularly followed an insurable occupation underground for 300 months, and is no longer emloyed in a mining undertaking. *Miners' Pesnions* are payable at the age of 50, if the insured person is no longer following an occupation comparable to his previous employment and has spent a period of 300 months in underground employment. Certain transitional conditions are applicable. *Miners' Special Scheme Adjustment Benefit* is payable to insured mine workers who have reached the age of 55 and opt to cease work in mining. The intention of this regulation is to render it unnecessary for workers with long years of service to change their occupation, which necessity had arisen in most cases during the last few years from rationalisation measures.

Conditions for the Payment of Survivors' Pensions

Survivors pensions are payable to widows, widowers, or orphans, and the former wife of deceased or missing insured persons. In the first three months after the death of the insured person, the widow or widower receives, in lieu of a survivors' pension, the pension, less children's allowances, to which the insured person was entitled at the time of his death, or, if the insured person was not entitled to a pension at the time of his death, the pension of the insured person less schildren's allowances, on the basis of which the survivors pension is assessed. A *Widows' Pension* is payable to a widow on the death of her insured husband. A former wife whose marriage has been divorced, annulled, or otherwise terminated, receives a pension if the insured person was under an order to pay her a maintenance allowance at the time of his death, or had paid such allowance during the year prior to his death. If there is no widow, the pension is still awarded if the deceased person had not been required to pay a maintenance allowance by reason of his own insufficient income or earnings. A *Widower's Pension* is payable on the death of the insured wife if she had been wholly or mainly maintaining the family. A former husband of a deceased insured person also has a claim to a pension in the same way as a former wife of an insured person.

Orphans' Pensions are payable to the children of deceased insured persons under the same conditions as those applying to Children's Allowances.

Qualifying Periods

A condition for the award of a pension is that the qualifying period has been satisfied, that is to say that contributions must have been paid for a certain number of months in order to secure entitlement. The qualifying period is, in gerneral, 60 calendar months. In the case of retirement pensions, including Miners' Special Scheme retirement pensions, the qualifying period is 180 months. Special regulations applicable to Miners' Special Scheme retirement pensions are given under the heading "Age Limits'. In calculating qualifying periods all reckonable periods are included (exception: only contributions prior to 1923). Amongst these are included periods for which pursuant to Federal Law, or to the former Imperial Statutory Pensions Insurance Regulations, contributions were actually paid (Contribution Periods), and periods for which no contributions were paid (Substitution Periods). Contribution periods are also allowed for periods in which non-contributors (Fremdrentner) had paid contributions to a foreign fund, or who, subsequent to 30. 6. 1948, had paid contributions in East Germany, or who, prior to their expulsion from an "expulsion territory", had been employed after their 16th year in a non-insurable occupation, but only under certain conditions.

The qualifying period is considered as satisfied if the insured person had become incapable of following his customary occupation, unemployable, capable only to a reduced degree of following a mining occupation, or had died, as a result of: an industrial injury, or during or as a consequence of military service, or similar service performed on the basis of a legal obligation, or during a war, as a prisoner of war, or as a direct consequence of war action, or as a victim of Nazi persecution, or during or as a consequence of internment or deportation, or as an expellee, or refugee from East Germany, or as a consequence of such expulsion or flight.

Assessment of insurance pensions

Pensions are assessed on the basis of earnings and the length of the insurance life: Four factors are taken into account:

the percentage of the personal basis of computation	(P).
the number of reckonable insurance years	(J).
the general basis of computation	(B).
the annual increment per reckonable insurance year	(St).

The personal labour performance of the insured person, assessed on the basis of his earnings and the number of his reckonable insurance years, is expressed by the factors P. and J. The general basis of computation B affects the amount of pension payable by reason of its relation to wage and salary levels at any given period. In the case of pensions already assessed and payable, account is taken of wage and salary movements by annual adjustments. In respect of each reckonable insurance year only a certain percentage of the personal basis of computation is reckonable for pension. This increment per insurance year varies as between different forms of pension insurance, but is fixed by law in such a manner that at the end of a normal working life a reasonable pension is payable. The personal basis of computation is a percentage of the general basis of computation, expressed in DM; the personal basis of computation is therefore also a DM amount. The number of reckonable insurance years is multiplied by the incremental scale. The percentage so arrived at is applied to the amount of the personal basis of computation, and the amount of the pension is thus determined. (R).

The formula for computing pensions (according to Hensen/Stegner can, with slight deviations, be shown in the following simplified form (w.e.f. 1971)

for 1970 : $R = P \times J \times 1.55$ for 1972 : $R = P \times J \times 1 78$

for 19711 : $R = P \times J \times 1.65$ for 1973 : $R = P \times J \times 1.92$

General Basis of Assessment

By virtue of the general basis of computation (B), the pensioner is enabled to maintain the standard of living to which he was accustomed during his working life. The general basis of computation for manual and non-manual workers is arrived at on the basis of the gross average annual earnings of all wage and salary earners, excluding apprentices and trainees, as the mean of the three calendar year period preceding the year in which the pension becomes payable. For example, on the basis of the average gross annual earnings in 1966, namely 9.893 DM, in 1967, 10.219 DM, in 1968 10.842 DM, there results an average of 10.318 DM for pensions which become payable in 1970. In fixing the general basis of computation in the case of the Miners' Special Scheme pensions, the gross average earnings of manual workers in this form of insurance are taken into account. It is somewhat higher than in the case of the manual and non-manual workers.

The following table shows developments in the field of the general basis of computation.

Movement of Average Gross earning from 1892 to 1974 in RM/DM per annum — extracts —

Year	ArV/AnV	KnV	year	ArV/AnV	KnV	year	ArV/AnV	KnV
1892	700	–	1933	1 583	1 604	1960	6 101	6 165
1900	796	–	1935	1 692	1 719	1965	9 229	9 326
1905	910	–	1940	2 156	2 179	1968	10 842	10 957
1910	1 078	–	1942	2 310	2 335	1969	11 839	11 965
1915	1 178	–	1945	1 778	1 797	1970	13 272	13 413
1920	3 729	–	1948	2 219	2 243	1971	14 559	14 714
1925	1 469	–	1950	3 161	3 194	1972	15 520	15 685
1930	2 074	2 110	1955	4 548	4 596	1973	16 544	16 720

from 1969 onwards — estimated

The incremental rates of the gross wages and salary amount per employed person amounted from 1949 to 1969 to 7.41 % and from 1957 to 1969 to 7.38 %.

The percentage of the personal basis of computation (P) reflects the relation in which, during the insurance life, the gross average earnings of all insured persons excluding apprentices and trainees, has stood to it. For instance, if an insured person whose pension becomes payable during 1970 had been in receipt of average annual eanrnings amounting to 160 % of the average annual earnings of all insured persons, then his personal basis of computation would amount to 160 % of 10.318 DM = 16.508,80 DM.

Earnings as the Personal Basis of Computation

The effect of the personal basis of computation is that the amount of pension payable is dependent on the position in the earnings scale which the insured person had occupied throughout his working life. In computing the amount of pension due this principle is applied in varying forms, and is subject to limitations.

1. Since 1942 the earnings of all insured persons have been entered in their insurance cards. This makes it possible to relate individual average earnings for each year to the average gross annual earnings of all insured persons. This is done by multiplying the earnings of the insured person, in so far as they form the basis of computation, by 100, and dividing the result by the average gross annual earnings of all insured persons for the same year, the result being the personal basis of computation. For the period prior to 1942 there are no records of earnings, but only of contributions. Contributions were paid by affixing stamps to the insurance cards, to a value corresponding to the wage, salary, or contribution category, as is still done to a certain extent in the case of voluntary contributors. From the value of contributions paid it is, of course, possible to estimate earnings. In order to simplify matters: the corresponding amounts have been laid down in tables; the number of contributions paid in each category, taken over longer periods of time, are multiplied by the values of the stamps affixed as shown in the tables for the different categories and the individual periods.

Anyone who, subsequent to 30.4.1961 has performed his conscript service (with the Armed Forces or as a conscientious objector) is treated for insurance purposes in respect of this period as though he had been in receipt of the average gross earnings under the Miners' Special Scheme.

2. The principle that actual wages or salaries are to be taken as the basis of computing pensions can be implemented only within limits. There are, for instance, no records of earnings in the following cases:

a) the insured persons was not in receipt of earnings, but he is credited with contributions, though none have in fact been paid, for substitution periods, excused periods, and/or credited periods (see below).

b) In lieu of the earnings which the insured person actually received, a different amount of earnings is assumed on social grounds. This amount, if it is higher, is credited in the following cases, namely, in periods of apprenticeship, in which, in certain cases, no earnings were payable, in the first five calendar years of comulsory insurance, during a longer period when payment in kind was made (board and lodging).

c) for periods during the inflation a different level of earnings is assumed.

d) The actual earnings are not acertainable because records have been destroyed, or are not accessible,

e) in the case of Non-Contributos' Pensions, actual earnings for periods of employment are not taken into account, even if records are available. But because of the difficulty of expressing earnings paid in a foreign currency notional earnings are assumed.

f) Special regulations apply in respect of supplementary contributions in substitute and excused periods, and in respect of double insurance in different branches.

For periods for which no contributions had been paid, but which were reckonable periods (a), special concessions in the case of very low incomes (b), for periods of currency inflation (c), the principle was applied between 1957 and 1965 that the position in the earnings scale, as shown by the personal basis of computation during the remainder of his working life was also to be assumed for the other periods. In this manner the insured person could, during the further course of his working life — but also by payment of voluntary contributions — improve or worsen the weighting of non-contributory periods. Since 1965, fixed weightings have been allocated to the periods in question, which are no longer influenced by the payment of voluntary contributions, as happened in a similar manner, namely on the basis of a fixed scale, in the case of the periods shown in d) and e).

On a) In the case of substitution and excused periods, as well as of additional reckonable periods, a percentage of the personal basis of computation, based on the following regulations is taken as a basis.

If the substitution or excused periods lie prior to 1.1.1965, a monthly average weighting is allocated, based on all contributions paid and earnings received up to 31.12.1964, to a maximum value of 16.66. In the process, the first five calendar years are disregarded if their weighting as a non-contributions period is more favourable. In the case of substitution and excused periods subsequent to 31.12.1964 there are various regulations. Substitution periods (which can occur only in rare cases after 31.12.1964), periods of sickness, of pregnancy, umemployment, inclement weather payments, and pensionable periods, are weighted at the monthly average of the period up to the end of the calendar year ending before the commencement of the allowable non-contribution period, but at the maximum of 16.66. In special cases special scales are applicable. School, technical school, and universitiy education periods, reckonable as excused periods, are weighted on the basis of special scales, which vary considerably.

Additional reckonable periods are weighted on the same principle as substitution periods; the decisive factor being the personal basis of computation resulting directly, before the commencement of the reckonable period, from all preceding periods.

On b) In respect of apprenticeship and training periods for which no contributions have been paid, credit is given according to tables corresponding to those applicable to school and technical school education periods prior to the 21st year. Remuneration received during the first five years of an insurance life is, generally, very low, and results in a decrease in the personal basis of computation. This is compensated for in such a manner that — if the first five years came to an end before 1. 1. 1964 — the first five years for which compulsory contributions have been paid are disregarded in calculating the percentage of the personal basis of computation, if the percentage is thereby increased, and — if the first five years came to an end after 31. 12. 1963 — the first five years are credited with certain average remuneration, as laid down in the tables applicable to the Non-Contributors Law, e.g. for 1970 10.764 DM per annum for men, and 7.728 DM for women. If, however, evidence is producted to show a higher remuneration, this higher amount is taken into account in calculating the pension.

Insured persons who are able to prove that, for a period of at least five years, they had received, in addition to cash payments, considerable payments in kind (e.g. board and lodging) are credited with certain weightings and emoluments as laid down in the tables, if these are more favourable than amounts proven.

On c) Contribution periods during the inflation (1. 10. 1921 to 31. 12. 1923 for manual workers; 1. 8. 1921 to 31. 12. 1923 for non-manual workers) are treated as substitution periods.

On d) and e) Non-Contributory Pensioners, and insured persons whose records were destroyed as a result of war action, are credited with contributions and remuneration on the basis of tables corresponding to the average earnings received by persons in the Federal Republic in the same occupational group to which these persons belonged.

On f) In the case of insured persons who, in the period between 1. 1. 1913 and 31. 12. 1922, were insured under both the manual and the non-manual workers schemes (double insurance), contributions to the non-manual workers scheme only are taken into account.

Contributions paid after 31. 12. 1956 during an excused or additional contributions period are weighted in a special manner. From the emoluments on which contributions have been paid, a further amount of 0.5 % of the emoluments is credited. This portion of the pension is treated in the same manner as a benefit deriving from the payment of higher contributions (see ref.).

3. The weighting units arrived at on the basis of individual calculations are added together, multiplied by 12, and divided by the sum of the months covering the full period (less additional periods). In this manner the percentage of the personal basis of computation of the insured person is ascertained. If the personal basis of computation results in a weighting in excess of 200, values lying higher than this weighting are disregarded in the normal computation of the pension. In return the insured person is granted a special rate of pension, which is treated in the same way as a benefit resulting from the payment of higher contributions (see ref.) This annual benefit is computed as follows: weightings in excess of 200 are multiplied by the number of calendar months taken as the basis of the computation of the personal basis of computation. The result in the case of a pension awarded because of inability to follow the customary occupation is multiplied by 0.02 DM, in the case of unemployability or retirement pension by 0.03 DM.

If contributions have been paid to both manual and non-manual workers insurance, the position is known as a *Transfer Insurance* (Wanderversicherung). Both contributions are linked together to arrive at a uniform rate of benefit. If contributions to the Miners' Special Scheme have also been paid, these contributions, together with those paid into the manual and/or non-manual workers schemes, are considered separately and are then added together to arrive at the pension payable.

Figures showing
Dimensions in Social Pensions Insurance

Year	Average Gross Earning		Increase compared with previous year	General Basis of Computation		Increase compared with previous year	Insurable Ceilings		
	ArV + AnV in DM/year	KnRV in DM/year	in %	ArV + AnV in DM/year	KnRV in DM/year	in %	ArV + AnV in DM/year	in DM/ month	KnRV in DM/year
1	2	3	4	5	6	7	8	9	10
1957	5 043	5 096	–	4 281	4 326	–	9 000	750	12 000
1958	5 330	5 386	+ 5,7	4 542	4 590	+ 6,1	9 000	750	12 000
1959	5 602	5 661	+ 5,1	4 812	4 862	+ 5,94	9 600	800	12 000
1960	6 101	6 165	+ 8,9	5 072	5 126	+ 5,4	10 200	850	12 000
1961	6 723	6 794	+ 10,2	5 325	5 381	+ 5,0	10 800	900	13 200
1962	7 328	7 405	+ 9,0	5 678	5 737	+ 6,6	11 400	950	13 200
1963	7 775	7 857	+ 6,1	6 142	6 206	+ 8,2	12 000	1 000	14 400
1964	8 467	8 556	+ 8,9	6 717	6 788	+ 9,4	13 200	1 100	16 800
1965	9 229	9 326	+ 9,0	7 275	7 352	+ 8,3	14 400	1 200	18 000
1966	9 893	9 997	+ 7,2	7 857	7 939	+ 8,0	15 600	1 300	19 200
1967	10 219	10 327	+ 3,3	8 490	8 580	+ 8,1	16 800	1 400	20 400
1968	10 842	10 957	+ 6,1	9 196	9 293	+ 8,3	19 200	1 600	22 800
1969	11 839	11 965	+ 9,2	9 780	9 883	+ 6,35	20 400	1 700	24 000
1970	13 272	13 413	+ 12,1	10 318	10 427	+ 5,5	21 600	1 800	25 200
1971	14 559	14 714	+ 9,7	10 967	11 083	+ 6,3	22 800	1 900	27 600
1972	15 520	15 685	+ 6,6	11 984	12 112	+ 9,3	24 000	2 000	30 000
1973	16 544	16 720	+ 6,6	13 223	13 364	+ 10,3	27 600	2 300	32 400

The figures below the line are estimated; they are based on forecast estimates made in October 1970.

Duration of Insurance

Pensions increase with the number of reckonable years. Reckonable years are the qualifying years for pension (contribution and substitution periods), excused periods and additional periods. If the qualifying period is regarded as satisfied because the insured person is no longer capable of following his customary occupation, or has died as a result of an industrial accident, at least five additional insurance years are credited. The number of insurance years which have had to be taken into account in pension insurance in recent years has amounted in the case of men to 35 to 36 years, of women to 23 to 27 years, in the case of widows' pension to about 31 years. Of these about 27 were contribution years, rather less in the case of women, roughly 3 years were substitution periods, and about 3 years were excused periods.

Substitution Periods

The object of crediting substitution periods is to safeguard the insured person against being placed at a disadvantage if he had been unable to pay contributions by reason of circumstances beyond his own control. Substitution periods are credited if preceded by a contribution period, and if payment of contributions was not obligatory during the substitution period, or if, within three years of the termination of the substitution period, or of a postponed or interrupted period of training following the substitution period, an insurable occupation had commenced. Substitution periods are:
periods of military or similar service performed on the basis of law, or during a war,
periods spent in mine clearance after 8. 5. 1945,
periods of internment or deportation if the insured person is a returnee,

in DM	Contri-butions ArV + AnV in %	Max. Contr. in DM/month	KnRV KnRV in %	Max. Contr. in DM/month	Standard Contributions in Artisans Insurance Class	in DM/month	Children's Allowances ArV + AnV in DM/month	KnRV in DM/month	Year
11	12	13	14	15	16	17	18	19	20
1 000	14	105	23,5	235,00	.	.	35,70	36,10	1957
1 000	14	105	23,5	235,00	.	.	37,90	38,30	1958
1 000	14	112	23,5	235,00	.	.	40,10	40,60	1959
1 000	14	119	23,5	235,00	.	.	42,30	42,80	1960
1 100	14	126	23,5	258,50	.	.	44,40	44,90	1961
1 100	14	133	23,5	258,50	XI	70	47,40	47,90	1962
1 200	14	140	23,5	282,00	XII	77	51,20	51,80	1963
1 400	14	154	23,5	329,00	XIII	84	56,00	56,60	1964
1 500	14	168	23,5	352,50	XIV	91	60,70	61,30	1965
1 600	14	182	23,5	376,00	XV	98	65,50	66,20	1966
1 700	14	196	23,5	399,50	XVI	105	70,80	71,50	1967
1 900	15	240	23,5	446,50	800	120	76,70	77,50	1968
2 000	16	272	23,5	470,00	900	144	81,50	82,40	1969
2 100	17	306	23,5	493,50	900	153	86,00	86,90	1970
2 300	17	323	23,5	540,50	1 000	170	91,40	92,40	1971
2 500	17	340	23,5	587,50	1 000	170	99,90	101,00	1972
2 700	18	414	23,5	635,50	1 200	216	110,20	111,40	1973

periods during which the insured person, without himself having taken part in the war, has been prevented by enemy action from returning from abroad, or from territories in the East of Germany now under alien administration, or has been detained or imprisoned there,

periods of incarceration if the insured person is a victim of Nazi persecution,

periods of incarceration as a political prisoner in East Germany, or the DDR, periods of expulsion or flight, at least during the period 1. 1. 1945 to 31. 12. 1946.

In respect of all these periods — with the exception of obstructed return from abroad, or from East German territories — periods of subsequent sickness or involuntary unemployment following return are also taken into account.

Excused Periods

In assessing pensions the excused periods compensate for periods during which the insured person was unable to follow an occupation, though not prevented from doing so because of any governmental measures (otherwise substitution periods may be applicable), or for personal reasons.

Excused periods are

periods of unemployability arising from illness or accident,

periods when undergoing rehabilitation,

periods when in receipt of Inclement Weather Benefit, and

periods of unemployment during which the insured person was registered for employment with a German Employment Exchange and was in receipt of statutory unemployment benefit, unemployment assistance, public assistance (Sozialhilfe), or family aid. In the case of non-contributory pensioners (Fremdrentner) these conditions do not apply.

These periods must cover at least one month in order to be reckonable.

Excused periods are also periods of pregnancy and child bed.

Periods following the attainment of the 16th year during which a successful apprentice-ship has been completed, without payment of contributions, and of a further course of education, or of a successfully completed technical school or university course, if immediately following such periods, or, if, on completion of a substitution period following such periods, an insurable occupation has been entered into within five years. In this connection school or technical school education is taken into account only as to four years, university study as to five years. Periods when in receipt of a Disablement Pension before reaching the age of 55, which terminated prior to 1. 1. 1957, and of a pension which coincided with a credited additional period are also excused periods.

The advantages arising from the crediting of an excused period are intended to benefit only such persons as are mainly dependent on employment as employees, and who have consequently been compulsorily insurable over a long period of years. Excused periods are therefore credited only in those cases in which the period from entering into insurable employment and the point at which the pension becomes payable amounts to at least one half, in any case not less than 60 months, of the periods for which statutory contributions have been paid. In calculating this period as a whole, certain periods are disregarded. Since the insured person will often not be able to produce proof of excused periods prior to 1957, a flat rate period is allowed without proof. This flat rate is calculated on the principle of an insurance period limited to a quarter of the difference between the whole period from the 16th year onward, up to, at the latest, the end of the month preceding 1. 1. 1957 in which the last statutory contribution was paid, and the insurance period covering the whole of the period, and the relation of these two periods to one another.

Additional Periods

Additional periods are the periods between the point at which the pension becomes payable and the completion of the insured person's 55th year. In the case of persons who have become incapable of following their customary occupation, or have become un-employable, before reaching the age of 55, the additional period is added to the contributions and excused periods in calculating the whole insurance period. A condition is that, of the last 60 months before the pension becomes payable, statutory contributions shall have been paid for at least 36 months, or for at least half the period between taking up insurable employment and the point at which the pension becomes payable, in respect of an insurable occupation. In computing the whole period certain periods are disregarded.

Annual Increments

Insured persons are credited with annual increments as follows.
Pension because of inability to follow the customary

occupation (Berufsunfähigkeit)	1,0 %	⎫
Pension because of unemployabilitiy	1,5 %	⎪
Retirement Pension	1,5 %	⎪ Of the
Miners' Pension	0.8 %	⎪ personal
Miners' Special Scheme pension because of inability		⎬ basis of
to follow his customary occupation, but whilst		⎪ compulation
continuing in mining employment	1,2 %	⎪
Otherwise	1,88 %	⎪
Miners' Special Scheme pension because of unemployability	2,2 %	⎪
Miners' Special Scheme Retirement Pension	2,2 %	⎭

In respect of Miners' Special Scheme pensions and Miners' Special Scheme retirement pensions, increments for 1971 will be at 1,.84 % and 2.1 %, from 1972 onwards at 1.8 % and 2.0 % respectively.

The insurance pension is increased by the increments for voluntary contributions at a higher rate to the amount of the contributions paid during an excused or additional period, and in respect of the percentages of the personal basis of computation in excess of 200. In addition, in the case of Miners' Special Scheme pensions, a bonus is payable, after at least 5 full years employment underground; in respect of every further full year it amounts to 1 per thousand annually of the Miners' Special Scheme insurance ceiling for the first 5 further years, 2 per thousand for the next 10 years, and 3 per thousand for each subsequent year.

The annual increment of 1.5 % results at the end of an insurance life lasting from the 15th to the 65th year in a retirement pension of 75 %, after 40 years to 60 %, of the personal basis of computation. The 75 % rate coincides exactly with the highest rate of pension payable in the Civil Service. The same increment is payable in the case of unemployability pensions, and of nearly all widows' pensions. The increment payable in the case of inabilitiy to follow the customary occupation is lower (1 %), since it is assumed that the residual ability to work can be utilised elsewhere.

Children's Allowances

In addition to the insurance pension, a children's allowance is payable for each child to the monthly amount of 1/120th (annual amount 1/10) of the current annual general basis of computation. The allowance is payable in respect of legitimate children, of step children resident in the pensioner's household, of children declared legitimate, of adopted children, of the illegitimate children of a male insured person, if paternity or the obligation to maintain has been established, of the illegitimate children of a female insured person, of foster children in cases where the relation has arisen before the pension became payable, of grand children and brothers and sisters under the conditions applicable to the Federal Children's Allowance Law, if the position existed before the pension became payable. Children's allowances are payable until the completion of the 18th year. Beyond this point allowances may be payable up to, at the outside, the 25th year in respect of children in full time education or vocational training, or performing a social service year, or if they are incapable by reason of physical or mental infirmity of maintaining themselves. In the case of a delay in education or training occasioned by the fulfillment of compulsory military or related service, the payment of children's allowances may be extended for a period equal to the period of such service. Payment of these children's allowances precludes payment pursuant to the Federal Children's Allowances Law. If such allowances are payable in addition to an orphan's pension, then the widow is entitled to a children's allowance pursuant to the Federal Children's Allowance Law.

Children's Allowances in Pensions Payments
— in DM monthly — extracts

Year	ArV/AnV	KnV	Year	ArV/AnV	KnV
1957	35.70	36.10	1967	70.80	71.50
1960	42.30	42.80	1968	76.70	77.50
1965	60.70	61.30	1969	81.50	82.40
1966	65.50	66.20	1970	86.00	86.90

ArV= Manual Workers' Insurance   AnV = Non-Manual Workers Insurance   KnV = Miners' Special Scheme Insurance

Assessment of Survivors' Pensions

Widows' and Widowers' pensions, as well as a pension payable to a former spouse, are assessed at the rate of six tenths of the pension to which the insured person would have been entitled, if, at the time of his death, he had been incapable of following his customary occupation. Children's allowances, and any additional period included in the pension, are disregarded. In the Miners' Special Scheme pensions insurance the basis of computation is the Miners' Pension payable because of inability to follow the normal occupation, plus the higher annual increments, but excluding children's allowance and any additional period. If the beneficiaries have reached the age of 45, or if they are incapable of following their normal occupation, or are unemployable, or have the care of at least one child entitled to an orphan's pension, the pension amounts to six tenths of the pension to which the insured person would have been entitled at the time of his death if he had been classified as unemployable. If the computation of the pension on this basis results in a widow's pension of less than six tenths of that of which the deceased was last in receipt, the pension is increased to that amount. If several persons in their capacity as widow, widower, or former spouse, have entitlement to a pension, each beneficiary receives only such amount of the assessed pension proportionate to the duration of the marriage with the insured person.

The orphan's pension amounts in the case of half orphans to one tenth, of full orphans to one fifth, of the pension to which the insured person would have been entitled, less children's allowance, if he had been classified as unemployable at the time of his death. It is increased by the children's allowance. The survivors' pensions taken together may not exceed the pension (Miners' Pension) including children's allowance to which the insured person would have been entitled at the time of his death if he had been classified as unemployable. The amounts will otherwise be reduced proportionately.

Integration of Expellees and Refugees

Expellees and Refugees, with the claims and entitlements acquired in their home countries, have now been integrated in the social pensions insurance of the Federal Republic.

The non-contributory pensioners (Fremdrentner) now include only manual and non-manual workers expelled from non-German expulsion territories, Germans who have returned from foreign countries who, for reasons arising from the war, are no longer able to make good their claims against the foreign insurance fund, refugees and migrants from East Germany, Germans who, after 8. 5. 1945, were deported for forced labour, as well as stateless foreigners resident in the Federal Republic. Pursuant to the principle of integration, Fremdrentner are now treated as though their working and insurance life had been spent in the Federal Republic. The principle of integration has consequences on the computation of periods of employment, the competence of the insurance fund, and the assessment of the pension.

The claims of insured persons against discontinued and no longer existent German insurance funds are dealt with according to general regulations. If no insurance records are available, the rules applicable to non-contributory pensioners are applicable.

Adjustment of Current Pensions

The annual adjustment of the gerneral basis of computation has its effect on pensions already payable. They are also amended by law. The drafting of the Adjustment Laws takes place in accordance with a prescribed process, in which a Social Advisory Council, consisting of four representatives of the insured persons, four representatives of the employers, three representatives of the social and economic sciences, and one representative of the German Federal Bank take part. The adjustment of pensions is designed to take account of the progress of economic efficiency and of productivity, as well as of the movements in the national income per employed person. The Federal Government annually submits to the legislative bodies the Pensions Adjustment Report, formerly the Social Report, which reports on the relevant facts and on the financial position of the pensions insurance schemes, and makes proposals for future measures. The Pensions Adjustment Report is linked with the Report of the Social Advisory Council. On the basis of the Pensions Adjustment Reports (Social Reports) of 1958 to 1969, and the proposals of the Federal Government, pensions have been increased annually since 1959. The Social Advisory Council and the Social Report also dealt, in 1963 for the first time, with an adjustment of cash benefits in Industrial Injuries Insurance. The 12th Pensions Adjustment, enacted in 1969, increasing pensions with effect from 1. 1. 1970. made it possible, as a consequence of timely legislation, to pay out the increased amounts at the end of 1969. A similar process is planned for the 13th Pensions Adjustment, taking effect from 1. 1. 1971. By virtue of a Law enacted in the early summer of 1970 it will in future be possible to pay the increased pensions on the first of January of each year.

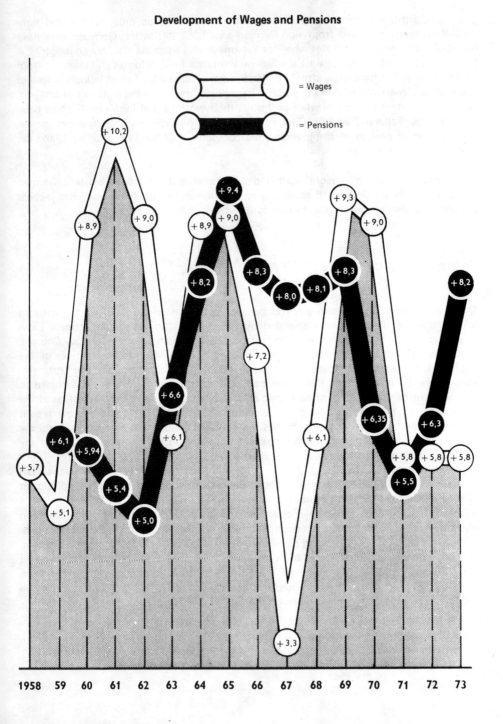

Development of Wages and Pensions

This diagram presents the development anticipated in July 1970 from 1969 onwards; for the latest values see pages 69/70.

Concurrence and Suspension of Pensions Payments

Pensions payable under Pensions Insurance are paid in lieu of the normal earnings of the insured person; pensions under Industrial Injuries Insurance are intended to compensate for the reduction in earning capacity consequent on the injury. This connection between pensions payable under Pensions and Industrial Injuries Insurance, based on customary earnings, can result in the payment to an insured person of a total pension exceeding his previous earnings. In order to obviate this socio-politically undesirable situation, special Pension Suspension regulations are in force, designed to ensure that, as a general rule, the pensioner shall not be in receipt of a higher total pensions income than his former net earnings. Similar regulations apply to survivors. We will refrain from giving details. The Suspension Regulations apply in number and effects only to a relatively small number of beneficiaries. In certain further cases of duplication of pension payments special regulations are applicable.

The Law as governing the Payment of Pensions Abroad

The Law here described does not apply in cases in which the Federal Republic of Germany has concluded an agreement on social security with the country in which the pensioner is resident, For details see the sector ,,International Security''.

If the beneficiary is not a German, and not a former German national, and if he normally and voluntarily resides outside the Federal territory, or if he is banned from residence in that territory, the payment of his pension is suspended. If he is only temporarily resident outside the Federal territory, the pension continues to be payable. An exception is made in the case of orphans whose parents or guardians are normally and voluntarily resident abroad; in these cases it is assumed that the residence of the orphans abroad is not voluntary, and the pension is payable.

If the beneficiary is a German, or a former German national, the payment of the pension is suspended in principle if he resides outside the Federal territory. There are certain exceptions:

In the event of temporary residence outside the Federal territory, the pension continues to be payable in full. Temporary residence is defined as residence of up to one year. This period may be extended for good and sufficient reasons. In the case of normal residence abroad, the pension continues to be payable in so far as it is payable in respect of insurance years actually spent in the Federal Republic. The pension also continues to be payable in respect of periods, excepting employment periods, under the pre 1945 insurance schemes, and of periods equated to the Non-Contributors Law (Fremdrentenrecht), if the insurance period credited had been spent mainly in the Federal territory, or if the pension had been assessed, or is being assessed, in respect of periods in which the beneficiary had normally been resident in the Federal territory. If these conditions are not satisfied, but if at least 60 contribution periods have been spent in the Federal territory, then the periods spent outside the Federal territory are taken into account to the same extent as contribution periods spent in the Federal territory. If these conditions are not satisfied, the pension can be paid, in so far as it is not based on periods equated to the Non-Contributors Law (Fremdrentenrecht) to insured persons resident in countries in which the Federal Republik of Germany has official representation. In the case of expellees from the territories incorporated in the German Empire in the period 1938 and 1939 to 1945, who are the victims of political persecution, pensions are payable under certain conditions, in so far as they are not payable in respect of periods falling under the Non-Contributors Law (Fremdrentenrecht). These benefits do not rank as social security benefits, an aspect which is of importance in the case of supra-national and bilateral social insurance agreements.

Former German nationals are treated in the same way in this respect as persons who, between 30. 1. 1932 and 9. 5. 1945, left Germany in order not to be compelled to live under conditions unacceptable to them, and as a result of the personal duress arising from the political situation, or who were unable or unwilling to return for the same reasons. The Draft Law for the Improvement of Reparations in Social Insurance provides for an easing of the conditions under which pensions may be paid to victims of Nazi persecution resident abroad. Members of German religious communities, who are former German nationals, may be paid pensions abroad if their employment, until the point at which the pension becomes payable, has been based mainly on religious or moral motives, is with the care of the sick, with education, with pastoral or other communal activities. Such pensions are payable in the territories of foreign States in which the Federal Republic has no official representation.

Persons entitled according to general rules to voluntary further insurance, may pay contributions from abroad. The insured person who wants to be further insured, applies to the Land Insurance Institute Rhine-Province in Düsseldorf if, before leaving the Federal territory, he was insured under pensions insurance for manual workers. In all other cases the Federal Insurance Institute for Non-manual Workers in Berlin Wilmersdorf is competent.

Non-manual workers who, because of their residence abroad on 31. 12. 1967, are exempted from insurance under Pensions Insurance for Non-manual Workers and, after having returned into the Federal Republic, become insurable on the basis of the unlimited insurance obligation in force since 1. 1. 1968, may apply for exemption. A prerequisite is that the application for exemption is filed with the Federal Insurance Institute for Non-manual Workers in Berlin Wilmersdorf within three months after having taken up an insurable employment in the Federal territory. Persons becoming insurable, or returning from abroad after the 31. 12. 1975, cannot successfully apply for exemption.

Commencement and Payment of Pensions

In principle pensions are payable from the end of the month in which the conditions are satisfied. If the pension (miners' pension), on account of reduced earning capacity in the customary occupation, or of unemployability, or retirement pension (Miners' retirement pension), has been paid in respect of the month of death, the payment of survivors' pension commences at the end of that month, otherwise from the time of death. The payment of provisional pensions commences 26 weeks after the occurrence of reduced earning capacity or unemployability. Miners' pensions or pensions (under the Miners' Special Scheme) on account of reduced earning capacity or unemployability are payable from the beginning of the month in which application has been made, if the application is made more than three months later than the satisfaction of the conditions; pensions to a former spouse are made in every instance from the beginning of the month in which the application is made. Payments are, as a general rule, made monthly by the Post Office, on production of an order to pay. Arrangements may be made for the post to pay the pension into the pension's account, and nearly half of them use this method. At the beginning of 1970 the post remited about 3.3 milliard DM to bank accounts in nearly 6 million cases (58 per cent of the approximately 10.3 million pensioners). In the case of non-manual workers' insurance the percentage is 70. Pension may be paid in the home if the beneficiary is over 75 years of age, or is infirm.

Commutation of Pensions and Refund of Contributions

In the event of remarriage the widow, the widower, or the former spouse, receives as commutation a sum amounting to five years pension payment. If compulsory payment of contributions in pension insurance ceases without the right to continue to pay voluntary contributions, or if an insured person, on the occurrence of unemployability has not satisfied a qualifying period of 60 months, and if it is no longer possible for him to satisfy the qualifying period before reaching his 65th year, the workers' portion of statutory and any higher rates of contribution paid subsequent to the Currency Reform in 1948 may be refunded on application. An application for refund of a part only of the refundable contributions is not permissible. A refund nullifies all claims in respect of past insurance periods and the right to continue to pay voluntary contributions.

If a beneficiary has a claim deriving solely from higher contributions, and if the resultant pension does not exceed 75 DM per annum, a lump sum may be paid in lieu of the pension. The formerly customary refund of contributions to female insured persons on marriage was discontinued at the beginning of 1968.

Transfer Insurance

A transferable insurance exists when an insured person during the course of his working life has been insured under the manual and non-manual worker's schemes, or under the Miners' Special Scheme, or under any two of these schemes. When the pension becomes payable, the overall amount due is assessed by the Fund into which the last contribution was paid, which Fund assumes responsibility for payments arising out of contributions made to other Funds. Special regulations apply to the competence of the Miners' Special Scheme.

Health Insurance of Pensioners

Since 1941 recipients of a pensions under pensions insurance are entitled to the benefits of social health insurance. In 1956 and 1957 this legal entitlement was amended (see section "Social Health Insurance"). All entitled pensioners are compulsorily insured for health insurance from the time they apply for payment. Compulsory insurance based on other grounds takes precedence over insurance as a pensioner, as does voluntary insurance based on other statutory regulations. Privately insured pensioners may contract out of statutory insurance. In all cases the Pensions Fund pays a health insurance contribution for the pensioner. Contributions are payable at the same rate as that applicable to an insured person entitled to continued payment of wage or salary for six weeks. This rate is applied to a basic wage reduced by 20 per cent in relation to those generally payable to the individual in the different Federal Lands. This basic wage may be further reduced according to the number of persons in receipt of a pension, that is to say, according to the proportion of employed persons to pensioners in any particular Fund. This is always the case when this relationship deviates from the Federal average.

This method is assessment can lead to a position in which the Sick Fund receives no contribution from the Pensions Fund. On the other hand the Health Insurance as a whole can be assured that all benefits payments must be refunded by Pensions Insurance, less a quota of 20 per cent.

The average amount payable throughout the Federal territory (w.e.f. 1. 7. 1970 = 49 DM) is also payable to members of private Health Insurance Schemes. The amount payable for voluntarily insured persons was fixed with effect from 1. 4. 1941 at 4 RM, has meanwhile been frequently increased, and stands since 1. 1. 1969 at 50 DM monthly. In the years 1968 and 1969, pensioners were required to pay 2 % of their pension, less children's allowances, into the health insurance fund.

Contributions to the Health Insurance of Pensioners
in DM per month

from	ArV/AnV	from	ArV/AnV	from	ArV/AnV
1. 8. 1941	3,30[1]	1. 7. 1959	17,20	1. 1. 1965	28.10
1. 4. 1950	4,20	1. 1. 1960	18,00	1. 7. 1965	28.60
1. 1. 1951	5,20	1. 7. 1960	18,50	1. 4. 1966	33.10
1. 4. 1952	5,85	1. 1. 1961	20,40	1. 1. 1967	38.10
1. 8. 1956	10,40[2]	1. 7. 1961	20,20	1. 7. 1967	40.40
1. 1. 1957	11,50	1. 1. 1962	25,00	1. 2. 1968	40.20
1. 7. 1957	13,00	1. 7. 1962	24,90	1. 7. 1968	39.30
1. 8. 1958	14,50	1. 1. 1963	26,00	1. 4. 1969	39.00
1. 7. 1958	15,50	1. 1. 1964	27,10	1. 2. 1970	43.60
1. 1. 1959	17,40	1. 7. 1964	27,20	1. 7. 1970	49.00

1) Up to 31.5.1949   1 DM was retained from every pension;   up to 31.7.1956   the amount applied to every pension
2) From 1.8.1965 the contribution applies to every pensioner insured for Health Insurance.

Additional Benefits

Pensions Insurance Funds are authorised, to the extent possible in their financial position, to carry out measures in excess of their statutory obligations, if such measures serve the maintenance of the employability of the insured persons and their dependents, or which serve to improve the general health of the insured population. These measures include: Provision for research into the causes of sickness threatening public health, for cancer research, school dental treatment, youth hostels and similar institutions. The Sickness Funds also receive additional payments from the Pensions Funds for dentures, medicines, and appliances. Over and above normal benefits, other expenditure for the benefit of pensioners and their dependents is permissible: this applies in particular to the promotion of house building for the insured population. Further, pensioners may, with their own consent, be accommodated in old persons' homes, or in orphanages, or similar institutions. Under certain conditions the Federal Miners' Special Scheme is obliged to pay, on application, a Miners' Special Scheme compensation benefit to an insured person if his customary occupation in a mining undertaking has been terminated after his 55th year for reasons for which he is not responsible. The compensation benefit is payable at the same rate as a Miners' Special Scheme pension payable on account of inability to follow the customary occupation, with annual increments per insurance year of 2 %. A Special Scheme pension is not payable in addition.

Finance

Coverages

Statutory regulations governing pensions insurance prescribed until 1957 the accumulation of very high reserves. However, these regulations have never been complied with over longer periods of time; the resultant reserves were lost in the 1923 inflation, and at the time of the Currency Reform of 1948 (to an amount of about 16 milliard RM). On the occasion of the Pensions Insurance Reform of 1957, the idea gained ground that, in consideration of the dimensions then reached, the expenditure of the Pensions Funds could no longer be covered by capital accumulation — which, it is estimated, would by now have reached 750 to 1000 milliard DM. For this reason a phased covering process was inaugurated. All expenditure arising in the 10 years phase beginning 1957 was to be covered, and at the end of the phase a reserve fund formed to the amount of the expenditure of the Funds in the final year of the first covering phase. The Third Amending Law of 25. 7. 1969 introduced a new covering procedure, namely a levy procedure with a high monetary reserve. It limits the growth of the reserves of Pensions Funds, which had risen to 26 milliard DM, and, in the long run, balances out the financial consequences of the increasing number of pensioners. Contribution rates were fixed for the period up to 1985 (from 1973 onwards at 18 %). Reserves will be held at about the present level, and will not increase in line with pensions expenditure. Financial forecasts, now replacing insurance actuarial balances, will now be made annually for the following 15 years, and will provide the legislative bodies with a more rapid survey of the financial progress of the Pensions Funds. If the reserves of the Pensions Insurance of Manual and Non-manual workers together on any occasion at the end of a least three consecutive years do not come up to the estimates of the expenditure for three months at the expense of the Funds, a uniform rate of contribution must be fixed in such a manner that the reserves from the deficit year onwards amount to at least the corresponding expenditure for three months.

In the case of the Miners' Special Scheme Pensions Insurance, this covering procedure is not expressly prescribed; any deficit arising will be met by the Federal Government.

Contributions

Current rates of contribution in manual and non-manual pensions insurance are 17 % of insurable earnings, up to the insurable ceiling. Insurable annual earnings are twice the general basis of computation for pensions payable during the same calendar year; earnings are rounded off upwards to an amount divisible by 1200. The result is that the maximum contribution for 1970 amounts to 306 DM monthly, i.e., 17 % of 1.800 DM. Contributions in the case of compulsorily insurable persons are normally paid as to one half each by the employer and the insured person.

Contributions are paid in full by the employer if monthly gross earnings do not exceed one tenth of the contribution ceiling for monthly earnings (1970 = 180 DM). Self-employed compulsory contributors pay themselves, whereas in the case of insurable members of religious communities, deaconesses, Red Cross nurses and members of similar communities, the contribution is paid by their organisation, and in the case of insurable persons serving with the Forces, by the government. In the case of Germans employed abroad in development aid, who have applied to become insurable, the contributions are paid by the employing body.

Contribution rates in Pensions Insurance
in % of insurable earnings

Manual Workers Period	Insurance %	Non-man. workers insurance Period	%	Miners' Period	Man. Workers Scheme	Non-man. workers Special
1891/1911	1,7	–	–	1924	11,6	10,0
1912/1916	2,1	–	–	1925	10,7	6,5
1917/1923	2,6	–	–	1926	11,0	9,3
1924	2,7	1913/1923	5,3	1927/1928	10,6	12,3
1925/1926	4,1	1924	3,0	1929/1930	8,5	10,3
1927/1942	5,0	1925/1942	4,0	1931/1937	9,8	10,9
ab 1.7.1942	5,6	ab 1.7.1942	5,6	1938/1941	9,0	16,0
ab 1.6.1949	10,0	ab 1.6.1949	10,0	1942/1948	18,5	21,5
ab 1.4.1955	11,0	ab 1.4.1955	11,0			
ab 1.3.1957	14,0	ab 1.3.1957	14,0			
ab 1.1.1968	15,0	ab 1.1.1968	15,0	from 1.6.1949	22,5	
ab 1.1.1969	16,0	ab 1.1.1969	16,0	since 1.6.1957	23,5	
ab 1.1.1970	17,0	ab 1.1.1970	17,0			
ab 1.1.1973	18,0	ab 1.1.1973	18,0			

Contributions in Manual Workers Insurance prior to 1927, to Non-manual Workers Insurance prior to 1942, and in the Miners' Special Scheme prior to 1938, are averages of the contribution rates for the seperate wages and salary groups.

Contribution rates for persons compulsorily insured under the Miners' Special Scheme amount to 23.5 % of earnings of the insured persons, in so far as they do not exceed the insurable ceiling; they are payable as to 8.5 % by the worker, and 15 % by the employer; they are payable by the employer alone if monthly gross earnings do not exceed one tenth of the contributions ceiling for monthly earnings (1970 = 210 DM). The insurance ceiling under the Miners' Special Scheme is higher, and is calculated on a different basis from that under Manual and Non-Manual Workers' Pensions Insurance.

The contributions of insured employees are paid in by the employer. He remits the contributions to Pensions Insurance, togehter with contributions to Health and Unemployment Insurance, to the collecting agency, the local Sick Fund, which, for its part transfers the amounts due to the other Funds. In the case of compulsorily insurable self-employed persons and voluntary contributors, contributions had so far been paid by affixing stamps, except in the case of compulsorily insured artisans. Since the beginning of 1970 they may be paid through a bank account. Since December 1969 voluntary contributors under the Manual Workers' Pensions Insurance Scheme may pay their contributions to the Land Insurance Institute through their bank. A condition is that they shall be paid promptly. A similar arrangement will apply in the case of non-manual workers with effect from the beginning of 1971.

Development of Contribution Classes

	Contribution Class	Year 1970	1971	1972	1973
a		17	17	17	18
b	100	– – 150	– – 150	– – 150	– – 150
a		34	34	34	36
b	200	150-250	150-250	150-250	150-250
a		51	51	51	54
b	300	250-350	250-350	250-350	250-350
a		68	68	68	72
b	400	350-450	350-450	350-450	350-500
a		85	85	85	✕
b	500	450-550	450-550	450-550	
a		102	102	102	108
b	600	550-650	550-650	550-650	500-700
a		119	119	119	✕
b	700	650-750	650-750	650-750	
a		136	136	136	144
b	800	750-850	750-850	750-850	700-900
a		153 ←	153	153	✕
b	900	850-950	850-950	850-950	
a		170	170 ←	170 ←	180
b	1 000	950-1050	950-1100	950-1100	900-1100
a		187	✕	✕	✕
b	1 100	1050-1150			
a		204	204	204	216 ←
b	1 200	1150-1300	1100-1300	1100-1300	1100-1300
a		238	238	238	252
b	1 400	1300-1500	1300-1500	1300-1500	1300-1500
a		272	272	272	288
b	1 600	1500-1700	1500-1700	1500-1700	1500-1700
a		306	306	306	324
b	1 800	1700-1800	1700-1850	1700-1900	1700-1900
a			323	✕	✕
b	1 900		1850-1900		
a				340	360
b	2 000			1900-2000	1900-2050
a					378
b	2 100				2050-2150
a					396
b	2 200				2150-2250
a					414
b	2 300				2250-2300

a = Contribution Class, and the contribution in DM; b= earnings falling under the indicated contribution class: average contribution for insurable self-employed craftsmen; minimum contribution for non-manual workers, whose voluntary contributions are to be paid to the same amount as those of insurable persons; half-heavy printed DM contributions = contribution class for higher contributions.

Government Subsidies

Government subsidies have at all times represented a form of financing typical for social pensions insurance. They have been paid without a break since 1891. The original amount of about one third of expenditure could not, however, be maintained. Subsidies and refunds paid by the Federal Government to the three branches of pensions insurance rose from 0.7 milliard DM in 1950 to 10.3 milliard DM in 1969, that is by almost fifteen times

Development of Governmental Subsidies and their Quota of the Expenditure of Pensions Insurance
— from 1970 estimated —

Year	ArV			AnV		
	Subsidy	Expenditure	%	Subsidy	Expenditure	%
1950	484	2551	19,0	179	998	17,9
1955	1784	4866	36,7	694	2192	31,7
1960	3517	12164	28,9	950	5719	16,6
1965	4961	18962	26,2	1120	9746	11,5
1968	6029	26266	23,0	698	13482	5,2
1969	6205	29608	21,3	786	15231	5,2
1970	6355	31729	20,0	848	16401	5,2
1971	6775	33922	20,0	1071	17790	6,0
1975	9601	46230	20,8	2161	28253	7,6
1980	12728	60692	21,0	2865	40021	7,2
1985	16873	77025	21,9	3798	51722	7,3

Year	ArV + AnV			KnV		
	Subsidy	Expenditure	%	Subsidy	Expenditure	%
1950	663	3549	18,7	176	605	29,1
1955	2478	7058	35,1	475	1274	37,3
1960	4467	17883	25,0	1235	2688	45,9
1965	6081	28708	21,2	2187	4046	54,1
1968	6727	39748	16,9	3060	5414	56,5
1969	6991	44839	15,6	3320	4860	68,3
1970	7203	48130	15,0	3685	5110	72,1
1971	7846	51712	15,2	3914	5416	72,3
1975	11762	74483	15,3	5773	7195	80,2
1980	15593	100713	15,5	7750	9377	82,6
1985	20671	128747	16,1	9379	11228	83,5

Note — Refunds from Artisans Pensions and Transfer Insurance have been deducted.

in 19 years. Despite this rapid absolute increase, other comparative figures reveal quite a different picture: In 1970 the Government is meeting one fifth of the total expenditure of Pensions Insurance; in 1953, in contrast, it was two fifths. Subsidies have continuously decreased relative to the total expenditure of pensions insurance. In manual and non-manual workers' pensions insurance, i.e. not including the Miners' Special Scheme, the government is paying one sixth during 1970, so that its quota has been halved in 18 years.

At the present time (1970/71) the quota of the Federal subsidy to the overall expenditure of Pensions Insurance has reached its lowest level. Even the increase in the subsidies to the Miners' Special Scheme Pensions Insurance cannot counterbalance this reduction. Between 1953 and 1961 about 10 to 11 % of the Federal Budget was devoted to subsidies to manual and non-manual workers insurance. Since 1957 the quota of subsidies from the Federal Budget had fallen from almost 12 % to 8.1 % in 1970. Only in the case of the Miners' Special Scheme has the quota risen continuously. Taking all these branches together, the amount has remained fairly constant for years at about 13 %. The period of the heaviest calls on the Federal budget was passed some years ago.

The payment of government subsidies must be regarded as a compensation for losses caused by the war. The premature payment of pensions arising from the war, the reckonability of substitution periods, and the loss of contributions, have occasioned losses for pensions insurance almost to the same amount as the subsidies. And there are other losses arising from the war which cannot be expressed in figures. In the new finance system operating since the Pensions Insurance Reform of 1957, the government subsidies amount to a (third) state contribution. Federal subsidies increase with rising wage levels, but the Federal Government is not taking over any part of the ever increasing cost of pensions.

Financial Adjustment

Manual and non-manual workers are insurable under pensions insurance, with equal contributions and benefits, but in different Funds. Since the number of non-manual workers has been on the increase for decades, but not that of manual workers, the non-manual workers Fund is able to reckon for this reason alone with a continuing increase of contribution income. In order to balance out the disparate development of these two branches of insurance — inevitable on the basis of existing economic conditions — the Pensions Insurance Finance Adjustment Law of 1964 cancelled the payments formerly made by the manual workers' Fund to the non-manual workers' Fund, based on the so-called "Transfer Insurance" (Wanderversicherung), and proposed a different distribution of the Federal Government subsidy. In lieu of such change, the Third Pensions Insurance Amendment Law of 1969 introduced direct financial adjustment changes in case the assets of one of the two branches of insurance should fall below two calendar months expenditure in the preceding year, less government subsidy, and those of the other should exceed 4 calendar months expenditure. It is to be anticipated that, as a result, the Non-manual Workers' Fund will be called on, for the first time about 1974, to make payments to the Manual Workers' Fund; in the following years these payments will increase rapidly from about 1.5 milliard DM to 3 to 4 milliard DM. The Funds were further placed under an obligation to accumulate the amounts of which other Funds are deficient, and mutual help is prescriebed in cases of emergency. In this manner it is anticipated that, without establishing a single uniform Fund, and without recourse to the capital market, the solvency of the Manual Workers' Pensions Insurance will be secured at all times.

Within the Manual Workers' Pensions Insurance, and because of the varied and strained financial position of the Insurance Institutes in 1969, an adjustment of existing assets to expenditure was introduced. It is true that the Common Burdens Procedure is operative, on the basis of which pensions, pensions commutations, contributions refunds, and contributions to the health insurance of pensioners, are borne jointly by the various Manual Workers' Pensions Insurance Funds, and distributed in respect of any calendar year in proportion to contributions income, but a so called Deficit-Spread-over-Procedure has also been inaugurated, pursuant to which deficits arising in separate Funds from the difference between expenditure and income are spread over in proportion to assets. This procedure led in 1969 (once only) to a spread over to an amount of nearly 15 % of total assets Further, administration expenses and expenditure for rehabilitation were fixed at uniform levels, and were limited only for administrative buildings. These measures are intended in their entirety to contribute to a uniform financial procedure in Manual Workers' Pension insurance.

In their relations with the Miners' Special Scheme Pensions Insurance, the Manual and Non-manual Workers' Schemes receive and refund the proportion of pensions arising from former insurance in the other branch of insurance (Transfer Insurance Adjustment). In addition, the Manual and Non-manual Workers' Schemes make an adjustment payment until 1973 for the decrease of insured persons under the Miners' Special Scheme, which has resulted in a corresponding increase in the number of their insured persons (Gain on transfer). Both types of payment amount in 1970 to about 1.3 milliard DM (balance).

Assets

The assets of Pensions Insurance rose between 1948 and the end of 1956 to 10.1 milliard DM, to rise again by 1966 to 27.3 milliard DM. As a consequence of the economic recession they declined in the years 1966 to 1968 to about 23.1 milliard DM. A subsequent reduction of the assets of Manual Workers' Pensions Insurance (by 1.3 milliard DM in 1969) stands in contrast to a growing increase in the case of Non-Manual Workers' Pensions Insurance, so that the assets of both branches taken together will rise to about 27 milliard DM by 1973.

Pursuant to the 3rd Amending Law to Pensions Insurance the assets have been redistributed, in order to accord better than hitherto with the different purposes of capital accumulation.

For the first time the Funds were required to retain a great part of their assets in cash. Until the required Liquidity Reserve has been reached, namely two months expenditure, the assets may not be invested long term.

The Liquidity Reserve is to be held in the form of cash, current accounts, fixed period and savings accounts, with credit institutes for a period of, or on notice of, up to 12 months, debenture stocks with a currency of up to 4 years, in so far as they have a remaining currency of up to 12 months, or in treasury bills, or interest free bonds. Further, the Funds are required, on a joint declaration by the Federal Government and the Federal Bank to immobilise up to 60 % of one month's expenditure in the form of finance bills and liquidity papers, if this is held to be necessary because of the state of the market, or for monetary reasons. The Liquidity Reserve had been calculated for 1969 at

Review of the System of the Investment of Assets

Type of Assets	Amount provided for in monthly expenditure charged against the Fund or branch	Period	Purpose
I. Reserves (Cash and investments	a) manual and non-manual ins. jointly at least 3	at 3 consecutive years ends	Security of benefits
	b) for each sepeately at least 2	at each years end	as the standard for the adjustment of liabilities
thereof			
1. Ready cash	permissible up to 1 (of the current calendar year	as required	cover of monthly expenditure
2. Liquidity Reserve	at least 1 1/2	at any time	medium term cover of expenditure without
3. Additional Liquidity Reserves	according to the deficits in the Liquidity Reserve of other Funds	at any time	realising assets on the capital market
4. Others, in particular long term investments	a) jointly: Difference in reserves up to 1 1/2	at 3 consecutive years ends	long-term cover of expenditure
	b) for each seperately: Difference in reserve up to 1/2	at each years and	
II. Administrative assets	As laid down in administrative regulations		Non-investment assets held for administrative needs

Cash and Investment Holdings on 31.12.1969, KnRV on 30.9.1969
in Mill. DM

Item	ArV[1]	AnV[2]	KnRV[3]
Cash and Credit a/c	134	25	160
Deposits with Credit Institutes	738	2 129	51
Interest free Exchequer Bills	25	–	–
Debenture Stocks			
maturing up to 4 years	7	151	1
more than 4 years	3 588	3 310	18
Credits with the Fed. Government	–	3 754	–
Loans	2 928	2 246	155
Mortgages, Land Charges	1 236	1 397	253
Land and Buildings	1 112	257	51
Inventory	145	16	5
Shareholdings	65	75	1
Total	9 993	13 360	696

1) Manual Workers Insurance   2) Non-Manual Workers Insurance   3) Miners' Special Scheme Insurance

an amount of about 4 milliard DM in manual and non-manual workers' insurance together, but in fact only about 2.3 milliard was available in a liquid form. Liquid funds amounted in the case of non-manual workers' insurance to 1.6 months expenditure, in the case of manual workers to only 0.4 months. The Liquidity Reserve is to be built up to about 6 1/2 milliard DM by 1973.

The amount of reserves is not limited in an upward direction. It is possible to accummulate them, however, only if the contribution rates permit of surpluses. Funds therefrom may be invested long term only when ready cash and liquid reserves are available in adequate amounts in all the Insurance Funds.

Administrative assets include in particular administrative office buildings and convalescent homes. They may not be taken into account as reserves, since, in case of need, they cannot be converted into cash to meet pensions payments. Administrative assets have been more closely circumscribed by an administrative Ordinance. In the case of manual workers' pensions insurance they were estimated at the end of 1969 at about 1.3 milliard DM, non-manual workers' at about 300 million DM.

Organisation

The administration of Manual Workers' Pensions Insurance is in the hands of 18 Land Insurance Institutes, covering the greater majority of insured persons, of the Federal Railways Insurance Institute for manual workers on the railways, and the Seaman's Fund for the mercantile marine, coastwise seamen and inshore fishermen. In 1969 these Funds employed about 34.000 persons. The Pensions Insurance Funds of Manual Workers are under an obligation to co-operate in the establishment or extension of hospitals etc., as well as the allocation of beds, in the interests of adequate, suitable, economical, and uniform treatment of all insured persons. Uniform equipment, with the requisite funds, is secured in the framework of the joint financial responsibility of all Manual Workers' Pensions Insurance Funds.

The administration of Non-Manual Workers' Pensions Insurance is in the hands of the Federal Insurance Institute for Non-Manual Workers, with a personnel in 1969 of about 10.000.

In the case of mine workers, the responsible body is the Federal Miners' Special Scheme — the Bundesknappschaft — with a personnel in 1969 of some 9.000.

All the administrations are corporations in public law, subject to overall governmental supervision. In this connection the position is that administrations whose scope covers only a single Federal Land are under the supervision of the supreme Labour authority in that Land, whereas those whose scope extends to several Lands, or to the whole of the Federal territory, come under the supervision of the Federal Government, which maintains a Federal Insurance Office for the purpose, an independent Federal authority. The administrations themselves have combined in the Association of German Pensions Insurance Administrations — a registered society. All administrations are self-governing bodies (see the sector "Self-Government").

Fed. Ins. Institute for Non-Manual Workers	in Berlin
Fed. Railways Insurance Institue	in Frankfurt
Seaman's Fund	in Hamburg
LVA Baden	in Karlsruhe
LVA Berlin	in Berlin
LVA Braunschweig	in Braunswick
LVA Hannover	in Hannover
LVA Free and Hansa City of Hamburg	in Hamburg
LVA Hessen	in Frankfort
LVA Lower Bavaria — Upper Palatinate	in Landshut
LVA Upper Bavaria	in Munich
LVA Upper and Middle Franconia	in Bayreuth
LVA Oldenburg-Bremen	in Oldenburg
LVA Rhineland-Palatinate	in Speyer
LVA Rhine Province	in Düsseldorf
LVA Saarland	in Saarbrücken
LVA Schleswig-Holstein	in Lübeck
LVA Swabia	in Augsburg
LVA Lower Franconia	in Würzburg
LVA Westphalia	in Münster
LVA Württemberg	in Stuttgart
Fed. Miners' Special Scheme	in Bochum

*LVA = Land Insurance Institute

Administrative expenditure consists of administrative costs and the costs of collecting contributions, and of providing benefits. It amounted in 1969 to a total of 654 mill. DM in the case of manual workers, and 270 mill. DM in the case of non-manual workers. The percentage since 1949 has been between 2.2 and 2.3 % in the case of manual workers, and

1,8 and 2 % in the case of non-manual workers. Percentages in the case of non-manual workers are lower than in the case of manual workers, but here the basis of comparison, namely the level of pensions, and consequently the vast bulk of expenditure, plays an important role.

Legislative bases

4th Book of the Imperial Insurance Regulations dated 19. 7. 1911 (BGBl, III − 820 − 1), last amended by the Law dated 23. 6. 1970 (BGBl. I S. 805).

Non-Manual Workers Insurance Law dated 26. 12. 1911 (BGBl. III − 821 − 1), last amended by the Law dated 23. 6. 70 (BGBl. I S. 805).

Imperial Miners' Special Scheme Law dated 23. 6. 1923 (BGBl. III − 822 − 1), last amended by the Law dated 23. 6. 1970 (BGBl. I S. 805).

Federal Miners' Special Scheme Errichtungsgesetz of 28. 7. 69 (BGB I S 974)

Non-Contributors Pension Law dated 25. 2. 1960 (BGBl. III − 824 − 2; 824 − 3), last amended by the Law dated 9. 6. 1965 (BGBl. IS 476).

insurance Records Ordinance of 3. 3. 1960 (BGBI 14 − 8232 − II) amended by Ordinance of 22.12.1965 (BGBI 1 − 2139).

Pensions Insurance of Self-employed Craftsmen

Introduction

Of the approximately 3 million self-employed persons, artisans, or craftsmen, are the second largest group after the farmers, with about 750.000 businesses and 708.000 owners (1964). The number of such businesses has declined by some 156.000 since 1949. In the coming years a further decline is to be anticipated, though at a somewhat reduced rate.

Retirement Pensions Insurance for self-employed craftsmen was first introduced in 1938. Pursuant to the Craftsmen's Self Provision Law, every craftsman affected was required to pay pension insurance contributions to the Non-Manual Workers' Scheme, but was permitted to contract out on condition that he took out a life insurance policy with a private company and paid the same amount in premiums as he would be required to pay to the Non-Manual Workers' Scheme. At that time a life insurance policy to the amount of 5.000 RM was regarded as adequate provision for old age. (In comparison: average gross annual earnings amounted in 1938 to 1947 RM).

Current legislation is based on the Craftsmen's Insurance Law (Handwerkerversicherungs-gesetz) which came into force in 1962. It limited the duration of compulsory insurability for all self-employed craftsmen to 18 years, but abolished the contracting out clause. It also limited the amount of the contributions payable. The Special Fund for Provision in Old Age for Craftsmen was closed down, and the assets transferred and earmarked from the Non-Manual to the Manual Workers' Pensions Insurance.

Since 1. 1. 1970 a special regulation has been in force for District Master Chimney Sweeps. They are now fully insurable under the Craftsman's Insurance Scheme. In addition, they are insurable in the Retirement Pensions Institute for District Master Chimney Sweeps, a self-governing corporation in public law. This is a case of overall provision, such as is customary in the public services; the pension from the Craftsman's insurance is taken into account. Administration is in the hands of the Bavarian Insurance Chamber, under the supervision of the Federal Minister for Economics.

The Functions of Insurance

Within the framework of the Manual Workers Insurance Schemes, the Craftsmen's Insurance Scheme accords to independent artisans largely the same benefits as those to which employed manual workers are entitled; the regulations are the same as those for other insurable self-employed persons (e.g. homeworkers), unless otherwise specified. The fact that Craftsman's Insurance is intended only to be a basic insurance is indicated by the limited compulsory insurance period, and in the amount of compulsory contributions. Both factors leave open to independent craftsmen the possibility of taking out additional voluntary insurance.

Scope

All self-employed craftsmen entered in the Roll of Artisans are compulsorily insurable under the Manual Workers' Scheme, without regard to the amount of their income, if they have paid less than 216 monthly contributions (18 insurance years) in respect of an occupation insurable under pensions insurance. Partners in a private company registered in the Roll of Artisans are also insurable if they themselves satisfy the conditions necessary for entry on the Roll. Insurability continues under certain conditions, even when the insured person is performing military service. Over and above the conditions for exemption from insurability applying under the Manual Workers' Scheme, the following are also exempt: owners of ancillary craftsmen businesses, if they are registered on the Roll of Artisans, general executors, executors, executors of bankrupt businesses, persons who as heirs, or in joint heirship, are entered in the Artisans Roll but are not actively employed in the inherited business, widows or widowers who continue to conduct the business, if this fact alone would render them insurable, Self-employed craftsmen are also exempt if they had been exempt under earlier legislation and had made adequate alternative provision for their old age. Pursuant to these regulations only 176.400 were insurable in the middle of 1969; the highest number ever was recorded in 1965, namely 195.000. Continued voluntary insurance is possible on the same conditions as those of Manual Workers' Pensions Insurance. If self-employed craftsmen fulfill the conditions for voluntary insurance by paying contributions to the Non-Manual Workers' Scheme on the basis of fomerly valid legislation, they may continue as voluntary contributors only to the Manual Workers' Scheme.

Benefits

Benefits are on the same scale as those under the Manual Workers' Scheme, with certain exeptions taking account of self-employment. For instance, periods of unemployment are reckonable as excused periods only if and so long as the person's name is deleted from the Artisans Roll. Periods of illness, disablement, pregnancy, or of confinement, are reckonable as substitution or excused periods only if the insured persons has not employed an insurable person — with the exception of an apprentice — during such periods. If a substitution period coincides with a period of compulsory insurability, such a substitution period is reckonable only if no contributions have been paid in respect of it. Contributions formerly paid into the Non-Manual Workers' Scheme are reckonable as contributions paid into the Manual Workers' Scheme, but in arriving at the personal basis of computation, the regulations of the Non-Manual Workers' Scheme are applicable. Pensions already payable continue to be paid by the Non-Manual Workers' Scheme.

Finance

The Funds to meet the expenditure of the Self-employed Craftsmen's Insurance are raised from the contributions of the insured persons, plus a government subsidy. In order to obviate the need for checking income, a standard rate of contributions is payable — in 1970 at 153 DM per month,an amount which will probably be amended annually. It corresponds to the average contribution for employed employees (see the sector "Manual Workers' Pensions Insurance"). There are exceptions to this rule, for example, master craftsmen and artisans, during the first three years following their entry in Artisans Roll, pay contributions only every second month, i.e. about 76 DM. They may, however, decide to pay contributions on the basis of their actual income if this amounts to less than one half of the ascertained average remuneration of all manual and non-manual workers — 1970 = 451 DM per month, though the minimum for each two monthly period is 68 DM.

Separate accounting for this scheme is not possible. Contribution income at some 250 mill. DM for 1970 is estimated.

The refunds in respect of craftsmen's pension payable by the Manual Workers' Scheme to the Non-Manual Workers' Scheme in 1970 amount to 647 million DM.

Organisation

The Self-employed Craftsmen's Scheme is administered by the Manual Workers' Scheme, which also collects the contributions; with effect from 1. 1. 1970 an insurance code number is being allocated to each craftsman. A certain amount of assistance is rendered by the Chambers of Artisans to the Insurance Funds.

Legislative Bases

Self-employed Craftsmen's Law dated 8. 9. 1960 (BGBl. III — 8250 — 1), last amended 18. 9. 1969 (BGBl. I.S. 1634). Chimney Sweeps' Law dated 15. 9. 1969 (BGBl. I.S. 1634).

Pensions Insurance for Farmers

Introduction

Under the designation "Old Age Assistance for Farmers", pensions and contributions were inaugurated for nearly a million independent farmers in 1957. This system of security has since been extended in scope, nature and extent, far beyond its modest beginnings, but has retained its original name. The award of an old age allowance has made it easier for the older generation to hand over the farm or holding to the young people and to go into retirement. Payment is dependent on the transfer of the farm. The law has both social and agrarian policy objectives. In addition, for the inauguration and extension of the system, a part was played by the desire to facilitate the integration of the farming industry as a whole, and farms on which several generations were living in particular, into modern industrial society, and into the European Common Market.

The Land Surrender Pension Scheme which came into force on 1. 4. 1969 is aimed at an improvement of the agricultural structure. Its purpose is to facilitate the surrender of smaller holdings by elderly owners, in order that the land so made available can be put to a more productive use. Such surrender is limited to the period between 1. 8. 1969 and 31. 12. 1973; the resultant pensions will be paid for an unlimited period. The number of independent farmers under the age of 45 rose between 1956 from 301.000 to 411.000; in the same period the number between 45 and 65 fell from 719.000 to 465.000. The number of those over 65 fell from 194.000 to 92.000. The "rejuvenating" effect of the allowances is particulary evident in comparison with the EEC territory. Whereas, in all the Member States of the EEC, 55 % of all independent farmers are over 57 years of age, the percentage in the Federal Republic of Germany is 31 %.

Old age allowances were introduced on 1. 10. 1957, and were considerably amended and improved in subsequent years. In 1961 the financing was regulated anew. If contribution income failed to cover overall expenditure, the deficit was to be met by the Federal budget. In 1963 benefits were increased by two thirds, and pensions became payable in the event of disablement. In 1965 pensions were again increased by one half. The scope was extended to include older employed family members, and measures for the maintenance, improvement and restitution of employability were inaugurated. At the same time, and also in 1966 and 1967, contributions were increased. 1969 saw further improvements

Contributions and Recipients
at the years and — in 1000s

Year	Independent Farmers	Insurable Farmers	Pensioners	Premature Recipients
1958	984	805	259	—
1960	919	772	320	—
1965	876	799	385	13
1968	844	778	445	36
1969*)	.	773	451	42
1970	.	762	458	47
1971	.	749	463	51
1972	.	735	467	54

* from 1969: estimated.

in benefits and the introduction of the Land Surrender Pension, but once again an increase both of contributions and of the government subsidies. Taking all amendments together, the old age allowances are now largely in line with all other pensions insurance schemes.

It is the intention of the Federal Government, in addition to the Land Surrender Pension, to take further measures to close down farms and holdings incapable of improvement. Farmers from such farms who take up permanent employment as workers are to be permitted to pay contributions retrospectively into social pensions insurance. The conditions for the award of the Land Surrender Pension are also to be eased. Of particular importance is the question of health insurance for farmers. A Working Party in the Federal Ministry of Labour and Social Order is looking into the possibilities, and their financing.

Functions of Agricultural Pensions Insurance

Old age allowances for independent farmers provide for them, their spouses, widows, and and older employed members of their families, basic security in their old age, and in the event of premature disablement. This is secured by a supplement to the allowance made by their successors on the farm — the Altenteil — mostly in the form of accommodation and payment in kind, and by rehabilitation measures, including the provision of a deputy. Payment of allowances accounts for the bulk of expenditure. The Land Surrender Pension will facilitate the abandonment of agricultural employment during the next four years to the benefit of the general agricultural structure.

Agricultural Old Age Allowances

Compulsory Insurability

Pensions insurance for farmers covers all farmers without regard to the amount of their income and the size of the holding, though there is a lower limit designed mainly to exclude persons engaged in farming only as a subsidiary occupation. Independent farmers are all persons engaged in agriculture and forestry, including viniculture, fruit, and vegetable growing, as well as horticulture, and pisciculture, whose holding, independent of the actual working of it, provides a livelihood based on the cultivation of the soil. That is in particular the case when the standard value, or the labour force requirements of a farm, have reached a defined minimum level, fixed by the Agricultural Old Age Pensions Fund in consultation with the General Association of Agricultural Old Age Pensions Funds, at their fair discretion on the basis of existing local conditions.

Exemption from Compulsory Insurability

Workers who have provided for themselves on some other basis may contract out of the scheme. This applies, on application, to farmers who have paid contributions to some other scheme for 15 years, or who, during the five years preceding their application, had followed some other occupation insurable under pensions insurance for at least 30 months in addition to their agricultural activities, or who have some other definite provision, or who, as self-employed craftsmen, are registered on the Artisans Roll, or when the predecessor on the farm and the spouse are deceased, or make a declaration in writing that they do not intend to claim an allowance from the Fund; in this event the exempted person is finally excluded from the Fund. On application, adult agriculturalists who belong to a joint heirship group conducting the business, but are not themselves mainly engaged in it, may be exempted for a maximum period of two years following inheritance; co-heir minors are always exempt. Farmers who first fulfill the conditions for compulsory insurance after reching the age of 50 are not insurable if, at that time, they are in receipt of a pension from some other scheme, or have a contingent entitlement to a Civil Service Pension. About 70.000 full time farmers are in fact exempt.

Voluntary Insurance

Former farmers and older employed members of their families can join the Old Age Pensions Funds voluntarily, though not as members, but as a concession. Farmers who have paid contributions for at least three years, or their widows or widowers, may voluntarily declare their desire to continue to pay contributions up to their 60th year, or up to the beginning of premature disablement. Expellees may pay 90 contributions retrospectively if they have already paid 90 contributions. Of employed family members those persons may join the Fund who had reached the age of 50 on 1. 5. 1965. In the case of younger persons it is assumed that they are compulsorily insurable as workers. These family members must have worked on the family farm for at least 5 years; the five years must have lain between 1. 5. 1955 and 30. 4. 1965, or in the ten years preceding the onset of unemployability. A further condition is that they must have been employed full time on the family farm. Employed family members can pay contributions retrospectively to 1957. In 1968 there were, of 3.8 million family members, 1.3 million employed full time, of whom 734.000 were wives (i.e. not entitled to be voluntarily insured). Of the 1.3 mill. 569.000 were over the age of 45.

Benefits

Standard benefits are: pensions, and premature pensions in the event of unemployability. Additional benefits may consist of a supplementary pension, and measures for the maintenance, improvement, or restoration of employability, of hospital treatment, and other benefits. With the sanction of the Supervisory Authority, the Funds may incur expenditure additional to their normal statutory obligations to promote or put into effect, other measures in the interests of the farmers.

Conditions for the payment of pensions

Pensions are granted in the event of unemployability, when the pensionable age has been reached, the qualifying period satisfied, and the farm or holding has been transferred to other hands.

Pensionable Age and Unemployability

Farmers and widowers receive a pension when they have reached the age of 65, widows at 60. Premature pension is payable if the farmer is incapable of work, i.e. if, as a consequence of illness or other infirmity, or of impairment of his physical or mental health, he is no longer able to follow any employment with a certain degree of regularity, or is able to earn only an inconsiderable amount. A premature pension is payable to widows under the same conditions. Widows and widowers also receive a pension, without regard to age and unemployability, if the deceased spouse was already in receipt of a pension, and the marriage had taken place before his (her) 65th year.

Qualifying Periods

The qualifying period for a claim to a pension is 180 calendar months during which contributions must have been paid into the Fund. The qualifying period for a premature pension is 60 calendar months. Employed family members are required to satisfy several conditions. During the 25 years preceding their 65th year they must have worked on the family farm for at least 180 calendar months, or, during the ten years preceding unemployability, for at least 60 calendar months. In addition, they must have paid contributions into the Fund for every month after 1. 10. 1957, or from the beginning of their employment, until their 65th year, or the onset of unemployability. Since, at the commencement of the scheme on 1. 10. 1957, it had not been possible to pay contributions, and since, later, until 1. 10. 1972, the qualifying period cannot be fully covered by contributions paid, other periods are reckoned as qualifying periods. For widows and widowers the same qualifying periods are reckoned as for the farmers themselves, as are also periods for which they have paid contributions after the death of the farmer.

Surrender of the Farm or Holding

Farmers and their widows receive old age or unemployability pension only on transferring the farm or holding to other hands, without the intention of resuming possession. Surrender is a transfer of the farm, or other surrender of ownership rights, whereby a transfer to a spouse does not rank as a transfer in the meaning of the law. If the transfer is not accompanied by a transfer of ownership rights, the statutory conditions are only then regarded as satisfied if the transfer is made in writing to expire not earlier than the farmer's 74th year, or nine years before the commencement of unemployability. If an owner has several holdings, he must transfer them all in order to qualify for pension. Married couples jointly running a farm must both retire. On surrender of a part only, a claim to pension lies only if the standard value, or the required labour force, of the portion not surrendered does not exceed 25 % of the minimum laid down by the Pensions Fund.

Amount of Pensions — Beginning of Payment

Pensions and premature pensions are payable as to the same amount to farmers, widows and widowers, the only exception being between married and unmarried recipients. Married persons receive 175 DM, unmarried persons 115 DM per month. Employed family members receive 57.50 DM per month, i.e. half the amount of an unmarried farmer. In general the following regulations apply: For the first three months following the death of the spouse, the survivor receives the full pension. If both spouses have a separate claim to pension, the survivor receives only the pension of an unmarried recipient. If one person has a claim to more than one pension, one amount only is payable.

Amounts of Pensions in DM per month

from	Farmer married	unmarried	Employed member of Family
1. 10. 57	60,00	40,00	—
1. 4. 63	100,00	65,00	—
1. 5. 65	150,00	100,00	50,00
1. 4. 69	175,00	115,00	57,50

The Representative Assembly of the Assosication of Agricultural Pensions Funds, can, on the resolution of a majority of two thirds of voting members, grant an additional pension. The percentage increase since the previous fixing of the amount of pensions may not exceed the percentage increase in the general basis of computation in the pensions insurance of manual workers during the same period. Pensions payable at the age of 65 begin in the month in which the conditions are satisfied; the same applies to the pensions of widows (widowers) and to 65 year old employed family members. For the rest, payments begin only in the month in which the conditions are satisfied if application is made within three months thereof, otherwise only in the month in which the application is made.

Measures for the Maintenance, Improvement, or Restoration of Employability

The Pension Funds are authorised to approve measures for the maintenance, improvement, or restoration of employability in the case of farmers, their spouses, widows and widowers, as well as for the recipients of premature pensions. Employed family members may also benefit from such measures if they have paid contributions into the Fund for at least five years. A condition is that employability has been endangered or impaired as a consequence of illness or some ailment or weakness, and that the treatment so sanctioned may be expected to lead to a considerable improvement, or to employability.

The treatment can include hospitalisation, sanatoria, specialist institutes, and spas. Since, in the case of farms run by a family, the absence of the farmer, or his employed wife, can impose a severe burden on the farm, and since this fact can lead to the refusal of rehabilitation treatment, the Fund provides a deputy for a farmer or his employed wife for the period of treatment, as a rule for up to three months. In the case of a farm which normally employs non-family labour, the provision of a deputy is limited to exceptional cases. The additional benefit consists, as indicated, in the provision of a deputy, alternatively in a payment of 20 DM per day. In the case of employed family members no deputy is supplied or payment made.

Finance

The funds for financing the scheme are raised from the contributions of the farmers and of employed family members, and from a government subsidy. If income is insufficient to cover expenditure, the Representative Assembly of the Association of Agricultural Pensions Funds may increase contributions. Expenditure is borne jointly by the Agricultural Pensions Funds; adjustments are made by the Association of Agricultural Pensions Funds. In the case of each Fund an amount of at least 5 % of annual expenditure is excluded from this process of adjustment; this amount is held in reserve to meet the costs of its legislative and statutory functions.

Income and Expenditure in 1.000 DM

Year	Income total	thereof Contributions	Subsidy	total	Expenditure — thereof Pensions	Curative Treatment
1958	164 618	89 238	75 1)3	164 618	158 446	–
1960	183 231	112 158	69 049	183 108	175 342	–
1965	491 982	128 239	363 271	495 975	474 256	8
1966	668 375	174 129	493 379	667 175	633 707	3 626
1967	708 332	205 680	501 062	704 270	670 510	9 661
1968	723 600	196 930	525 243	723 973	685 841	13 654
1969	850 000	213 000	635 000	838 000	791 000	23 000
1970	892 000	251 000	639 000	888 000	838 000	27 000
1971	908 000	246 000	660 000	911 000	856 000	30 000
1972	907 000	240 000	665 000	932 000	873 000	33 000
1973	903 000	236 000	665 000	952 000	889 000	35 000

Contributions

Contributions amount to 27 DM per month for farmers, and 13.50 DM per month for employed family members. Every farmer is insurable in principle, but pays only one contribution, even if he is running several farms, or if a married couple is jointly so engaged.

In the latter instance the partner mainly responsible for the running the farm is insurable. Persons who have been insurable as farmers for at least three years, as well as their widows or widowers, may, within two years following the termination of such insurability, make a declaration to the Fund to the effect that they are desirous of continuing to pay contributions. In certain

from	Farmers	Employed Family members
1.10.57	10	5,00*)
1. 1.59	12	6,00*)
1. 1.66	16	8,00
1. 1.67	20	10,00
1. 1.69	22	11,00
1. 1.70	27	13,50

+ in respect of contributions which are paid retrospectively

circumstances contributions to the Pensions Fund may be made retrospectively. A corresponding arrangement applies to employed family members.

Federal Government Subsidy

The comparatively unfavourable relation between contributors and beneficiaries under the Pensions Scheme is due to the change in the structure of the agricultural industry, as a consequence of which the number of farms and holdings is constantly declining. Since the desired improvement in the structure of the industry is being facilitated by the increased number of transferred holdings consequent on the payment of the pensions, the Federal Government pays a subsidy to the Pensions Fund. The money is provided from the budget of the Green Plan; the amount for 1970 has been fixed at a maximum of 639 mill. DM.

Land Surrender Pension

Land Surrender Pensions are payable to farmers who have reached the age of 60, or who are unemployable in their own occupation in the meaning of Manual Workers' Pensions Insurance regulations. Further, contributions must have been paid into an Agricultural Pensions Fund for at least 60 calendar months, and, in addition, the farmer must have been mainly engaged in running his farm in the 5 years preceding the surrender. During this period his holding may not have exceeded a defined maximum size (about 20 to 25 acres). The object is, of course, to provide, in particular for smaller farmers, an incentive to surrender their holdings. The surrender must have been effected at the latest by 31.12.1973, and must serve the purpose of structural improvement. Farmers at the age of 55 may also be awarded a pension if there is no prospect of placing them in alternative employment. All other conditions (see above) must be satisfied. With effect from 1.4.1969, the Land Surrender Pension amounts to 275 DM per month for married persons, and 180 DM for unmarried persons. Any pension payable by the Agricultural Fund will be taken into account. Further, amounts payable from other forms of social pensions insurance, from industrial injuries insurance, or as Civil Service pension, are taken into account to a certain amount. If the farmer was in receipt of a Land Surrender Pension, the widow or widower will continue to be entitled. The costs of this scheme are borne by the Federal Government.

Organisation

Each separate Agricultural Industrial Injuries Institute has established an Agricultural Pensions Fund. These Funds are corporations in public law under government supervision. The 19 separate Funds are joined together in the Association of Agricultural Pensions Funds, itself a corporation in public law, which has its headquarters in the offices of the Federal Association of Agricultural Industrial Injuries Institutes, which is also under government supervision. The self-governing bodies of the Pensions Funds are the organs of Agricultural Industrial Injuries Institutes to which they are attached (see the sector "Self-Government"). In matters affecting farmers' pensions, employees have no representation. The Agricultural Pensions Funds are also competent for the award of Land Surrender Pensions.

Association of Agricultural Pensions Funds	in Kassel
Schleswig Holstein Fund	in Kiel
Hannover Fund	in Hannover
Oldenburg — Bremen Fund	in Oldenburg
Brunswick Fund	in Brunswick
Rhine-Hessen/Palatinate Fund	in Speyer
Baden Fund	in Karlsruhe

Württemberg Fund	in Stuttgart
Upper Bavaria Fund	in Munich
Lower Bavaria/Upper Palatinate Fund	in Landshut
Westphalian Fund	in Münster
Lippe Fund	in Detmold
Rhine-Agricultural Fund	in Düsseldorf
Hessen-Nassau Fund	in Kassel
Government District Darmstadt Fund	in Darmstadt
Lower Franconia Fund	in Würzburg
Upper and Middle Franconia Fund	in Bayreuth
Swabian Fund	in Augsburg
Horticultural Fund	in Kassel
Saarland Fund	in Saarbrücken

Legislative bases

Law on Old Age Pensions for Farmers dated 27. 7. 1957, in the version of 14. 9. 1965 (BGBI. I.S. 1448), last amended by the Law dated 29. 7. 1969 (BGBI. I.S. 1017).

Security in Old Age for the Free Professions

Introduction

The free professions, numbering about 250.000 persons, are the smallest group within the three million self-employed persons. Their common characteristic vis-a-vis the remaining self-employed persons is the lack of any considerable working capital, and their dependence on their income from their own personal efforts. The need to make some provision for the exigencies of life in the form of a claim to cash benefits independent of their professional activities follows logically, and is self-explanatory.

The free professions display, as between different groups, very considerable differences in income, in the course of their profession, and in organisation. These differences are particularly pronounced in the matter of provision for old age and for survivors, There would, therefore, be little purpose in attempting to make any statement applicable to the whole group. On the other hand, any attempt at a seperate presentation for each individual group would only lead to confusion, and it is also unnecessary, since there are so many points of resemblance. On the one hand there are those free professions which, since the inauguration of Statutory social policy, have always been regarded as standing in need of special protection, since, financially and socially, they occupy a similar position to that of workers — for instance, private teachers and tutors, musicians, actors, variety artists etc.; on the other hand there are those free professions organised in Professional Chambers in public law, who, on the basis of State regulated incomes have a guaranteed practice in their professions and a secure income. In between there are groups whose incomes are, it is true, not inadequate, but are not secured in public law.

These three groupings have always sought and found solutions for their security in old age, characteristic for each sector. The free professions bearing a close resemblance to the workers have long been compulsorily insurable in the Non-Manual Workers' Pensions Insurance Scheme under Reichs, later Federal law; the so-called "Chamber organised" free professions have set up their own schemes, mostly on the basis of Land legislation; for the remaining free professions there is no special statutory provision; in many instances their members are entitled to continue to be voluntarily insured under the Manual or Non-Manual Workers' Schemes.

Free Professions in Non-manual Workers' Insurance

Compulsorily insured under the Non-Manual Workers' Scheme are: Teachers, instructors, tutors (Piano, singing, drawing, swimming, riding etc.) (since 1922), music (since 1929), free nursing (since 1932), child bed nursing (since 1943), babies' and children's nursing (since 1945), midwives (since 1929), seagoing pilots (since 1. 1. 1970), variety artistes (since 1938). With the exception of the last three named groups, members are compulsorily insurable only if they themselves do not employ other persons — a restriction of little significance.

Compulsorily insured members of the free professions receive the same benefits as non-manual workers, i.e., in addition to pensions, measures for the restoration of employability (rehabilitation), and contributions to pensioners' health insurance. On reaching pensionable age, i.e. at 65, pensions are payable even in the event that full employment continues, despite the fact that in their case more frequent advantage is taken of this concession. There is no seperate accountancy for the income and expenditure in respect of self-employed persons in Non-Manual Workers' Insurance.

All members of the free professions who, in addition to their free professional activities, regularly follow a salaried occupation to a not inconsiderable extent, are compulsorily insurable. This is usually so in the case of veterinary surgeons, of whom four fifths are employed as meat inspectors in slaughter houses, and also in the case of hospital doctors. If, in the case of professional groups, statutory insurance or pensions schemes are operative, members may contract out of Non-Manual Workers' Insurance. At the moment 31 such schemes are known, membership of which entitles individvals to contract out on application. If a member of one of these professions refrains from submitting an application for exemption, he is subject to double insurance and payment of contributions (into Non-Manual Workers' Insurance, and into his professional pensions scheme); only some 18.000 regularly pay contributions. Income is under 16 mill. DM. The majority of contributions actually paid are paid at the minimum rate. Midwives are required to pay at the contribution rate of 400 (1970 = 68 DM) per month. Pilots responsible for the safety of the sea routes on the German North Sea and Baltic coasts pay contributions at the same rate as the average earnings of a deep sea captain, that is to say, normally at the highest rate.

Insurance and Pensions Schemes

For the professional groups: Doctors, dental surgeons, veterinary surgeons, pharmaceutical chemists, solicitors, tax advisers, officially approbated tax advisers, architects (though only in part), there is, pursuant to legal regulations, a form of self-administration in corporations in public law, with compulsory membership (Chamber Constitution). Such organisations are — as developments have shown — a condition pre-requisite for the establishment of insurance and pensions schemes based on Land regulations.

The following list detals the insurance and pensions institutes whose members, if they are (also) salaried employees, may claim exemption under the Non-Manual Workers' Scheme. Over and above these organisations there are, in union with Health Insurance Doctors Associations and Professional Chambers, pensions forms which are in effect insurances, but which figure under the title "Distribution of Honoraria", or as "Welfare". Such arrangements which, a decade ago, were more widely distributed than to-day, but which have since been transformed into modern pensions schemes, or have been absorbed by them, have been included in this list, but are distinguished by an asterisk.

Insurance and Pensions institutes in Public Law of the Free Professions organised in Chambers

Doctors

Pensions Institute for Doctors, Dental Surgeons, Veterinary Surgions in Baden Württemberg;
Bavarian Medical Pensions Scheme, including Dental Surgeons, Dentists and Veterinary Surgeons;
Berlin Medical Pensions Scheme;
Medical Pensions Scheme of the Bremen Chamber of Doctors;
Hamburg Medical Pensions Scheme;
Pensions Scheme of the Hesse Land Chamber of Doctors;
Lower Saxony Medical Pensions Scheme;
Pensions Scheme of the North Rhine Chamber of Doctors;

Pensions Scheme of the Westphalia-Lippe Chamber of Doctors;
Pensions Scheme of the District Association of the Land Chamber of Doctors in Coblenz-Montabaur;
Pensions Scheme of the District Association of the Land Chamber of Doctors in Mayence;
Pensions Scheme of the Trier District Association Chamber of Doctors;
Pensions Scheme of the Saarland (including Dental Surgeons);
Pensions Scheme of the Schleswig Holstein Chamber of Doctorss.

Dental Surgeons

Pensions Scheme of the Chamber of Dental Surgeons Berlin, associated with the Chamber of Dental Surgeons Bremen;
Pensions Scheme of the Chamber of Dental Surgeons Hamburg;
Old Age Pension Scheme of the Chamber of Dental Surgeons Lower Saxony;
Hesse Dental Surgeons Pensions Scheme;
Pensions Scheme of the Chamber of Dental Surgions, North-Rhine;
Pensions Scheme of the Chamber of Dental Surgeons Chamber Rhineland-Palatinate;
Pensions Institute of the Health Insurance Dental Surgeons Association Schleswig Holstein*;

Veterinary Surgeons

Pensions Scheme of the Land Veterinary Surgeons Chamber Hesse;
Pensions Scheme of the Land Veterinary Surgeons Chamber Lower Saxony;
Pensions Scheme of the Land Vertrinary Surgeons Chamber North Rhine;
Pensions Scheme of the Land Veterinary Surgeons Chamber Westphalia-Lippe;
Pensions Scheme of the Land Veterinary Surgeons chamber Rhineland-Palatinate;
Pensions Scheme of the Land Veterinary Surgeons Chamber associated to the Saarland;
Pensions Scheme of the Land Veterinary Surgeons Chamber Schleswig-Holstein;

Pharmaceutical Chemists

Bavarian Apothecaries Pensions Scheme;
Extended Welfare Organisation of the Apothecaries Chamber Hamburg*;
Old Age Welfare Scheme of the Land Apothecaries Chamber Hesse*;
Old Age and Survivors; Pensions Scheme of the Apothecaries Chamber Lower Saxony*;
Pensions Scheme of the Apothecaries Chamber North Rhine*;
Pensions Scheme of the Apothecaries Chamber Westphalia-Lippe*;
Pensions Scheme of the Land Apothecaries Chamber Rhineland Palatinate*;
Welfare Institute of Apothecaries of the Saarland*;
Apothecaries Pensions Scheme of the Apothecaries Chamber Schleswig-Holstein*;

Solicitors
Bavarian Solicitors Fund;
Hesse Darmstadt Solicitors Emergency Fund;
Coblenz Solicitors Emergency Fund;
Pensions Fund of the Solicitors in the Chamber of Solicitors in Saarbrücken;
Pensions Fund of the Rhine Chamber of Solicitors*;
Pensions Fund of the Hamburg Chamber of Solicitors*;

Other Professional Groups

Pensions Scheme of the Chamber of Tax Advisers and Approbated Tax Advisers for the Saarland;
Pensions Scheme of the Solicitors Chamber of the Saarland;
Pensions Scheme of the Architects Chamber of the Saarland.

In the still operative Insurance and Pensions Schemes based on Land legislation an estimated 100.000 members of the free professions are compulsorily insured (i.e., excluding voluntarily insured and employees).

Insured Persons

The demarcation line for membership of the insurance and pensions schemes is in general dependent on membership of the Professional Chambers, even when special laws are in force. In the case of medical practitioners it is, in part, only the Health Insurance doctors who are compulsorily insurable, whereas the remaining doctors may elect to be voluntarily insured. Not only persons engaged whole time in the free professions are included in the schemes, but also other persons exercising the profession on the basis of a special licence. This includes, for instance, public officials and salaried employees. Whereas established officials are not normally required to pay contributions, salaried employees normally need pay only a small contribution, fixed under consideration of their compulsory insurance under the Non-Manual Workers' Scheme, though they may also apply for exemption under that scheme.

Amounts of Contributions

Contributions payable are dependent on the levels of benefits and on coverage, and are payable in part on the basis of net income, in part of gross income, in part graded according to age. In no case are flat rate contributions payable. Contributions are not inconsiderable. In so far as contribution rates are based on net income, they reach in many cases the contributions payable in Non-Manual Workers' Insurance, i.e., they amounted in 1969 to 16 % of income, and in some, though not many cases. were even higher. Only in the case of veterinary surgeons are contributions relatively low. In the case of pharmaceutical chemists, contributions are dependent either on turnover, or on the number of assistants employed; it is here impossible to make any comparisons. The total income of all these schemes probably amounted to 150 mill. DM in1969.

Benefits

In nearly every case these insurance and pensions schemes award pensions on the ground of a reduced standard of occupation, and on retirement, and survivors' pensions; they also pay death benefits and other benefits of minor importance. In connection with pensions payable to insured persons, two types of insurance and pensions schemes are to be distinguished. The one type provides benefits in respect of a reduced standard of occupation, the other type provides, in addition, retirement pensions. In the first instance no proof of a reduced standard of occupation is required on reaching a certain age e.g. 68 or 70, whereas on the other hand it is usually a condition for the award of a pension that the National Health practice in the case of medical practitioners and dental surgeons, the meat inspection practice in the case of veterinaries, and the solicitors practice, be relinquished. Pensionable age is usually higher than in the case of employed employees, i.e. at 68 to 70 years of age. It is however clear that about half the schemes have now introduced the 65 year age limit.

It is in the method of assessing pensions, and in their amount, that perhaps the gratest differencies are evident. In the matter of assessing pensions two methods are distinguished. The older established schemes, in particular those associated with the Bavarian Chamber of Insurance, grant fixed pensions, whereas the more recently established schemes adapt pensions more or less automatically to rising incomes, in much the same way as has happened in Workers' Pensions Insurance since 1957. For the rest, pensions are in part gradated according to insurance years, in part addiionally according to the level of income, whereas other schemes award uniform pensions, that is to say, they practice a more pronounced social balance. Generally speaking, minimum pensions are payable, in some case also maximum pensions, usually based on the fact that minimum and maximum contributions are payable.

In view of the highly varied nature of the assessment of pensions it is very difficult to make any statement as to their absolute amount. They vary between 100 and 1500 DM per month, and are in some cases even higher.

Corresponding to the amount of income and the particular situation of the professional groups, the lowest pensions are, on an average, payable to veterinary surgeons, who are, of course also insurable as meat inspectors under the Non-Manual Workers' Pensions Scheme. The highest pensions are payable to medical practitioners, whereas in the case of dental surgeons considerable differences occur. In the case of solicitors and notaries the amount of pension is oriented, for example, on that of a comparable established official. It will be necessary to reckon with some 10.000 to 12.000 pensions payable to former members of the free professions and their widows, entailing an annual expenditure of 30 to 40 million DM.

Organisation

Most insurance and pensions schemes exist in the legal form of a Special Fund within a corporation in public law, namely the Professional Chamber. The Bavarian institutes and the Baden-Württemberg Doctors' Pensions Scheme are independent corporations. In the case of the remaining institutes, the Special Fund is administered, for example, by the Chamber, and is controlled by specially elected members of the profession who are not members of the Executive Committee of the Chamber; in part, in complete contrast, it is administered by such persons, whilst control is exercised by the Chamber. The statutes contain numerous regulations on the internal organisation of the insurance and pensions schemes, usually in a three phase system, comprising the administration through a management committee, a supervisory committee, and a representatives' or delegates' meeting, which resolves on the statutes, and elects the other bodies.

Overall supervision is usually the responsibility of the Land Ministers of the Interior, technical supervision sometimes of the Minister of Economics.

There are in many instances transfer agreements between the insurance and pensions schemes in the Lands, which, in the event of a change of residence, guarantee the members of the free professions the right to continue in insurance, as well as maintaining their pensions entitlement.

Special Aspects of the Professional Groups

The different types of insurance and pensions schemes find varying degrees of favour in the eyes of different professional groups. The veterinary surgeons have organised their scheme as a kind of group insurance, on the model of industrial life insurance, and have contented themselves with relatively low contributions and benefits. The explanation for this procedure is that four fifths of all veterinary surgeons are employed as meat inspectors in abattoirs and similar installations, and are therefore compulsorily insurable under the Non-Manual Workers' Scheme. This group is consequently already insured under a "dynamic" scheme, and its members require only an additional amount of benefit corresponding to their income from their private practice.

Pharmaceutical chemists also find themselves in a special position. Whereas independent apothecaries, thanks to the former ruling restricting the issue of licences, could rely on an adequate livelihood in their old age, and for their survivors, from the income of the business they had taken over, employed apothecaries ran a very considerable risk, in that they were frequently compelled to wait to an advanced age before they could acquire a business of their own. For this reason the self-employed apothecaries have organised an insurance scheme to cover their employees against the risk that they might have to remain employees all their lives, and have to remain dependent on a pension in their old age. In this instance the indepddendent apothecaries are the "insurers", and their employees the beneficiaries, that is to say, the employers pay the premiums, the employees draw the benefits. In this manner provision is made for members of a professional group from funds not deriving from the income from their own business. For the independent apothecaries, moreover, this is an insurance against the danger that they themselves may lose their business and, as employed employees, find themselves in need of insurance cover.

The greatest varieties in this field are to be found in the schemes of the medical practitioners and the dental surgeons, but also of the soicitors. The doctors' schemes demand the highest contributions, and have the highest reserve funds.

Other Free Professions

To the third group of free professions not compulsorily insurable either under the Non-Manual Workers' Scheme or under statutory Land insurance and pensions schemes must be counted principally the technical free professions, as follows: Architects, engineers, chemists, etc. to a total of 45.000 to 50.000 persons, authors, lecturers, artists, to a total of some 30.000 persons. In addition, in respect of the free professions for whom Professional Chambers in public law exist, there are, in most Lands, no insurance institutes; these are: solicitors, patents lawyers, chartered accountants, tax advisers, and approbated tax advisers.

In lieu of the absence of compulsory insurance, voluntary insurance in social pensions insurance offers a certain substitute. In the technical, economic, and tax advisory professions, the quota of those persons who are voluntarily insured under the Manual and Non-Manual Workers' Schemes is higher than in most of the other free professions. The proportion of members of these professions continuing as voluntary contributors (mainly) under the Non-Manual Workers' Scheme varies between 65 and 85 %. It is to be anticipated that this proportion will increase with the growing numbers of the younger generation. The extent to which the free professions avail themselves of the opportunity of continued voluntary insurance is unknwon. In the economic and tax advisory professions, it may be gathered from enquiries that on the average about two thirds of the potential professional life are covered by insurance contributions. In the case of the other free professions the duration of contribution payments will be a shorter one, so that, at a later period, gaps will be evident in staturoy retirement pensions provision.

A special situation occurs in the case of solicitors, authors, and artists.

Solicitors were, up to a decade ago, only as to a quarter insurable. In the meantime this situaation has changed for younger solicitors for three reasons: The Lands now have a duty to insure solicitors retrospectively under the Non-Manual Workers' Insurance Scheme in respect of the period they spend as juniors undergoing practical training in the courts, when they were temporary Civil Servants subject to recall (auf Wiedderruf), in general, that is, for two and a half to three and a half years. Further, conscripts are compulsorily insurable for the period of their military service, i.e. for eighteen months. Finally, very many more solicitors are nowadays in the employ of firms and organisations in an employee status, and are therefore, above all since the raising of the compulsory insurance ceiling, also compulsorily insurable for this period. It is therefore quite possible that the quota of silicitors remaining voluntarily insured under the Non-Manual Workers' Scheme will, in the course of a generation, reach almost the same level as that customary in the case of other advisory professions.

In consideration of these developments, former plans to establish a special Solicitors' Insurance (Draft Law, Parliamentary Paper III 2656, IV 2298) have not been pursued.

Of the artistic and literary professions, as already stated, musicians and variety artists are compulsorily insurable under the Non-Manual Workers' Scheme. Musicians and actors can also enter into voluntary membership with the Pensions Institute of the German Stage, an institute in public law, and the Pensions Institute of German Cultural Orchestras, which, however, are intended, and have been established, primarily as a supplementary provision for actors and musicians in fixed employment; both institutes are administered by the Bavarian Insurance Chamber.

In consequence of the irregular careers of artists and authors, and the fact that these carrers are often exercised as subsidiary occupations, little progress has been made with proposals to establish some form of compulsory insurance or pensions insurance for them. In lieu therefore, the Federal Government and the Lands have provided funds in varied ways to provide for artists who have fallen into need, and for their old age. These are in the main welfare arrangements. Of these the following are worthy of mention: Aid to Artists, in the Office of the Federal President. Its object is to pay tribute to important artistic works in the form of an honorarium. Conditions for the award are old age or illness, need, and the greater importance of the artist. This Aid Fund makes awards to some 600 artists regularly, and to 400 occasionally, or once only. In most Federal Lands, some artists and authors receive a sinecure. The total number probably does not exceed 300.

Legislative bases

Baden-Württemberg
Law on the Pensions Institutes for Doctors, Dental Surgeons, and Veterinary Surgeons dated 2.12.1951, in the version of 28.7.1961 (BGBl. S.299).
The Amending Law on the Chambers Law, the Architects Law, etc. of 2.4.1968 (GBl. S. 134).

Bavaria
Law on Public Insurance Schemes of 7.12.1933, in the version of 29.5.1957 (GVBl. S. 105), last amended by the Law of 23.11.1965 (GVBl. S. 356).

Berlin
Chambers Law of 18.12.1961

Bremen
Chambers Law for Curative Professions of 9.6.1959, in the version of 4.11.1968 (GBl. S. 151)

Hamburg
Apothecaries' Chamber Law of 28.7.1949 (GVBl. S. 141). Dental Surgeons Chamber Law of 28.7.1949 in the version of 3.2.1964 (GVBl. S. 28).
Medical Doctors Chamber Law of 28.7.1949 - all Laws amended by the Law 13.3.1961 (GVBl. IS. 91).

Hesse
Law on the Professional Representation and Professional Jurisdiction of medical doctors, dental surgeons, veterinary surgeons, and apothecaries of 10.11.1954, in the version of 18.4.1966 (GVBl. S. 101).
Law on the National Health Doctors Association of Hesse, and the National Health Dental Surgeons Association of Hesse of 22.12.1953 (GVBl. S. 206).

Lower Saxony
Law on the Professional Representation of medical doctors, apothecaries, veterinary surgeons, and dental surgeons of 1.12.1950, in the version of 17.4.1967 (GVBl. S. 107).
The Architects Law of 23.2.1970 (GVBl. S. 37).

North-Rhine;Westphalia
Law on the Chambers and the Professional Jurisdiction of medical doctors, apothecaries, veterinary surgeons and dental surgeons of 5.2.1952, in the version of 3.6.1954 (GVBl. S. 376).

Rhineland Palatinate
Law on the Chamber of medical doctors, dentists, apothecaries and veterinary surgeons of 1.4.1953, in the version of 17.4.1967 (GVBl. S. 127).
Solicitors Pensions Law of 22.7.1965 (GVBl. S. 153).

Saarland
Law No. 860 on the Medical Doctors Chamber of the Saarland of 15.5.1968 (Amtsbl. S. 310);
Ordinance on the Establishment of a Pensions Scheme for Tax Advisers and approbated Tax Advisers in the Saarland of 19.12.1961 (Amtsbl. S. 648), amended by the Ordinance of 24.6.1968 (Amtsbl. S. 648).

Schleswig-Holstein
Laws on the Medical Doetors, Dental Surgeons, Veterinary Surgeons, and Apothecaries Chambers in Schleswig-Holstein of 18.12.1953, in the version of 14/16.11.1967 (GVBl. S. 245).

Civil Service Pensions

Introduction

Civil Service Pensions in the Federal Republic of Germany are not normally shown under public social benefits; they are, as a rule, reported on and accounted for seperately. In international compendiums, and in comparisons with other countries which have no specific legislation applicable to public officials, or in which pensions schemes are still in an undevolped state, their inclusion is, however, necessary, for instance for purposes of the compensation of expenditure on social security. A survey of the bases on which these pensions are paid rounds off the picture of social security in the Federal Republic of Germany in the widest sense of the word. Consequently, Civil Service pensions have been included in the Social Budget 1969/70, which the Federal Government submitted to the legislative bodies in April 1970. A comparison with Social Pensions Insurance is not applicable without certain reservations, since non-manual and the manual workers in the public services - and not only these - receive additional superannuation payments. A connection between Civil Service pensions and Social Pensions Insurance exists in the matter of the maximum amount of pension payable when a Civil Service pension is payable at the same time as a pension arising from subsequent insurable employment after premature retirement from the Service. In ruling as to whether the illness of a civil servant is an industrial disease, the Service applies the Industrial Diseases Regulations of the Industrial Injuries Insurance Institutes. The amount of compensation payable to a civil servant injured on duty is based on the amount of the basic rent payable under War Pensions regulations.

Pensions law is based on regulations under the law applicable to permanent civil servants. Its bases are also applicable to judges, soldiers, police officials of the Federal Government, and to established officials of the Federal Lands, municipalities, and municipal associations, as well as corporations in public law. The special conditions of certain groups of civil servants are not taken into consideration. The total number of civil servants of the Federal Government, the Federal Lands, and the local authorities is about 1.3 million.

Benefits under the Pensions System

Benefits include pensions, survivors' pensions, accident compensation, maintenance contributions, commutation and transitional payments. In December of each year a special payment is made to the amount of one half, from December 1971 onwards two thirds, of the current month's pensions entitlement. Benefits payable during sickness are not included in this report.

Civil Service pensions are presently payable to about 500.000 pensioners, and survivors' pensions to about 400.000.

Pensions

Conditions

On reaching the prescribed age limit the civil servant is retired. The age limit is, as a general rule, 65 years; for some groups of established officials(police officials, soldiers, and judges) the law prescribes different retirement ages.

An official must be retired if, because of a bodily ailment, or of weakness of his physical or mental health, he is permanently incapable of performing his duties - is unfit for duty. Without submitting proof of his unfitness for duty a permanent official may apply for retirement at the age of 62.

The payment of a pension is dependent on a qualifying period of at least ten years. This does not apply if the official has become unfit for duty by reason of illness, wounds, or other injury, resulting without any serious fault on his own part, from the performance of his duty, or as a consequence of his official duties.

Assessment

Pensions are assessed on the basis of pensionable salaries and years of pensionable service. Pensionable salaries consist of the end basic salary, the provincial differentials applicable to the place of residence, and other pensionable emoluments. If the official has retired bacause of unfitness for further service, his pension is assessed on the basic salary of the salary stage he could have reached on reaching normal retirement age. Pensionable years are the years which the official has served as an established official from the day of his first appointment following his 17th year in the employ of an authority in public law in the Federal or former Reich territory. Periods of political persecution increase the pensionable years. Pensionable also are periods after the age of 17, and prior to appointment as a permanent official, spent in compulsory military service, or professionally in the service of the new German army (Bundeswehr), the previous German army (Wehrmacht), in civil defence, in the former Reichs Labour Service (Reichsarbeitsdienst), or as an acive police official. Periods of employment in the public services prior to establishment may be pensionable, in certain cases only as to one half. Other periods may also be pensionable, though in some circumstances only to a limited extent, e.g. under certain conditions periods of private employment in defined occupations and in training, as well as periods of study in a university or college of advanced technology.

Amounts

Pensions amount to at least 35 % of pensionable emoluments, rising after ten years service by annual increments of 2 % until the completion of the 25th year, thence by 1 % to a maximum of 75 % of pensionable emoluments. Minimum pensions are payable to the amount of 573 DM per month for an official, 381 DM for a widow, 76 DM for a half orphan, and 127 DM for a full orphan. If an official is disabled and retired as a result of an accident on duty he receives an accident pension to the amount of at least 66 2/3 % of pensionable emoluments. If his pension as assessed amounts to 47 % or more, it is increased by 20 %, but may not exceed 75 %. In this case, too, minimum amounts are payable.

Adjustment

If the emoluments of established officials are increased or decreased, in general, or for certain groups of officials, pensions are correspondingly re-assessed at the same time. Since 1957 basic salaries and local differentials, and pensions, have frequently been adjusted in line with changing economic conditions, the latest occasion being on 1.1.1970 by about 8 percent.

Benefits in the Case of Accidents

An official is entitled to certain benefits in respect of an accident sustained on duty, or arising out of service. Certain illnesses may also be regarded as accidents sustained on duty: the criterion here is the Industrial Diseases Regulations in Social Accident Insurance.

In addition to the replacement of damaged articles, the official is entitled to curative treatment, and all necessary and reasonable expenditure to this end is refunded. If, as a result of the accident, the official is so helpless that he cannot manage without care and attendance, the costs of a nurse are refunded; if an official has been retired, a supplement to pension is payable on application for the period for which he requires care and attendance, up to an amount equal to his pensionable emoluments.
If, as a result of the accident, the earning capacity of the injured person is considerably reduced, he receives, in addition to his emoluments or pension, accident compensation to the amount of the basic war pension.

Children's Allowances

Childrens allowances to the amount of 50 DM per month are payable for legitimate children, children declared legitimate, adopted children, step children, if the official has taken them into his household, foster children and grand children, if the official has taken them into his household, and if he is not in receipt from some other source of a sum in excess of 150 DM per month for their maintenance and education, and the illegitimate children of female officials.

Children's allowances are payable up to the age of 27; after the age of 18, however, only if the child is engaged in education or training occupying the bulk of his working capacity, and if he is not in receipt of a salary, wage, or other remuneration in respect of such education or training. If education or training is delayed for a period beyond the 27th year for reasons for which neither the official nor the child are personally responsible, the allowance continues to be payable for a period corresponding to the period of proven delay. For a child permanently incapable of earning its own livelihood by reason of a physical or mental ailment, the allowance continues to be payable without regard to its age if the condition was present before the age of 27, but after the age of 18 only if the child is not in receipt of a personal income in excess of 150 DM per month; orphans allowances and orphans' pensions in these cases are taken into account as income.

Benefits for Survivors

Death Benefits

On the death of an official his survivors receive death benefits, if, at the time of death, they were members of his household. Death benefit amounts to twice the monthly emoluments of the deceased, less children's allowances and allowances for official expenditure; on the death of a pensioner, twice the amount of his monthly pension or maintenance allowance.

Widows' pension

The widow of an official who would have been in receipt of a pension at the time of his death, and the widow of a pensioned official, receive a widow's pension. A widows' pension is not payable if the marriage with the deceased had lasted less than 3 months (exceptions are possible in special circumstances), or if the marriage had taken place after retirement, and the official was more than 65 years old at the time of the marriage, or if the marriage had been dissolved at the time of death.

The wife of a deceased official whose marriage had been dissolved, the guilty party, or the party adjudged mainly guilty being the husband, and who, in the event that the marriage had continued would have been entitled to a widows' pension, is entitled to a pension to the same amount as the widows' pension, in so far as the deceased had been obliged to contribute to her maintenance. For the rest. a maintenance allowance to the same amount as a widows' pension is payable, unless there are special reasons for with-holding it; income from other sources is taken into account as to a reasonable amount.

A widows' pension amounts to 60 % of the pension of which the deceased was in receipt, or of which he would have been in receipt if he had retired on the day of his death. If the widow was more than 20 years younger than the deceased, and if there is no child of the marriage, the pension is reduced by a certain amount. If an official, or a pensioner who was in receipt of an accident pension, dies as a result of an accident sustained on duty, the widows' pension payable amounts to 60 % of the Accident Pension.

A widower has a claim to a widowers' pension if there was a legal claim to maintenance against the deceased female official.

Orphans' Pension

Orphans' pensions are payable in respect of the bodily heirs and adopted children of a deceased official who, at the time of his death, was in receipt of a pension, or of the children of a deceased pensioner. No pension is payable in respect of an adopted child if the pensioner was already in retirement at the time of the adoption, and was already over 65 years of age. A maintenance allowance to the same amount as an orphans' pension may, however, be payable

The claim to an orphans' pension terminates at the end of the month in which the orphan reaches the age of 18 or dies.

An orphans' pension is payable beyond the 18th year up to the 27th year, if the orphan is engaged in full time education or vocational training, or if, by reason of a physical or mental ailment, the orphan is incapable of earning his own livelihood, beyond the 27th year. If the period of education or vocational training has been interrupted or delayed by a period of compulsory military service, the orphans' pension continues to be payable for a corresponding period beyond the 27th year.

The orphan's pension amounts in the case of a half orphan to 12 percent, of a full orphan to 20 % of the pension of which the pensioner was in receipt, or of which he would have been in receipt if he had retired on the day of his death, in the case of death as a result of an accident whilst on duty, to 30 %. If the mother of the child of the deceased is not entitled to a widow's pension, and is not in receipt of a maintenance allowance, the orphan's pension is that payable in respect of a full orphan.

Maintenance Allowance

If there is no entitlement to a pension, or to widows' and/or orphans' pension, and if the refusal of such benefits would result in hardship for the official or his survivors, a maintenance allowance is payable if certain conditions are satisfied.

Pensions payable at the same time as other Benefits and Suspension of Payments

If, in assessing pensionable service, periods of insurable employment under one or other of the statutory pensions insurance schemes have been taken into account, that part of the pension deriving from the statutory pensions scheme must be reckoned against the Civil Service pension due, corresponding to the period in which the pensionable service stands in relation to the years of insurable employment for which compulsory or voluntary contributions have been paid, in the payment of which the employing authority participated. This regulation applies only to established posts to which the official had been appointed prior to 31.12.1965.

In the case of appointments subsequent to 31.12.1965, the co-incidence of a Civil Service pension with a pension from social pensions insurance results in a reduction of the Civil Service pension in cases in which a defined upper limit has been exceeded. The upper limit is the amount resulting from the pension, plus children's allowance, if it is based on the end salary of the salary scale on which the pension is assessed. The upper limit is based on the pensionable years of service from the completion of the 17th year of life until the date the pension becomes payable, plus any subsequent years of insurable employment or activity. Any part of the pension based on voluntary continued insurance, or voluntarily paid higher contributions, is disregarded. In the case of widows and orphans, the above regulations apply as to the same percentage on which survivors pensions are based.

If a Civil Service pensioner is in receipt of a wage or salary in respect of employment in the public service, the pension is payable only up to a certain maximum amount. That is, in the case of pensioners up to the age of 65, the pension that would have been payable if it had been based on the maximum of his salary scale. In the case of pensioners over 65 years of age, and of widows, the above assessed amount is increased by 60 % of the total income from pension and other sources, less the amount applicable to pensioners under 65 (for orphans: 40 %).

The payment of pension rests if the entitled person is not a German national, or if he is permanently resident abroad. In the case of residence abroad lasting more than three years, the payment of pension may be suspended; continued payment to entitled persons resident in the Federal territory is permissible.

Retrospective Insurance and Settlements

If an established official resigns without having acquired a claim to a pension, he is retrospectively insured for the period of his employment, since, on the basis of his contingent right to a pension, he had been exempt from insurance under Social Pensions Insurance for that period. This retrospective insurance is itself contingent on certain insurance law conditions (see the Sector "Retrospective Insurance" Page 55).

A married female official allowed to resign on request receives a cash settlement which, based on her length of service, amounts to between twice and sixteen times her final monthly salary. The claim may be waived in favour of retrospective insurance under Social Pensions Insurance. Settlement may take the form of a pension.

Finance

The pensions of established officials and their survivors are financed from the budgets of the Federal Government, the Federal Lands, and the local authorities, as well as of the corporations in public law. Some employing authorities secure the financing of pensions by their membership in Pensions' Funds.

Expenditure for Civil Service Pensions
in mill. DM

1950	1956	1960	1965	1969	1970	1971	1972	1973
2 241	5 010	6 512	10 205	13 600	15 200	16 400	17 700	19 100

Legislative bases

Federal Established Officials Law of 14.7.1953 in the version of 22.10.1965 (BGB. I S. 1776), last amended by the Law of 15.4.1970 (BGB. I S. 339). Federal Civil Service Salaries Law of 27.7.1957, in the version of 14.12.1969 (BGB. I S. 2201), last amended by the Law of 15.4.1970 (BGB. I S. 339).

Supplementary Provision for Old Age

Introduction

Statutory prescribed pensions insurance, and other provision for old age, cover the needs of the pensioners and other recipients for adequate incomes in their old age, in the event of disablement, and for provision for their survivors, in highly varying degrees. Comparatively low benefits are payable in the case of agricultural pensions, since this pension was originally intended only as a cash supplement to the provision normally made for the old folks on a family farm (board and lodging). The insurance for self-employed craftsmen, in so far as it is based on compulsory insurance, also barely suffices to cover the minimum cost of living. Pensions insurance of manual and non-manual workers provide, after a full working life of decades, pensions amounting to about one half of normal average earnings, although in the case of non-manual workers who have had rapid promotion this percentage is not reached, amongst other reasons because of the insurability ceiling. Under the Miners' Special Scheme, on the other hand, retirement pensions amounting to between two thirds and three quarters of average earnings are payable. Comparatively the highest are the pensions of Civil Servants, which are usually 75 % of the final salary, whereas professors in ordinary receive their full salary after retirement. In view of such generous provision it is understandable that other pensioners endeavour to obtain comparable supplementary pensions. The gap between statutory pensions insurance and the ideas of what is a reasonable provision for old age is closed in part by provision made by corporations in public law, in part by superannuation payments based on collective and works agreements.

Supplementary Pensions in Public Law

Supplementary Pensions in public law are payable by:

1. The Supplementary Pensions Institute of the Federal Government and the Federal Lands, covering about 1 mill. manual and non-manual workers.

2. The Federal Railways Insurance Institute, Department B, covering about 190.000 manual and non-manual workers in the employ of the Federal Railways.

3. The Supplementary Pensions Institute of the Federal Post, covering about 180.000 manual and non-manual workers in the postal services.

4. The Pensions Fund of German Railways and Tramways, with about 5.000 insured persons.

5. The Supplementary Pensions Institute of the German Stage, covering about 21.000 members of the stage, in theatres, opera houses, and private theatres.

6. The Supplementary Pensions Institute of German Cultural Orchestras, covering 5.000 musicians employed by public orchestras.

7. Pensions Insurance for Steel Workers, based on Federal Law, covering about 30.000 workers in steel works and similar enterprises in the Saarland.

8. Supplementary Pensions Institute covering about 5.000 District Master Chimney Sweeps.

9. Pensions Fund for the widows and orphans of about 1.700 journeyman chimney sweeps in Bavaria.

10. Supplementary Pensions Fund of the Bavarian Municipalities, covering about 81.000 manual and non-manual workers.

There are probably similar institutes to those shown under No. 10 in some other Federal Lands. In addition, the Federal Government has also come to the assistance of super-annuation funds in those enterprises affected by certain consequences of the war. Help was granted as follows:

Federal grants to alleviate hardship arising in works superannuation funds — by the Federal Insurance Institute.

Retrospective insurance for holders of the former Pensions Fund Reserves (Versorgungs-stockkonten), and, by the Pensions Institute of the Federal Government and the Federal Lands, to meet benefits payable by the former Pensions Fund of the Administrations of Imperial Insurance.

It is estimated that about 2 mill. employees are covered by supplementary pensions provided by corporations in public law. These pensions are administered by the corporations in public law and the institutes. They are based in part on formal Federal laws, in part on Tariff Orders of the former German Reich, in part on collective agreements, and the last two on Land Legislation. In the case of nearly all these pensions it is characteristic that compulsory contributions are payable, as to one half each by employers and

Public Law Supplementary Pensions

Institute	Year	Insured in 1000s	No. of Pensions in 1000s	Income in mills.	Expenditure in mills.	Reserves in mills.
Pensions Institute of the Fed. Gov. and the Fed. Lands	1969	986	216		310	
The Fed. Railways Insurance Insitute – Department B	1966	190	170		150	
The Pensions Fund of the Fed. German Post	1968	180	56		85	
The Pensions Institute of the German Railways	1961	9	7	36	29	20
The Pensions Institute of the German Stage	1962	21	4	12	7	
The Pensions Institute of German Cultural Orchestras	1962	5		5	1	
The German Steel Workers Pensions Insurance	1969	31	30	25	17	138
The Pensions Institute for German District Master Chimney Sweeps	1968	5	3	23	17	116
The Pensions Institute for Journeyman Chimney Sweeps	1962	2	0,2	0,1	0,3	
Supplementary Pensions Fund. for Bavarian municipalities	1961	83	8	39	6	

Circa 1520

workers, with the exception of the steel works pensions insurance in the Saarland, which receives a historically based Federal supplement to the amount of 34 %, and the Pensions Fund of German Railways, in respect of whose prior obligations the funds are provided by the Federal Government. The form these supplementary pensions takes is very varied. The Federal Government and the Federal Lands and District Master Chimney Sweeps Fund guarantee, since the reform of 1965, together with Pensions Insurance, a pension largely in line with Civil Service pensions. In contrast, the institutes organised in the Bavarian Chamber of Insurance (nos. 5,6,9,10 — exception no. 8) continue to pay benefits based on contribution units.

In contrast to the above table, the following figures include the Supplementary Pensions Funds of Local Authorities.

Supplementary Pensions in the Public Services
in mill. DM

Year	Total Expenditure	including Cash payments	Administrative Costs	Total Income	incl. Conts. paid	others	Assets	Balance
1963	422	400	22	1 100	570	280	250	+ 678
1965	486	460	26	1 380	720	360	300	+ 894
1966	518	490	28	1 510	780	390	340	+ 992
1967	570	540	30	1 380	730	300	350	+ 810
1968	772	740	32	1 480	770	320	390	+ 708
1969	714	680	34	1 670	880	370	420	+ 956
1970	777	740	37	1 860	990	410	460	+1 083
1971	830	790	40	1 990	1050	440	500	+1 160
1972	992	850	42	2 110	1120	460	530	+1 218
1973	974	930	44	2 240	1190	490	560	+1 266

Health Insurance

Introduction

As a consequence of sickness, the family budget finds itself faced with the costs of medical treatment, medicines, and hospital charges. If the breadwinner is ill and unfit for work, the family must go without its accustomed income. In order to cover the costs of sickness, and to replace the loss of income, social health insurance was inaugurated. In the course of time the benefits provided have been very considerably expanded.

Owing to their very considerable numbers, and their decentralisation, the Sick Funds are able to maintain close contacts with insured persons throughout their working life, as well as with employers. They also collect the contributions to statutory pensions insurance and unemployment insurance, and perform various services for other branches of social insurance.

The system of Health Insurance stands in close interrelationship with the whole public health system. Changes in this sphere (e.g. medical advances) have a decisive influence on the tasks facing statutory health insurance. On the other hand, every change in the sphere of health insurance has its repercussions on public health policy.

The form and manner of services provided is also determined by the attitude of the medical practitioner, the Health Insurance, and also by other public and private services, as shown in the Section "Overall Economic Background."

The Growth of Health Insurance

Year	The Number of Sick Funds	The Number of Insured Persons — Millions —
1911	22 000	10,0
1914	13 500	16,0
1932	6 600	18,7
1938	4 600	23,2
1951	1 992	20,0
1955	2 070	22,7
1960	2 028	27,1
1965	1 972	28,7
1966	1 955	28,9
1967	1 919	28,7
1968	1 883	29,1
1969[1]	1 846	30,1

1) Position as at 1.10.1969

Historical survey

Social Health Insurance is the oldest branch of social insurance. Its forerunners were the Industrial Providence Funds (under the Prussian Law of 1854), and the Assistance Funds (Law of 1876). Health Insurance for manual workers was inaugurated in 1883, on the present basic principles (compulsory insurance, free services, sick benefits), though only for industrial workers. In the course of the so-called Revisionary Legislation (1885—1903), workers from the transport branch and commercial — or office — employees were included (1903). A total of about ten million persons were insured. Contributions were payable as to two thirds by the workers, as to one third by the employers. Sick benefit to the amount of at least one half of earnings was at first paid only for three months, later (1903) for up to six months. The Reichs Insurance Code of 1911 extended insurance to agricultural and forestry workers (6 to 7 million), domestic servants, and home workers, and reduced the existing 22.000 Sick Funds by 8.500. Following the reduction of benefits and contributions on the outbreak of the first World War, maternity benefits to cover the period before and after confinement were increased during the war, including members of the families of insured persons. It was again improved in 1919 and 1926. In 1927 Health Insurance was extended to seamen. The economic crisis of the early 30s led to severe cuts, for example to the introduction of a fee for a doctor's certificate, and of the Insurance Fund Medical Control Service (Emergency Decree of 1930), but also to free medical care for dependants as an obligatory service. The so-called Consolidating Legislation (1934/39) dealt primarily with questions of the organisation of Health Insurance, its financial aspects, and supervision. The administration of hospitals and institutes, preventive medical care, the Insurance Funds medical control service, the administration of financial reserves, and the auditing of the finances of Health Funds, were concentrated as a joint responsibility in the hands of the Land Insurance Intitutes. It was only within the framework of war time legislation in 1941/43 that an extensive improvement of benefits was introduced; above all, since that time, medical care has been provided for an unlimited period. Maternity benefits were also improved. At the same time the Health Insurance Funds commenced to collect contributions from wages to Pensions Insurance, Health Insurance, and Unemployment Insurance.

After the end of the second World War (1945) health insurance was very largely in a position to maintain its services. In 1949 the Social Insurance Amendment Law brought benefits and contributions into line with the changed economic conditions. In 1955 the law applying to Associations of Sick Funds, in 1956 the law applying to Sick Fund medical practitioners and to pensioners, was reformed. Social Health Insurance was also affected by many other laws passed in the first decade of the Federal Republic of Germany. A decisive point was reached by the Law for the Continued Payment of Wages during sickness enacted in 1957, which increased sick pay, obliged the employer to pay a supplement thereto in respect of manual workers, and so brought the position of manual workers during sickness largely into line with that of non-manual workers; the position was further improved in 1961 by the abolition of waiting days. In 1965 sick pay and household allowances were considerably increased, even for the period after the first six weeks of sickness; the insurable ceiling for non-manual workers was raised, as were the upper limits of insurable earnings, and the benefits. However, a fundamental reform of the whole law governing Health Insurance, such as has taken place in the case of Pensions Insurance and Industrial Injuries Insurance, is still outstanding. A relevant draft was submitted in 1958, and again in 1962, but was not adopted by the Federal Parliament; the principle points in dispute are the payment by the insured person of a part of the costs arising from sickness, and the honoraria of the medical practitioners.

In 1965 maternity benefits were reformed. At the same time pensioners were required to pay health insurance contributions. This clause was again deleted with effect from January 1st 1970.

The efforts to achieve a reform of Health Insurance led in 1969 to the introduction of Continued Payment of Wages to manual workers during sickness. This brought the position of manual workers completely into line with that of non-manual workers — a long outstanding demand. At the same time, the maximum rate of contribution was reduced with effect from 1.1.1970, and the insurable ceiling was raised to 1.200 DM per month. Further, a rebate for unused sick certificates was introduced, and the fee payable for medical prescriptions was raised to 20 % of the costs (though to a maximum of 2.50 DM). In 1967 the fee payable had already been raised. Further improvements in the law governing Health Insurance are in the course of preparation. The Federal Government has appointed a Committee of Experts to make relevant proposals. In addition it is intended to raise the insurable ceiling for non-manual workers to bring it into line with the higher salaries, and toaccord to independent farmers and the members of their famalies the protection of health insurance.

The Functions of Health Insurance

The purpose of Health Insurance is to ensure that, in the event of sickness or accident, there shall be available for the insured person and his dependants: adequate treatment by medical practitioners and dental surgeons, and in hospitals, supplies of medicines and other medical requisites and appliances. In addition, insofar as wages or salaries do not remain payable, cash benefits are payable. Similar services are available during maternity; further, precautionary medical examinations are also provided. Measures for the prevention of sickness, and convalescent treatment, are designed to maintain health. In the event of death, death benefits are payable.

Scope

In March 1970 the following were compulsorily insurable under Health Insurance: 17.8 mill. employed employees, and 7.9 mill. pensioners. About 4.6 million persons were voluntarily insured. These approximately 30.3 mill. persons, with almost 24 mill. dependants, comprise about 88 per cent of the total population. Of the approximately 30.3 mill. insured persons (1970) 17.7 mill. are men, 12.6 mill. are women. Of every 100 insured persons, 59 are compulsorily insurable, 26 are compulsorily insured pensioners, and 15 are voluntary insured persons.

In addition, further recipients of social benefits receive their medical treatment through statutory Health Insurance (acting on behalf of the other branches) namely:

> War injured persons, the dependants of severely war injured persons, war survivors,
> Recipients of Social Aid — based on local arrangements,
> Industrial injuries and industrial diseases sufferers,
> Returnees,
> Recipients of reparations benefits.

According to the microcensus of 1968, 98.6 per cent of the total population (about 59.6 mill. persons) were insured against sickness. 87 per cent were covered under statutory Health Insurance.

Of the total population, 16.7 mill. or 28 per cent were compulsorily insured; 7.3 mill. or 12.1 per cent as pensioners, and 5.6 mill. or 9.2 per cent were voluntarily insured. 25.1 mill. or 37.6 per cent of the total population are included as dependants. In other forms of insurance under legislation some 0.8 mill. persons or 1.3 per cent of the population are insured. 5.9 mill. persons were privately insured. Of the latter, some 1.1 mill. were established officials (not counting dependants); these persons receive a part refund of the costs of sickness from their authorities, that is to say, from public funds. About 0.8 mill. persons, or 1.4 per cent of the population had no insurance cover.

Compulsory Insurability

By virtue of law some 26 mill. persons are compulsorily insurable
Employed employees (18 mill.)
Unemployed
Pensioners (8 mill.)
Female pupils in certain types of vocational training, and self-employed persons in occupations resembling part-employment.

It will be seen that all persons are insurable who are members of the groups working for pay, those who are desirous of doing so (the unemployed), who have done so (pensioners), or who are undergoing training (apprentices, certain female pupils).

Population in April 1968 according to Insurance Funds/-Insurance and Type of Insurance Cover — Thousands —

Insurance Fund/-Insurance	Total	Compulsorily Insured	Voluntarily Insured	Insured Pensioners	Insurance Cover[1]	Medical Care for Police and Armed Forces	Insured Dependants	Without Cover
General Local Sick Funds, District, Trade Associations, Land Sick Funds	30 238	10 391	1 823	5 249	–	–	12 775	–
Works Sick Funds, including Posts and Railways, Established Officials Funds, and the Ministry of Transport Fund	8 526	2 625	1 008	791	–	–	4 102	–
Miners' Special Scheme Fund	2 019	381	27	614	–	–	997	–
Mutual Benefit Funds	10 956	3 282	2 550	581	–	–	4 543	–
Private Health Insurance	5 945	–	3 312	/	–	–	2 633	–
Students' Health Insurance	211	–	200	/	–	–	11	–
Other Insurance Cover[2]	844	25	10	/	729	60	19	–
Without Insurance Cover	842	–	–	–	–	–	–	842
Total	59 580	16 703	8 928	7 238	729	60	25 080	842

1) Insurance cover as recipient of Social Aid, War Damages Pensioner, etc.
2) Including Foreign Health Funds, and Social Insurance in the Soviet Sector of Berlin

In detail:

Employed employees are those working for renumeration, in particular manual workers, e.g. journeymen, tradesmen's mates, domestic servants, seamen, apprentices (even if they are not in receipt of pay), without regard to the amount of their annual earnings, as well as non-manual workers with a regualr annual salary of up to 14.400 DM. Amongst the non-manual workers are counted, in particular, senior employees in industry and commerce, works foremen, clerical workers, commercial employees and apprentices, actors and musicians, employees in educational and training occupations, in welfare, in the care of the sick, ship's masters and ship's officers in inland waterways. Ship's masters and ship's officers as non-manual workers in deep sea vessels are insurable without regard to the amount of their annual earnings. On the basis of the statutes of the Miners' Special Scheme, all non-manual workers insurable under the Miners' Special Scheme Pensions Insurance have been declard insurable for health insurance purposes.

The fixing of a rigid ceiling for the insurability of non-manual workers has always led to a position in which, when the general level of salaries rose, numbers of non-manual workers ceased to be compulsorily insurable, continued as voluntary contributions, and then again became insurable at irregular intervals when the insurable ceiling was raised (see above table); the numbers of voluntary contributors then always again declined. There are at present two draft laws before the Federal Parliament on the basis of which the insurability ceiling in statutory Health Insurance will be fixed at 75 per cent of the general basis of computation in pensions insurance (= 1.425 DM per month). Both laws are intended to come into force on 1.1.1971.

Insurable Ceiling for Non-Manual Workers in Health Insurance*)

from	Marks/per Year
1. 1. 04	2 000
1. 1. 14	2 500
12. 1. 25	2 700
1. 10. 27	3 600
1. 6. 49	4 500
1. 9. 52	6 000
1. 10. 57	7 920
1. 9. 65	10 800
1. 8. 69	11 880
1. 1. 70	14 400

*) Also the amount on which contributions are payable

Unemployed persons are insured if they are in receipt of unemployment benefit or unemployment assistance. Similarly, those taking part in vocational further training courses, or re-training courses, are insured if they are in receipt of maintenance allowances. The membership of insurable workers is continued as long as they have a claim to short time working benefits or inclement weather benefits.

Health insurance for pensioners was first introduced in 1941, and reformed in 1956 and 1967. The contribution to Health Insurance payable by pensioners under the 1967 regulations was cancelled with effect from 1.1.1970. At present, some 8 mill. pensioners are insured under Health Insurance.

In principle all recipients of pensions from the manual and non-manual workers pensions schemes are insurable under Health Insurance. On application, exemption may be granted to a person taking up a private insurance for himself and his entitled dependants providing services comparable with those of statutory insurance. However, any insured person who was insured under statutory insurance for at least 52 weeks during the 5 years before claiming a pension may not claim such exemption. The same rule applies in the case of survivors of a deceased person who had been insured under statutory Health Insurance at the time of his death. Application must be made within one month of the beginning of compulsory insurability.

The insurance of pensioners under statutory Health Insurance begins on the day the application for pension is made (formal membership). Until the pension has actually been awarded, the pensioner is required to pay the contributions himself; they are refunded from the beginning of the payment of the pension. This does not apply in the case of the widow or of an orphan of an insured person claiming a widow's pension, or an orphan's pension before reaching the age of 18. If a pension is refused, formal membership also terminates. Pensioners under the Miners' Special Scheme Pensions Insurance are insured unconditionally for Health Insurance. If pensioners are in employment, and consequently still insurable, this insurance has priority.

Student nurses, infant-, children's-, midwifery- and maternity nursing *students* are insured under special regulations, since as a general rule, they enter into insurable employment on completion of their training.

Membership in Groups of Insured Persons
— Thousands as a Yearly Average —

Year	Totals	Compulsory Members less Pensioners	Insurable Pensioners	Voluntary Members
1938	23 222	19 769	–	3 453
1950	20 200	13 245	4 734	2 464
1955	24 900	16 292	6 663	2 982
1960	27 060	17 655	5 504	3 901
1965	28 740	17 201	5 885	5 654
1966	28 924	17 791	6 023	5 110
1967	28 698	17 019	6 241	5 439
1968	29 123	16 697	7 384	5 042
1969[1]	29 766	16 501	7 767	5 497
1970[2]	30 287	17 769	7 913	4 604

1) Position at 1.7.1969
2) Position at 1.3.1970

Of self-employed persons the following are compulsorily insurable: homeworkers, variety artists, midwives, private teachers, instructors and musicians, persons privately engaged in sick, maternity, infant and children's nursing, who do not themselves employ labour; their regular annual income may not exceed 14.400 DM. Amongst the latter are included nursing sisters, therapeutic gymnastics instructors, day nursery nurses, and masseurs, if they work independently (they are otherwise in general insurable as employees.).

Membership according to Different Types of Insurance Fund
— Thousands as a Yearly Average —

Year	OKK	LKK	BKK	IKK	SeeKK	KnK	EK Ar	EK An	Total
1938	13 524	1 817	4 097	676	59	762	2 287		23 222
1950	13 838	670	2 300	398	21	1 128	81	1 764	20 200
1955	16 143	540	2 960	660	46	1 335	145	3 071	24 900
1960	15 433	469	3 600	936	70	1 402	231	4 919	27 060
1965	15 442	418	3 874	1 244	71	1 318	290	6 082	28 740
1966	15 373	420	3 869	1 294	72	1 286	302	6 307	28 924
1967	15 115	426	3 766	1 329	74	1 229	309	6 452	28 698
1968	15 332	434	3 832	1 367	75	1 153	319	6 615	29 123
1969[1]	15 715	438	3 995	1 385	76	1 126	328	6 783	29 845

1) Provisional Figures

OKK — General Local Health Insurance Funds;
LKK — Land Health Insurance Funds;
IKK — Trade Association Health Insurance Funds;
SKK — Seamen's Health Insurance Funds;
KnK — Miners' Special Scheme Health Insurance Funds;
EK — Manual Workers Mutual Benefit Funds;
EK An — Non-Manual Workers Mutual Benefit Funds.

Exemption from Insurability

There are, basically, four grounds for exemption from insurability, namely:
inconsiderable employment,
in the case of established public officials, and employees having a comparable status, or whose position is otherwise secured,
in the case of employment generally preparatory to establishment in the public services, and
in the case of an employment relationship between married persons.

In addition some forms of employment of aliens, particularly of border crossers, are exempt.

A subsidiary employment is exempt for purposes of Health Insurance under the same conditions as those applying to Pensions Insurance.

Exempt from Health Insurance are: established public officials, other employees in the public services, and clergymen of religious communities officiallly recognised as corporations in public law, insofar as their contingent rights to pensions and survivors' pensions are guaranteed, or during any period in which they are undergoing training as public officials, or as clergymen, or are temporarily so employed. As in the case of statutory Pensions Insurance, exemption is possible on application in certain cases in which pensions comparable to those in the public services are payable. Also exempt in certain circumstances are members of religious communities, deaconesses, red cross nurses, and similar persons, if they are engaged primarily for religious or ethical motives in the care of the sick, or in other activities for the public good. Teachers employed full time in private state registered special schools are exempt if they have contingent rights to pension and survivors' pension on the basis of Civil Service or similar regulations.

In contrast to statutory pensions regulations, administration students, and other employees, are exempt who, for the purpose of, or during their period of, training for their future profession are actually employed, whether as work students during vacation, as scientific assistants, medical assistants or as junior barristers or solicitors.

Finally, a married person employed by the other partner to the marriage is exempt under Health Insurance; the Federal Constitutional Court has held that this special regulation is not incompatible with the Basic Law, since such exempted married persons are entitled to be voluntarily insured.

Non-manual workers, home workers, private teachers, instructors, musicians, variety artists, midwives, persons working on their own account in nursing — sick nursing, maternity, infant, or children's nursing — are able to apply for exemption. On the occasion of the raising of the insurability ceiling on 1.1.1970 only about 1 per cent of the approximately 1.025 mill. persons affected in fact applied for exemption. Such persons can be exempted if they become insurable as a result of the raising of the insurability ceiling, and if they have private insurance cover for themselves and their dependants providing for benefits and services corresponding to those provided under statutory insurance. That is to say, that at the point in time at which the persons affected become compulsorily insurable, they must have comprehensive full insurance for themselves and their dependants providing all services provided under statutory insurance (including cash benefits). Persons becoming insurable by reason of the raising of the insurability ceiling who had been previously insured with a private company are entitled to terminate their contract with that company at the end of the month in which they can prove that they are covered by statutory insurance.

Entitlement to Insurance

On condition that their total income is not in excess of 14.400 DM per annum the following are entitled to become voluntary contributors to statutory Health Insurance: manual workers exempted from compulsory insurance, employed family members working for an employer without any formal contract of employment or fixed remuneration, tradesmen and owners of businesses, as well as persons who, on the termination of their period of service in the Armed Forces, or as police officers in the Federal Border Forces, are engaged in a period of training or further training in preparation for their future occupation. Insurance Funds are not entitled to impose an age limit for entry into insurance in respect of the latter group, or to require a certificate of health. The Insurance Funds are, therefore, not empowered to reject such persons on account of an existing illness. In other cases the Funds have these powers.

Benefits

Statutory Health Insurance provides for a whole range of benefits, which are laid down in detail in legislation, and which are traditionally provided according to different principles. The following table gives a general survey. Under benefits in kind are to be understood in the main treatment by medical practitioners and similar services. Help is provided in the case of sickness, confinement, maternity benefit, and in the form of death benefits. Certain benefits are designated as standard benefits, and no Insurance Fund is permitted to provide benefits below the standard laid down; they are, however, authorised, on the basis of their statutes, to provide additional benefits within legally defined limits. Such benefits may be either obligatory or discretionary.

Benefits are granted in principle to all insured persons and their depehdants, though cash benefits, which are paid in lieu of wage or salary, are naturally payable only if an actual loss of earnings occurs, that is to say, not in the case of pensioners or family dependants.

Benefits in kind to meet the needs of the insured person are provided directly by the Insurance Fund in the form of medical treatment and medicines. That is to say, insured persons are not required first to pay and then obtain a refund. The Funds conclude contracts for the provision of the services needed with medical practitioners, dental surgeons, pharmaceutical chemists, opticians, etc. The nature and extent of benefits in kind provided must be such as are necessary to cure the illness. They must therefore be suitable and adequate in each particular case, but must not be in excess of what is essential. This principle applies explicitly, or in a similar form, to all benefits in kind.

Originally sick pay was the most important financial benefit provided under Health Insurance, whereas at the present time, and despite increases payable under the 1957, 1961 and 1965 legislation, benefits in kind occupy the forefront. The relation between expenditure on treatment and cash benefits was:

1885 = 0.6 : 1   1955 = 4 : 1   1965 = 3.3 : 1
1925 = 1 : 1   1961 = 3 : 1   1968 = 4.5 : 1.

As a result of the introduction of the continued payment of wages to manual workers during the first six weeks of sickness, the quota of benefits in kind will further increase. The quota of cash benefits will probably fall to one eigth of the costs of benefits in kind by 1973. The main emphasis of expenditure has accordingly shifted to benefits in kind and their costs, in particular as a result of advances in medical science, and of the continued payment of salaries to non-manual workers and of wages to manual workers during sickness.

Prevention of Illness

General and special measures for the prevention of illness are financed by Health Insurance as a joint measure undertaken by all Insurance Funds, and are implemented by a

Type	Benefits in kind or cash	Insurance law title of benefit general	special	Obligatory or discretionary benefit	Standard benefit or additional benefit
Medical treatment	Kind	Sick aid	Nursing	Obligatory	Standard
Dental treatment	Kind	Sick aid	Nursing	Obligatory	Standard
Medicines	Kind	Sick aid	Nursing	Obligatory	Standard
Minor medical aids	Kind	Sick aid	Nursing	Obligatory	Standard
Major aids	Kind or cash	Sick aid	Nursing	Obligatory	Standard only in Hamburg, Schleswig-Holstein, Lower Saxony, North Rhine Westphalia
Dentures	Kind or cash	Sick aid	Dentures	Discretionary	Standard
Sick pay	Cash	Sick aid	Sick pay	Obligatory	Standard
Household Allowance	Cash	Sick aid	Sick pay	Obligatory	Standard increase: additional
Hospitalisation	Kind	Sick aid	Alternative benefit	Discretionary	Standard
Home nursing and Attendance	Kind or cash	Sick aid	Nursing	Discretionary	Standard only in Hamburg, Schleswig-Holstein, Lower Saxony, North-Rhine Westphalia
Mdical aids	Kind or cash	Sick aid	Nursing	Discretionary	see "Major aids"
Convalescent Treatment	Kind	Sick aid	Nursing	Discretionary	Standard only in Hamburg, Schleswig-Holstein, Lower Saxony, North-Rhine Westphalia
Medical treatment inclusive per examinations	Kind	Maternity services		Obligatory	Standard
Medicines, bandages bandages and other aids	Kind	Sick aid		Obligatory	Standard
Midwifery	Kind	Sick aid		Obligatory	Standard
Lumpsum on confinement	Cash	Sick aid		Obligatory	Standard
Maternity allowance allowance	Cash	Sick aid		Obligatory	Standard
Death benefit	Cash	Sick aid		Obligatory	Standard increase: additional

special department of the Land Insurance Institutes. These measures include, for example, advice to insured persons on hygiene, and on dangers to health, mass examinations, and, when necessary, preventive immunisation.

Individual measures for the prevention of illness may be approved by Insurance Funds at their own discretion, for instance, spa treatment for children, anatomical jaw bone treatment, or cash supplements thereto.

Benefits for the Cure of Illnesses

In the event of illness, Health Insurance grants medical and dental treatment, the provision of medicines and medical aids, or contributions towards the cost thereof, and home nursing; these benefits are lumped together under the designation ,,Care in Sickness'', and are granted indefinitely. If a member ceases to be insurable during the course of an illness, benefits cease at the latest 26 weeks after termination of membership.

Medical Treatment

Medical treatment of a sick person by a medical practitioner includes all consultations, visits, operations, and other special services, as well as medico-technical examinations, ray treatment, and all other so-called medical special treatment suitable and adequate on the basis of the most up-to-date medical knowledge to effect a cure or an amelioration of the illness. If this condition is satisfied, expensive methods of treatment may be approved, e.g. the use of a heart-lung machine during an operation. On the other hand the doctor is not permitted to give or to prescribe any treatment that is unnecessary, or too expensive. He may refer patients to other doctors, usually specialists, or send them to hospital, and he prescribes medicines and other medical aids.

Only so-called Insurance Fund doctors who are members of an Insurance Fund Association are permitted to practice under social insurance, others only in cases of emergency. Lay medical practitioners, speech therapists, and similar persons, are permitted to practice only on the instructions or under the supervision of a doctor. Every doctor may be registered as an Insurance Fund doctor if he satisfies certain personal conditions. The insured person has free choice of doctors; only under the Miners' Scheme is he required in the first instance to report to his own district doctor. An insured person and his entitled dependants may change their doctor at will, but should not do so during a current quarter without good and sufficient reason. The doctor will give them a transfer certificate whenever necessary, e.g. to a specialist.

Proof of membership of an Insurance Fund is the sick certificate, which must be handed to the doctor. In urgent cases the certificate may be handed in later. Every insured person receives in respect of himself and his entitled dependants a refund of 10 DM for each quarter during which he has been insured for at least 60 calendar days, though to a maximum of 30 DM per annum, but in which he has not handed in a sick certificate for medical treatment, has not claimed any nursing services, and in which he has received no other refund in respect of medical treatment. Sick certificates are issued free of charge and hold good for three months.

The Insurance Fund is under an obligation to provide medical treatment free of charge. The Insurance Fund Doctors' Association undertakes this responsibility on behalf of the Fund. Treatment provided by the Fund is, within the framework of legislative provision, regulated by written contracts with the Association, in such a manner as to ensure uniform, adequate and suitable treatment for sich persons. Honoraria are also regulated by similar contracts. In this connection, due consideration must be given to the financial position of the individual Funds. The choice of the type of honoraria is left to the free decision of the contracting partners. The law permits lump sum payments, as well as payment for individual items of treatment; and other forms. If no agreement is reached, the terms of the contract are laid down in a binding form by Arbitration Boards. Payment is made by the Insurance Fund to the Association to cover the whole amount due. The Association then distributes the amount amongst the registered medical practitioners on the basis of a scale agreed between the Association and the Association of Insurance Funds. Payment for medical treatment is made by local, land, works and trade association funds, in part by lump sum payments, and by Mutual Benefit Insurance Funds, mainly by individual items.

The number of registered doctors increased between the end of 1959 and the end of 1965 from 36.864 to 43.765, to increase further to 44.188 by the end of 1969. In addition, by the end of 1969, 2.478 doctors (chiefs and heads of departments in hospitals) were engaged in Insurance Fund practice. The costs of medical treatment per member of a Social Insurance Fund (less pensioners) increased from 17.25 RM in 1937, over 26.19 DM in 1950, 71.26 DM in 1960, 129.07 DM in 1964, to 149.80 DM in 1968.

In respect of income from Insurance Fund practice, including the Mutual Benefit Funds, varying average amounts are quoted. Average income is estimated at 80.000 DM per annum, from which necessary expenses must be met. A further 20 % of this income comes from private practice.

Dental Services

Dental treatment includes the treatment of every from of dental decay, as well as oral surgery and, above all, conservative treatment. A special benefit is the provision of dentures, crowns, and pegs. The Fund may either meet the whole cost, or may make a part allowance. The general rule is that the Fund pays one third of the costs, and may pay a further third on behalf ot the Pensions Fund. Prior approval is necessary.

Insurance Fund dental surgeons only are authorised to provide treatment. Treatment is given only on production of a special certificate. Treatment is remunerated on the same basis as that of medical practitioners, as a general rule on the basis of individual items of treatment.

In 1959 registered dental surgeons numbered 23 821; in 1960 25 038, at the and of 1968 26 134. Annual expenditure per member, which amounted in 1937 to 4.82 RM, increased by 1951 to 7.56 DM, to 20.24 DM by 1960, and to 61.71 DM in 1968. The increase in the annual cost of dentures per member tok the following course: 1951 − 5.58 DM, 1960 − 10,40 DM, 1964 − 15,66 DM, and 1968 − 20,35 DM.

Provision of Medicines and Medicinal Aids

The insured person has a claim to any medicines prescribed by his doctor, including new and expensive medicines. However, in prescribing medicines, the doctor has a duty not to exceed what is absolutely necessary, and to pay regard to the cost thereof. If a cure can be affected by medicines which are equally good, but cheaper, these must be given preference. Guide lines are laid down by the Federal Committee of Doctors and Insurance Funds. The Insurance Funds Doctors Associations supervise the manner of prescribing by their members, in order to check the costs and suitability. If it transpires in the course of such checks that prescriptions have not been within the framework of those indicated by general experience, the doctor is required to justify the cost and suitability of the more expensive medicaments. In this connection it is less a question of an individual case of treatment than of the customary practice of the particular doctor. That is to say, the doctor is not debarred from prescribing an expensive item if it is really necessary.

The insured person is required to pay a prescription charge of 20 % — though to a maximum amount of 2.50 DM — towards the costs of prescribed medicines, dressings and médical aids. The remaining cost is refunded to the pharmaceutical chemist by the Insurance Fund on the basis of agreements between them. No payment is required of compulsorily or voluntarily insured pensioners, nor of insured persons with a reduced standard of employment of at least 50 %, if such is not a temporary condition, or if insured persons are in receipt of such pay, household allowance, injury allowance, or transitional allowance.

Medical aids include spectacles, trusses, medicinal baths, arch supports, massage etc. In contrast to medicines, medical aids have their effect on the organism not internally but externally. Minor medical aids are those costing as a rule less than 100 DM; the amount is laid down by the Fund. They are granted on the same terms as medicines, namely on payment of a small charge. In many instances prior sanction is required; this is granted in the form of a stamp affixed to the prescription.

In the case óf larger items the Fund generally makes an allowance, at least to the amount granted in the case of minor items, in the Lands Hamburg, Schleswig-Holstein, Lower Saxony and North Rhine-Westphalia on the basis of Land Laws (standard benefit), elsewhere on the basis of the Statutes. As a ruie the allowance amounts to one third of the costs, a further third may be paid on behalf of the Pensions Fund, so that the insured person is required to pay only one third.

Per year and member the following sums were paid out in respect of medicines, curative and medicinal aids purchased in apothecaries: 1951 — 15.76 DM, 1960 — 34.96 DM, 1964 — 51,65 DM, 1968 — 89,54 DM.

Hospital Treatment

The question as to whether a sick person is entitled to hospital treatment is one for medical opinion. It depends on the nature of the illness, the course it is taking, and the prospects of a cure offered by hospitalisation. The Fund must normally sanction hospital treatment if the illness requires care and attention which cannot be provided in the home, if it is infectious, or if it is of such a nature that it requires constant obervation. In other cases the Fund decides at its own discretion whether hospitalisation is medically necessary.

Hospital treatment includes treatment, food, and accommodation. The treatment includes medical treatment remunerated at standard rates, nursing services, medicaments, and the use of medical aids and apparatus. In principle, the insured person has a free choice of hospitals, but the Fund may impose certain restrictions. The hospitals have a duty to provide adequate, suitable, and economical treatment, under reasonable conditions. Standard rates are still subject to official price control. The Funds normally sanction hospitalisation in the third class. If, however, the nature of the illness renders it necessary to accommodate the patient in a single room, this must be done. If the patient asks for a higher class of his own accord, the Fund will, as a rule, pay only the third class rates.

Hospital treatment is conditional on the agreement of the insured person. In many cases such agreement is refused, e.g. in cases of infectious diseases; if a patient refuses to go to hospital on medical instructions, he receives no benefits for the duration of the illness, e.g. no sick pay.

Hospital treatment in respect of one and the same illness is granted to a maximum of 78 weeks in a three year period; at the end of this period entitlement is renewed. In the case of several illnesses, the period obtains in respect of each, though it is not extended in respect of new illnesses occurring during treatment.

Periods spent in hospital in the Federal Republic of Germany are above average as compared with other countries, though they are becoming shorter. They still amounted in 1963 to 28.2 days per case. In 1968 they had fallen to 25.9 days. Under Statotory Health Insurance, however, the periods were shorter than the Federal average. They amounted in 1963 to 23.4 days, over 22.8 days in 1965, to 22.1 days in 1968. The following table shows the number of hospital cases, hospital days, duration and cost per day in Statutory Pensions Insurance. Expenditure in respect of hospital and spa treatment rose from 24.84 DM per member in 1951, over 81.60 DM in 1964, to 132,12 DM in 1968.

Hospital Cases, Hospital Days, Duration and Cost per Diem

Year	Cases Thousands	Days Thousands	Duration in days	Costs in Mill. DM	Costs per Diem in DM
1950[1]	2 929	68 261	23,3	438	6,50
1955	3 555	81 833	23,0	777	9,50
1960	4 093	90 991	22,2	1 568	17,20
1965	4 445	101 324	22,8	2 947	29,10
1966	4 578	103 605	22,6	3 397	32,80
1967	4 751	106 607	22,4	3 851	36,10
1968	5 012	110 815	22,1	4 384	39,50

1) Less Berlin

The costs of hospital treatment are dependent on the cost falling on the hospital. In calculating these costs it is of considerable importance to ascertain whether the costs of the purchase, or the replacement of essentials whose useful life is shown by experience to be longer than three years, including the costs of maintenance and repair, or only the costs of administration have been taken into consideration in fixing the standard daily rates paid to the hospitals. In order to provide assistance to the hospitals in the matter of necessary investments, a draft law before Parliament — the Law on the Security of the Financial Position of the Hospitals — provides that financial assistance shall be granted from public funds. For this purpose the Emergency (Akutkrankenhäuser) Hospitals are to be awarded non-repayable advances. Alternatively it is intended to take over the debt service (interest and amortisation) on loans which have been taken up for investment purposes. The costs of maintenance and repair are to be included in investment costs.

Home Nursing

Insurance Funds can provide help and attendance by male and female nurses, in the home for example, if the patient is bedridden and hospitalisation is indicated but cannot be carried out, or if there is an urgent reason for leaving him with his family. Since, however, such personnel is scarcely available, this benefit can only seldom be granted.

Post Illness Benefits

It is often the case that, following an illness and curative treatment, the insured person and his family are in need of care. The Funds grant convalescent treatment and provide necessary medical aids.

Convalesecent home treatment

In practice convelescent care almost always takes the form of accommodation in a convalescent home, where the insured person is able to recover from his illness before resuming work. Such treatment is at the discretion of the Fund. During the stay in a convalescent home, household allowance is payable.

Appliances

Following the cure of his illness the insured person often requires medical appliances in order completely to restore his working capacity. This includes artificial limbs (protheses) hearing aids, invalid chairs, etc. The Funds make allowances towards the costs, as a rule to the same amount as in the case of major medical aids. Generally speaking the insured person is required to meet one third of the cost.

Cash Benefits

During the last few years the average number of sick persons unfit for work has amounted to between 600.000 and 700.000. The relation between unfit sick persons and the total number of insured persons is known as the sickness quota. In practice it can be ascertained only in the case of manual workers. The quota rose from 5.4 per cent in 1957 to 6.1 per cent in 1961; in order to reach a correct appraisal of the increase, the amendments to the law and the differing methods of compiling statistics must be taken into account. Since 1963 the quota has been somewhat lower. It stood at 6.1 per cent in 1962, 5.9 per cent in 1963, 5.5 per cent in 1965, 5.6 in 1966, 4.9 per cent in 1967 and 5.4 per cent in 1968. In 1969 it again rose to 5.6 per cent, and thus again reached the annual average of 1965 and 1966.

The Average Sickness Quota of Coumpulsorily Insured Members with an Immediate Claim to Cash Benefits
— Annual Averages —

Year	Total	OKK	LKK	BKK	IKK	SeeKK	KnV	Mutual Benefit Societies	
								Man.	Non-Man.
1951	3,92	3,78	2,47	4,41	3,72	4,16	5,97	2,97	2,75
1955	4,52	4,44	2,57	5,03	3,90	3,89	5,69	3,67	3,82
1960	5,95	5,98	2,95	6,33	5,00	3,57	6,32	5,37	6,65
1965	5,58	5,50	3,02	5,88	4,73	3,53	8,15	5,07	6,26
1966	5,66	5,58	3,12	5,96	4,74	4,05	8,43	5,22	6,22
1967	4,90	4,85	2,92	5,11	4,34	4,31	6,98	4,55	5,39
1968	5,46	5,36	3,20	5,96	4,74	4,01	8,00	4,96	5,96
1969	5,65	5,52	3,28	6,25	4,68	3,86	8,64	5,07	6,68

About one half of the sickness quota of manual workers is due to illnesses lasting from one to 14 days. One fifth is unfit from 15 to 21 days, three tenths longer. In the course of a year the sickness quota is usually highest in March, lowest in June.

Payment of Earnings by Employers during Unfitness for Work

In the event of sickness resulting in unfitness for work the question arises as to who is to take care of income during the sickness.

Until the introduction of the continued payment of wages during sickness, unfit manual workers received sick pay from their statutory funds. In addition, they received from their employers an allowance to the amount of the difference between their previous net earnings and sick pay, for a period of six weeks.

Since the introduction in 1970 of continued payment during sickness, all employees now receive the same income for the first six weeks as they did before falling sick. The disbursements of the Insurance Funds, formerly a quid pro quo for loss of wages, are, therefore, now of considerably less importance; it is only in the event of a prolonged illness that they are of importance to the financial position of the worker.

Since 1.1.1970 all employees unfit for work have an unconditional legal claim against their employer to continued payment of their gross wage for a period of 6 weeks, as also in the case of spa treatment approved by an Insurance Fund, the Fund bearing the full costs thereof. No waiting days are required, but the worker must have actually taken up employment. Exceptions are, temporarily and inconsiderably employed persons, and women in receipt of maternity benefits.

During the first six weeks of unfitness for work, or of spa treatment, the full gross wages are payable which the employee would have received had he been fit for work. (Loss of wage principle). Waiting days entailing loss of pay or benefit are no longer imposed. In the event of sickness, the payment of wages continues without interruption. Previously, payment of sick pay and employer's supplement ware made only from the day on which the doctor certified unfitness for work.

It was only in the case of industrial injuries and certain industrial diseases that waiting days were not required.

The sick worker is required to notify his employer of his unfitness for work within three calendar days by submitting a medical certificate. A similar certificate, showing the nature of the illness is sent to the relevant Insurance Fund.

Cash Benefits Payable by Insurance Funds in lieu of Wages

In cases in which the insured person is unfit for work for more than six weeks, statutory social insurance has a duty to provide substitute for wage or salary. The following benefits are payable in the case of
Unfitness for Work — Sick Pay
Hospitalisation — Household Allowance
Employment barred because of Pregnancy — Maternity Allowance (See 'Maternity Aid')

Sick Pay

Cash benefits are payable to manual and non-manual workers, but not to pensioners and family dependants; voluntary contributors may be debarred from receipt of sick pay by the Statutes of the Fund. Payment of sick pay is, in general, of importance to an employee only after the lapse of six weeks of unfitness for work. In the event that an employer refuses to pay, the claim to sick pay commences from the day of unfitness for work, but the claim to payment is then transferred to the Insurance Fund, to the amount paid by the Fund.

Conditions

Sick pay is payable to an insured person who is unfit for work as a result of illness. Unfitness is, as a rule, certified by the Insurance Fund doctor providing the treatment. The Insurance Funds are under an obligation to ask for an opinion from their own confidential medical service if such is necessary to dispose of justified doubts as to the unfitness. On the other hand, the insured person, his doctor, and his employer, are also entitled to claim an opinion from the confidential medical service. The obligation to provide such an opinion applies to all Insurance Funds. Such opinion is, in the future, to be called for in order to ensure the success of curative treatment, and to inaugurate suitable measures of rehabilitation.

The confidential doctor is not bound by any instructions from the Fund. The Fund can withold sick pay, wholly or in part, if an insured person fails without good and sufficient cause to report to the confidential doctor after receiving a written request to do so; a good and sufficient cause would be, for instance, that the insured person is confined to his bed. Sick pay may also be witheld in the case of guilty involvement in a brawl. Sick pay is not due in cases in which unfitness for work has not been properly notified. This rule does not apply if notification is received within a week of the commencement of sickness. In special exceptional cases the manager of a Fund is empowered to authorise payment for, at the most, one week prior to the receipt of the notification. Further, the claim to sick pay rests if the insured person receives wages or salary for the period of sickness.

Amounts

The amount of sick benefit payable is dependent on the wage or salary regularly earned before the illness (customary earnings). It is less for the first six weeks of unfitness than later, and amounts in the case of an insured person without dependants to 65 per cent of the customary wage; if there is a dependant to maintain 69 per cent, and for every further dependant to 3 per cent more. The maximum amount may not exceed 75 per cent of the customary wage. From the 7th week onwards sick benefit is fixed at 75 per cent of the customary wage. With dependants' allowances it can amount to 85 per cent of the customary wage, but it may not exceed customary net income.

The customary wage is the regular remuneration of which the insured person was in receipt before becoming unfit for work. It is based on the method of payment, i.e. either by the hour or the calendar day. In the case of insured persons whose payment is not made by the month, the amount earned in the last wages period (which must amount to at least 4 weeks) is divided by the number of hours worked and of hours of absenteeism. This results in an hourly wage rate which, multiplied by the number of normal hours of work, corresponds to the customary wage. The Fund is empowered, in the case of firms normally working a five day week, to require earnings to be calcualted on a daily basis. In such cases the hourly wage is multiplied by the number of the hours regularly worked on each day. In the case of all other insured persons the earnings in the month before unfitness for work are divided by 30. Customary earnings are calcualted to a maximum amount corresponding to the maximum contribution payable. If sick benefit is calcualted and paid by the calendar day, earnings up to 40 DM are taken as a basis. If benefit is paid for 6 working days, the maximum amount is 46.67 DM per day. If the Insurance Fund has prescribed calculation on the basis of a working day, the highest amount reckonable for a working day is 56 DM.

Duration

In the case of an industrial injury, or an industrial disease, benefit is payable from the first day on which unfitness for work is certified, in all other cases from the following day. In the case of one and the same illness it is payable for a maximum period of eighteen months (exactly: 78 weeks) within a three year period. If a further illness occurs during unfitness for work, the benefit period is not thereby extended. If the insured person has become fit for work, and then again becomes unfit because of some other illness, he again has a renewed claim to benefit for eighteen months.

The claim to sick benefit terminates when a retirement pension, or an unemployability pension has been awarded. Unemployability pension is reckoned against the payment of sick benefit. If pensioners continue in employment insurable under Health Insurance they receive both the pension and sick benefit, though recipients of unemployability pension and retirement pension to a maximum of six weeks. In order to prevent claimants taking undue advantage of the extensive period for which sick benefit is payable, the Funds are empowered, after 6 weeks of unfitness for work, to set a period in which they must make application for the payment of a pension.

Household Allowances

A household allowance is payable in respect of periods of hospitalisation. It is intended to cover expenses which continue during such periods, e.g. the rent. It is calcualted as a percentage of the sick benefit payable. In the case of an insured person without dependants, it amounts to 25 per cent, increases if there is one dependant to two thirds of sick benefit, plus 10 per cent for every furhter dependant. The Statutes of an Insurance Fund may increase the household allowance to 80 per cent of sick benefit, but it may not in any case exceed the sick benefit due.

Death Benefit

On death, a death benefit is payable. It amounts, as a standard benefit, to twenty times the basic wage, at least to 100 DM. It can consequently amount, as a standard benefit, to

800 DM. The statutes can increase the amount, as an additional benefit, to forty times the basic wage, and can fix the minimum amount at 150 DM. In the first instance the benefit is used to pay the costs of burial, and is paid to the person or persons responsible for the funeral arrangements. If any surplus remains, entitled recipients are: the spouse, the children, the father, the mother, brothers and sisters, in that order, if they were resident in the household of the deceased at the time of his death.

On the death of the spouse, a child, or other dependants of an insured person who were resident in his household, and wholly or mainly maintained by him, the insured person is entitled to death benefit amounting to one half of the amount payable according to the statutes in respect of a member, to a minimum amount of 50 DM. The amount is reduced by the amount of death benefit payable in respect of which the deceased was himself compulsorily insured.

Maternity Benefits

The Health Insurance Law of 1887 already provided for the payment of a confinement grant to insured women for the period immediately following confinement. The period for which it was payable was extended in the subsequent decades. In 1914 the benefit was extended to the wives of insured persons. In 1927 the Law for the Protection of Motherhood was enacted, and was amended and extended in 1942.

Art. 6 (4) of the Basic Law gurantees for every mother the protection and care of the community. In order to implement this principle, a new Law on the Protection of Motherhood was enacted in 1952, and was considerably amended in 1965. At the same time the confinement grant under Health Insurance was changed into Maternity Benefit and was comprehensively revised. It is true that the amendments did not, as originally intended, come into effect on 1. 1. 1967, but not until 1. 1. 1969.

The Law on the Protection of Motherhod provides for restrictions on the nature of employment, for pre-natal and post-natal care, as well as for a ban on dismissal by the employer. In the arrangements at the place of work, the employer is required to have special consideration for expectant and nursing mothers. In the case of restrictions on the nature of employment there is no loss of earnings. In respect of family members entitled to benefits under Health Insurance, the insured person receives a maternity benefit, though only a once and for all payment of 35 DM. The Statutes of an Insurance Fund are, however, authorised to increase this amount to 150 DM.

Benefits in Kind under Maternity Benefits

Every woman insured under statutory Health Insurance receives maternity benefits in the event of pregnancy. These include medical care and aid, medical examination to determine pregnancy, and other precautionary examinations, laboratory tests, a midwife, and, if necessary, medical aid during confinement, the supply of medicines, dressings and appliances in the event of complaints during pregnancy or during confinement; the insured person is not required to pay any charge toward the costs of medicines, dressings, or appliances. The Insurance Fund must provide the insured person with accommodation and care in a maternity home or hospital for the period of the confinement, though to a maximum period of ten days. The insured person has a free choice of hospitals, though the Fund may restrict the choice to certain hospitals. During the period spent in a hospital or maternity home, the insured person has a claim to household allowance. Further, and in lieu of the former confinement grant, a confinement costs lump sum of 50 DM is payable to cover incidental costs arising. The Statutes of a Fund may increase this amount to 100 DM.

Maternity Allowance

In addition, insured women still in employment six weeks before confinement, or who are home-workers, or whose employment has been permissibly terminated by the employer during pregnancy, receive a maternity allowance in lieu of wage or salary. Allowances are payable only on the condition that in the tenth to the fourth month inclusive before confinement the woman has been insurably employed for 12 weeks or if a contract of employment had existed. Maternity benefit is calcualted on the basis of the average earnings, less statutory deductions, of the last three calendar months (in the case of weekly payments: the last 13 weeks) prior to the six weeks protective period before confinement. It amounts to a minimum of 3.50 DM, a maximum of 25 DM per diem. It is payable for six weeks before and eight weeks after the birth, in the case of a premature birth, or of more than one child at a birth, for twelve weeks after confinement. The probable date of birth must be certified by a midwife or a doctor; if they prove to be in error, the period is extended accordingly. Other insured persons who have a claim to sick benefit when unfit for work receive maternity allowances to the same amount as sick benefit, if they have been in insurable employment for at least twelve weeks between the tenth and fourth month before confinement.

Insured persons who have no claim to materinity benefits, receive a single payment of 150 DM on confinement, but no sick benefit or household allowance in addition to maintenance allowance; if, and insofar as wages continue to be payable, maternity allowance is withheld.

Finance

Health Insurance is financed from contributions. Employees and employers pay equal amounts. The employer pays the full amount if the worker earns up to 65 DM per month, or 15 DM per week, and also in the case of a person performing a voluntary social year. Certain limits are set for the fixing of the amount of contributions payable. Within these limits each Insurance Fund fixes contributions according to its own needs; in general the limit is set at between 6 and 9 per cent of insurable earnings up to 14.400 per annum or 1.200 DM per month, the average being 8.2 per cent. For compulsorily insured contributors without a claim to continued payment of earnings, the average contribution is 10.8 %. Voluntarily insured persons pay the full contribution themselves. Contributions in respect of insurable pensioners are paid by the Social Pensions Insurance Funds. Voluntarily insured pensioners must pay the contributions themselves, but they receive a refund from the Pensions Fund equal to the amount paid in respect of compulsorily insured pensioners. In the case of recipients of unemployment benefit, unemployment assistance, and maintenance allowances, the contributions are paid by the Federal Institute for Labour. Special regulations apply in the case of the recipeints of short-time working allowances and inclement weather benefits. The Federal Government makes a refund of 400 DM to the Health Insurance Fund in respect of every case of the payment of a maternity allowance.

Average Amounts of Rates of Contributions in Health Insurance in Percentage of Basic Wages for Compulsorily Insured Members with a Claim to Immediate Cash Benefits

Date appli- cable	Total *	OKK	LKK	BKK	IKK	SeeKK	KnV	Mutual Benefit Funds	
								Man.	Non-Man.
1. 4. 60	8,4	8,6	6,9	8,2	7,8	5,8	8,2	8,8	7,9
1. 4. 65	9,8	9,9	8,7	9,7	8,8	6,6	10,7	9,9	11,5
1. 4. 66	9,9	10,0	9,2	9,6	9,0	6,6	10,0	10,0	12,0
1. 4. 67	10,1	10,2	9,7	9,9	9,2	6,6	11,0	10,3	13,1
1. 4. 68	10,2	10,3	9,8	9,8	9,3	6,6	10,9	10,6	13,8
1. 4. 69	10,4	10,5	10,0	10,0	9,8	7,8	12,0	10,8	14,1

* See Footnote on page

Under the Miner's Special Scheme Health Insurance contributions are also payable on the above basis. In addition, the Federal Goverment pays a supplement to the amount of 1 per cent of the insurable earnings of manual workers. Further, the expenditure for benefits paid under Health Insurance are refunded by the Miner's Special Scheme Pensions Insurance Fund.

Average Amounts of Contributions in Health Insurance in Percentage of Basic Wages for Compulsorily Insured Members with a Claim to Immediate Cash Benefits

Date appli- cable	Total *	OKK	LKK	BKK	IKK	SeeKK	KnV	Mutual Benefit Funds	
								Man.	Non-Man.
1. 4. 1969	8,5	7,8	8,6	7,3	7,4	6,6	10,0	7,9	9,1
1. 4. 1970	8,2	8,2	8,8	7,5	7,8	6,6	9,6	8,1	9,1

The financial situation of statutory Health Insurance has deteriorated; in contrast to 1967 expenditure exceeded income in 1968 and 1969. This trend will continue.

Income and Expenditure in Mill. DM

Year	Income	Total	Medical and Dental Treat- ment	Expenditure — thereof — Medicines Appliances Dentures	Hospital Treatment	Cash Benefits
1938	1 803	1787	526	205	205	397
1950	2 422	2 278	568	438	438	469
1955	4 617	4 627	1 276	826	709	938
1960	9 524	9 513	2 342	1 568	1 362	2 572
1965	15 961	15 785	4 148	2 947	2 422	3 501
1966	18 554	18 362	5 109	2 940	3 397	3 791
1967	19 738	19 236	5 400	3 325	3 851	3 301
1968	21 195	21 513	5 844	4 390	4 384	3 967
1969	23 315	23 734	6 284	4 989	5 042	4 186
1970	24 120	23 583	6 598	5 660	5 748	1 530
1971	25 863	26 322	7 047	6 422	6 553	1 607
1972	28 404	28 695	7 526	7 288	7 470	1 687
1973	31 245	31 550	8 038	8 272	8 516	1 771

The financial situation of statutory Health Insurance has deteriorated; in contrast to 1967 expenditure exceeded income in 1968 and 1969. This trend will continue.

Adjustment of Employer Expenditure consequent on the Law on Continued Payment of Wages during Sickness

Since the costs falling on wage intensive firms, especially smaller firms and independent artisan enterprises, can entail an additional financial burden, an adjustment procedure has been inaugurated to balance out the resultant expenditure. The implementation of this procedure has been entrusted to the Local, Land, and Trade Associations Health Insurance Funds, the Federal Miners's Special Scheme, and the Seamen's Health Insurance Fund; the offices of the General Insurance Funds are also associated in this procedure, though only the employer's representatives in the self-governing bodies take part.

Employers are affected by this form of adjustment only if they employ, as a rule, not more than 20 employees. Employees are both manual and non-manual, not counting apprentices and trainees. At the beginning of each calendar year the competent Insurance Fund is required to ascertain which employers are entitled to participate for the coming calendar year. Decisions are binding on employers, unless they are disputed in the Social Courts. Decisive for participation is whether the employer has employed not more than 20 employees in a period of eight calendar months in the calendar year preceding the ruling.

Exempted from this procedure are: certain institutions in public law, units and similar institutions of foreign troops stationed in the Federal Republic, home-workers and similar workers, as well as the Central Associations of Voluntary Welfare Services, their sub-sections, institutes, and homes.

Employers benefiting receive from the competent Health Insurance Fund 80 per cent of the wages paid during sickness, as well as the employer's portion of Social Insurance contributions. Payment is due immediately the employer has paid the wage. It is payable only on application. Claims lapse two years after the end of the calendar year in which they arose. Only certain defined claims by the Insurance Fund may be deducted from payment due.

The funds needed to meet these adjustments are raised by a levy on all employers affected, based on the earnings of the workers employed by the firm. In order to mitigate the burden falling on the firms, the Federal Government grants a subsidy, as follows:

in 1970 — 200 mill DM
in 1971 — 150 mill DM
in 1972 — 100 mill DM
and in 1973 — 75 mill DM
a total of 525 mill DM.

Employers in branches of industry and commerce are authorised to make voluntary arrangements to cover the additional expenses arising, in which arrangements employers may participate who are not covered by the statutory arrangements. Such arrangements require the sanction of the Federal Ministry of Labour and Social Order.

Organisation

Health Insurance Funds and Mutual Benefit Insurance Funds number 1831 (mid 1970). They are financially and organisationally autonomous, and each is responsible for balancing its own income and expenditure. They are subject to official supervision. They are organised as follows: 401 Local Health Insurance Funds (General Scheme Funds), 107 Land Health Insurance Funds for agriculture, 1133 Works Health Insurance Funds operating in the larger enterprises, 178 Trade Association Health Insurance Funds for small scale artisan firms, 1 Seaman's Health Insurance Fund for seagoing employment, the Miners' Special Scheme, 7 Mutual Benefit Funds for non-manual workers, 8 Mutual Benefit Funds for manual workers. At the beginning of 1970 the Insurance Funds employed about 77.000 persons.

The Insurance Funds are self-governing bodies (see sector ,,Self-Government''), with an Executive Committee and a Delegates' Assembly, comprised of equal numbers of representatives of workers and employers. Exceptions are the organs of the Mutual Benefit Funds, which are comprised solely of representatives of the insured persons, and the organs of the Miners' Special Scheme Fund, which are comprised as to two thirds of workers' representatives, and one third of employers' representatives. The Delegates' Assembly resolves on the Statutes of the Funds, in which contribution rates and additional benefits are laid down.

For the purpose of safeguarding supra-local and common interests the Insurance Funds are organised in Insurance Fund Associations.

Federal Association of Local Health Insurance Funds   in Bad Godesberg

Federal Association of Land Insurance Funds   in Hannover

Federal Association of Works Health Insurance Funds   in Essen

Federal Association of Trade Association Health Insurance Funds   in Cologne

Association of Manual Workers Mutual Benefit Funds   in Hamburg

Association of Non-Manual Health Funds   in Hamburg

Miners' Special Scheme   in Bochum

Working Community for Common Problems of Health Insurance   in Frankfort

Federal Association of Insurance Fund Doctors   in Cologne

Federal Association of Insurance Dental Surgeon   in Cologne

Legislative bases

Second Book of the Reichs Insurance Code of 19. 7. 1911 (BGBl. III—820—1), last amended by the Law of 14. 4. 1970 (BGBl. I.S. 337)

Reichs Miners' Special Scheme Law of 23. 6. 1923 (BGBl. III—822—1), last amended by the Law of 23. 6. 1970 (BGBl. I. S. 805).

Protection of Motherhood of 24. 1. 1952 in the version of 18. 4. 1968 (BGBl. I.S. 315), amended by the Law of 24. 5. 1968 (BGBl. I. S. 503).

Law as applied to Insurance Fund Doctors of 17. 8. 1955 (BGBl. III—8230—22)

Law on the Associations of Statutory Health Insurance Funds and Mutual Benefit Funds of 17. 8. 1955 (BGBl. III—8230—23).

Ordinance on the Miners' Special Scheme Health Insurance of Pensioners of 8. 6. 1942 (BGBI. III—822—4—1), last amended by Ordinance dated 22. 12. 1968 (BGBI. I. S. 1324).

Law on the Continued Payment of Wages during Sickness, and on the Amendment of the Law on Statutory Health Insurance of 27. 7. 1970 (BGBI. I. S. 946).

Improvements in Health Insurance

In November 1970 the Federal German Parliament enacted the following improvements in Social Health Insurance:

1. Insured persons and the members of their families are entitled to medical examination for the early detection of certain illnesses. This is of great importance for health. There is a free choice of doctors.

Entitled are:

— children up to the age of 4, to examination for the early detection of illnesses which can endanger the normal physical or mental development of the child to a pronounced extent;
— women from their 30th year onwards to annual examination for the early detection of cancer;
— men from their 45th year onwards to annual examination for the early detection of cancer.
Entitlement to these examinations commences with effect from July 1st, 1971.

2. From January 1st, 1971 onwards the reduction of sick pay hitherto operative in the case of hospitalisation is abolished.

3. From January 1st, 1971 all non-manual workers have a claim to the employer's portion of their health insurance contribution. In the same way as compulsorily insured persons; those continuing voluntarily in Social Health Insurance, and those privately insured are now entitled to this portion.

4. The insurance ceiling has been made "dynamic". It will be adjusted annually to wage and salary movements. It will amount at any one time to 75 % of the contributions ceiling from 1.200 DM per month to 1.425 DM per month.

5. All non-manual workers who are not already compulsorily or voluntarily insured may now enter into insurance under the statutory health scheme.

6. New entrants into employment whose monthly salary is in excess of 1.425 DM monthly may elect to become insured under the statutory health scheme within three months of commencing employment.

7. Self-employed persons with a monthly income of up to 1.425 DM may also voluntarily enter into insurance.

8. In the case of pensioners who did not take up insurance under the statutory scheme before the last permitted date in 1968, they again have the opportunity to do so up to March 21st, 1971.

Industrial Injuries Insurance

Introduction

If a worker suffers an accident arising out of and in the course of his employment, he would, on the basis of his contract of employment, have a common law claim for compensation against his employer, if the accident was due to the employer's fault. This employer's liability has been replaced by Industrial Injuries Insurance, which is in so far a liability insurance of the employer. It is also an insurance to the benefit of the workers, who have a claim to benefits if the accident was not due to the employer's fault, if it occurs on the way to or from work, and in the case of a prescribed industrial disease. In the course of the development of industrial injuries insurance, the number of cases in which the employer's liability has had to be replaced have declined in importance. The number of accidents sustained on the way to and from work, in particular fatal accidents, has also declined in recent years. According to an enquiry conducted by the Industrial Injuries Insurance Funds, a considerable number of accidents are due to causes to be found in the persons of the injured themselves, i.e. for which they are themselves responsible. The Funds are constantly endeavouring, with the support of legislation, to improve industrial safety and hygiene, to prevent accidents, or, when they occur, to mitigate their effects, for example by First Aid, further, so far as possible, to enable the injured person to return to his job. These endeavours are to be stepped up in the future.

Since its inception (1884), Industrial Injuries Insurance has been less subject to alteration than other branches of social insurance. Nevertheless, and in particular since 1949, a whole range of improved benefits and services have been introduced. The year 1963 brought a Reform of Industrial Injuries Insurance, which, above all, prescribed that, in establishments employing more than 20 workers, a Safety Steward was to be appointed, that the Federal Government should annually submit an Accident Prevention Report, and that the Funds should be empowered in the case of industrial diseases, and outwith the Statutory Register of Industrial Diseases, to acknowledge such diseases if, on the basis of the most up-to-date medical knowledge, they are held to have arisen out of, and in the course of, employment. Since 1967 pensions have been adjusted to wage and salary movements in the same manner as in the case of social pensions insurance (Social Council — Pensions Adjustment Report). In the course of the 1963 Reform, the Federal Government assumed responsibility for a part of the burden of pensions, above all those of the Mine Workers Industrial Injuries Insurance Institute. This arrangement ceased with effect from 1. 1. 1968; the position now is that, only in the case of the industrial institutes and the mercantile marine institute, a financial adjustment is made if the relation between the cost of pensions and the wages bill becomes too unfavourable.

In order to direct the constant attention of the public and the legislature to the importance of accident prevention, the Federal Government has a duty to submit an annual Accident Prevention Report. The last (4th) Report, submitted in respect of 1967, showed a considerable reduction in the number of accidents (14 % less than in 1966), but a slight increase (1 %) in industrial diseases. The number of fatal accidents was also down (6 % less than in 1966). Fatal accidents in the narrower sense fell by almost 7 %, accidents on the way to and from work by about 4 %, and industrial diseases by 6 %.

In order to step up the efforts to humanise working life, the existing Federal Institute for Safety at Work has been transformed into a Federal Institute for Accident Research and Safety at Work, with its seat in Dortmund.

147

Functions of Industrial Injuries Insurance

The object of industrial injuries insurance is to prevent industrial accidents and industrial diseases; in the event of their occurrence, however, to compensate the injured person, his dependants or survivors, either by restoration of his employability, by vocational aid, or by cash payments to him, his dependants, or his survivors.

Accident Prevention

The administrations of the accident insurance Funds have a duty to prevent accidents by every possible and appropriate means, and to ensure effective First Aid, and in so doing, they set themselves the following aims: They are to intensify technical supervision, further improve medical care following an accident, jointly to conduct research into the causes of accidents, and to direct the attention of the public to accident prevention. The interest of the enterprises themselves in ensuring safety at work to be further intensified. Accident prevention arrangements are to be inaugurated at the place of work.

The Accident Insurance Funds are under an obligation to issue regulations laying down the arrangements, the rules, and the measures employers are required to take to prevent accidents, and the behaviour required from the workers themselves for the same purpose.

Reported Accidents
in 1000s

Year	Industrial accidents	to and from work	Industrial diseases	Year	Industrial accidents	To and from work	Industrial diseases
Industrial Accident Insurance Institutes				Municipal Accident Insurance Associations			
1950	879,1	69,2	35,3	1950	30,2	3,6	1,0
1955	1 701,9	209,7	48,6	1955	48,9	8,2	0,8
1960	2 262,9	248,5	31,5	1960	53,4	9,4	0,6
1965	2 223,3	217,1	25,6	1965	62,9	12,4	0,6
1966	2 114,2	203,3	24,0	1966	63,2	12,5	0,7
1967	1 754,2	172,9	23,7	1967	63,7	12,8	0,7
1968	1 873,3	192,5	23,4	1968	65,4	13,0	0,8
1969	1 960,3	204,7	22,4	1969	54,0	13,5	0,9
Agricultural Accident Insurance Institutes				Executive Authorities			
1950	244,4	1,3	0,1	1950	104,4	12,6	1,2
1955	307,4	2,7	0,6	1955	121,6	24,4	1,4
1960	277,3	2,6	0,8	1960	117,5	23,1	0,8
1965	249,8	2,6	0,5	1965	119,4	23,2	0,8
1966	250,5	2,5	0,6	1966	114,4	21,6	0,8
1967	253,3	2,7	0,9	1967	110,4	21,2	1,1
1968	253,2	2,8	0,8	1968	126,1	26,8	1,3
1969	244,9	2,8	0,6	1969	104,0	21,7	1,4
Overall Accident Insurance							
1950	1 258,2	86,6	37,6				
1955	2 179,8	244,9	51,3				
1960	2 711,1	283,6	33,7				
1965	2 655,4	255,3	27,5				
1966	2 542,3	239,9	26,1				
1967	2 181,5	209,5	26,3				
1968	2 317,9	235,1	26,2				
1969	2 363,1	242,6	25,4				

These regulations are also intended to lay down in how far medical inspections of insured persons are to be carried out prior to employment entailing for them or for third persons exceptional accident or health hazards. The Funds are also empowered to require employers to ensure effective First Aid in the event of accidents. About 1.100 specially trained technical supervisory inspectors control compliance with accident prevention regulations, and give advice to employers on the most effective relevant measures. They are empowered, on the first sight of threatened danger, to give immediately effective directions for its elimination. In addition, some 2.000 employees of the Funds are employed in the supervision of accident prevention in the enterprises themselves. The number of Safety at Work Stewards inside the enterprises, first legally appointed in 1963, amounted in 1967 to about 250.000. The managements of the Funds are empowered to impose fines of up to 10.000 DM on employers guilty of deliberately or grossly infringing safety regulations; in minor cases smaller fines may be imposed.

Scope

More than 26 mill. persons are insured under Accident Insurance. The number of so-called fully employed workers amounts to about 24 mill. The term ,,fully employed workers'' is a calculation value which is generally used for statistical returns, reached by extracting from the number of insured persons those fully employed, i.e. employed throughout the whole year. About 6.7 mill. persons are included in accident insurance by virtue of certain types of employment usually performed only for short periods.

Compulsory Insurability

Statutory accident insurance covers many different groups of persons. By far the biggest majority are workers and similar categories. Pursuant to the Law, all persons are insurable who are employed on the basis of a contract of employment, service, or apprenticeship, without regard to the amount of their remuneration, further homeworkers, middlemen, pedlars, spouses employed in the business, and other employed persons.

Also insurable are persons in show business, and artistes, as well as unemployed persons, in so far as they fulfill their legal obligations, or the requirements of the labour administration.

Certain self-employed persons are also insurable, namely farmers, the owners of small enterprises in coastwise shipping and inshore fishing, and their spouses employed in the business. Accident insurance also covers persons active in the interests of the community. For instance, in June 1969, development aid helpers were included if they were employed for a limited period abroad, or during their period of training in Germany. Also included are persons engaged in health, veterinary, and welfare services, in an organisation rendering aid in catastrophies, air raid wardens, lifesavers, and persons requested by a public official to render assistance in an official matter, as well as persons who render assistance in the pursuit or arrest of a person suspected of a crime, or who render assistance to a person wrongfully assaulted. Further, blood donors, donors of tissue, and persons undergoing medical examination on the grounds of industrial safety and accident prevention regulations. Finally, all persons are insured who are active in an honorary capacity on behalf of the Federal Government, the Lands, the municipalitites, municipal associations, or other corporations, institutions, or foundations in public law, in so far as they have no legal claim to continuing compensation designed to secure their livelihood, also all persons summoned as witnesses by a court, a public prosecutor, or other authorised office.

Cover is also provided for persons engaged in vocational training and further training in official institutes, and persons engaged in teaching in an honorary capacity in such institutes, those who, under the Self-Help Schemes, are engaged in house building, and the preparation and cultivation of land, the erection of industrial plant and of communal services if, as a result of the building operations, publicly promoted and tax rebate dwellings are erected.

Even in cases where these conditions are not fulfilled, a person may, in certain circumstances, be covered by insurance if he is engaged in one of the above-mentioned activities in the same way as others.

Also covered are persons sentenced to imprisonment, and employed in the same kind of activities as the above-named persons, as are persons performing task work imposed by the courts.

The Funds are also empowered to extend insurance cover to self-employed persons not enumerated above, and to their spouses employed in the business, but not to heads of households or to shipowners not members of the crews of their ships.

Exemptions

Exempt from insurance are, in particular, public officials in the performance of their duties, or in employment, to which Civil Service Accident Provisions or similar provisions apply, further, persons who, in the case of accidents receive benefits under the Federal Pensions Law, members of religious communities, sisters in convents, and similar persons, for whom life-long care and maintenance are guaranteed; further, doctors, lay medical practitioners, dentists, and apothecaries in the exercise of their free professions, relatives and in-laws of heads of households employed in the household without remuneration, with the exception of agricultural households.

Voluntary Insurance

Self-employed persons and their spouses employed in the business may insure voluntarily, but not heads of households.

Benefits under Accident Insurance

Accident insurance compensates for losses suffered as a result of bodily injury or death. No compensation is payable in principle in respect of material damage; an exception is made in the case of damage occurring in the course of the accident to artificial limbs, major orthopaedic aids, and similar applicances. An industrial accident is an event due to external circumstances, orrcurring in a limited period of time, and resulting in a physical injury, arising out of and in the course of employment. Industrial accidents within this meaning are accidents sustained in proceeding to and from the place in which the insured employment is performed, accidents arising out of the storage, transport, maintenance, or renewal of working gear, even if such gear is the property of the employed person. Compensation in respect of industrial diseases is also paid in accordance with accident insurance regulations. These are diseases, as defined in a legal register, arising out of and in the course of employment. If, in accordance with the most up to date medical knowledge, the conditions for entry into this register have been fulfilled, compensation is to be paid in individual cases, even prior to such entry. Benefits payable under accident insurance are fixed officially; no application from the injured person or his dependants is required. Employers are obliged to report every serious accident. Prohibited actions or carelessness on the part of the insured person do not result in loss of benefits. On the other hand, no claim for compensation lies if the beneficiary has deliberately caused the accident.

Services for the restoration of employability

Rehabilitation services include, primarily, curative treatment, cash allowances (e.g. Injury Allowance) during treatment, and labour and occupational promotion measures.

Curative Treatment

A claim to curative treatment and injury allowance lies in the case of an injured person who is insured under Social Health Insurance only in so far as the Fund is not itself the responsible body. Here it must be noted that, in the relation between the Accident and Health Insurance, a refund must be made by the Accident Insurance Fund to the Health Fund - with the exception of Death Benefit - of all costs arising after the 18th day following the accident, if the injured person is insured under Health Insurance.

The purpose of curative treatment is to eliminate by all means available the ailment or bodily injury, and the reduced standard of employment, arising out of the accident or the industrial disease, and to prevent any further deterioration. Its object is the rapid and complete restoration of the health of the injured person, so far as this is possible, and his re-integration into working life. Curative treatment is granted from the day of the accident, and continues for so long as an improvement and an increase of employablility are to be anticipated, or so long as special measures are necessary to prevent a deterioration of the condition, or to remedy physical complaints. Treatment is granted even in cases in which there is no reduced standard of employment. Curative treatment includes medical treatment, both as out-patients and in-patients, the provision of medicines and other medical supplies, and the fitting of artificial limbs and so on, orthopaedic and other appliances, necessary to ensure the success of the treatment, or to mitigate the effects of the accident. Aids supplied include artificial limbs, dentures, artificial eyes, guide dogs, invalid chairs. Also included are group gymnastic exercises under medical supervision, as well as any other appropriate curative measure. If an artificial limb or a large orthopeadic applicance has been damaged during the course of the accident, it will be repaired or replaced by the Fund during treatment or hospitalisation; special allowances may be paid to the injured person and his dependants to eliminate the hardships which can arise during protracted treatment.

Attendance Allowances

Curative treatment also includes provision for attendance. This is granted so long as the injured person, as a result of the accident or industrial disease, is so helpless that he cannot manage without care and attendance. An injured person is helpless if he is regularly dependent on the help of other persons for the performance of every day actions. Attendance consists of attendance in the home (help and attendance by a male or female nurse, or in some other suitable form), or in admission to a suitable hospital (hospitalisation). In lieu of attendance, an attendance allowance is payable to an amount of 133 to 534 DM per month, according to the degree of helplessness. On the basis of the 13th Amendment to the Law, attendance allowances are to be increased with effect from 1.1.1971, and otherwise amended in line with other cash benefits.

Amounts of Attendance Allowances	
from	DM per month
1.1.26	20 bis 75
1.6.49	25 bis 100
1.6.51	50 bis 150
1.9.57	75 bis 275
1.1.61	100 bis 350
1.1.70	133 bis 534
1.1.71	145 bis 583

Occupational Aid

Occupational aid includes vocational training to the point of the restoration or increase of earning capacity in the event of reduced standard of employment in the customary occupation; if necessary the injured person can be trained for some other occupation of, so far as this is possible, an equivalent standard, whereby the financial position of the injured person and his dependants must be adequately secured during the period of training.

Cash Benefits for Injured Persons

Injury allowance

Injured workers normally receive their wage or salary for the first six weeks of unfitness for work arising from an industrial accident. In so far as they do not receive such payment at the time, or later, they are paid injury allowance. However, no injury allowance is payable if the injured person has a claim to sick pay from statutory Health Insurance to the same amount as the injury allowance. Allowance is payable from the first day on which the injured person is medically certified unfit for work. Allowances are assessed on the amount of regular earnings lost. This may be based on an amount of up to at least 36.000 DM per year.

If a subsequent illness occurs as a result of the accident, leading to renewed unfitness for work, injury allowance is payable in addition to injury pension. It is assessed on the basis of the earnings of which the injured person was in receipt prior to the renewed illness.

Pensions for injured persons

The pension is intended to secure the living standard of the injured person and his dependants in the measure in which his earning capacity has been reduced as a consequence of the accident or the industrial disease. A condition for the award is, as a rule, that earning capacity shall have been reduced by at least 20 % beyond the 13th week following the accident. Earning capacity is the ability of the insured person to earn his livelihood by the use of all opportunities open to him throughout the whole of the economy on the grounds of his skill and knowledge, and of his physical and mental qualities. Generally speaking, his earning capacity prior to the accident is taken as 100 %. His residual earning capacity, which covers all employment in the general labour market he can reasonably be expected to accept, is the basis taken as reduced earning capacity on which the pension is assessed. The 'limb compensation rate' which plays a role in the public consciousness, calling for a fixed percentage compensation for certain injuries, can only serve as a guide, since, in assessing the degree of earning capacity, the individual repercussions of the accident on the injured person must be taken into consideration.

Basis of assessment of pensions

Cash benefits under Accident Insurance are, generally speaking, assessed on the basis of the annual earnings of the injured person, normally his earnings in the year preceding the accident. There are minimum and maximum limits. In how far an amount in excess of the statutory annual limit of 36.000 DM may be taken into account may be laid down in the statutes of the individual Funds. Minimum annual earnings are assessed on the basis of 300 times the fixed local wage at the place of employment. In the case of Seamen's Accident Insurance, average wages are taken as the basis of annual earnings; in agriculture this is also partly the case. Other variations take account of the special circumstances of certain groups of persons. For instance, if average earnings are expressed in a foreign currency, or if the amount cannot be proved, average annual earnings are taken as the amount earned by a comparable worker in the Federal territory at the time of the accident. Annual average earnings may be taken at an amount higher or lower than actual earnings, if the latter amount appears to be particularly unfavourable.

Amount of pensions

Pension amounts to two thirds of annual earnings if the injured person is totally unfit for work (Full Pension). If his employability is diminished as a result of the accident, the pension payable is that portion of the full pension corresponding to the degree of reduced employability. In certain cases supplements to the injuries pension are payable. For example, the pension of a severely injured person (employability reduced by 50 % or more) is increased by 10 % if, as a result of the accident he is unable to work, and is not in receipt of a pension from statutory Pensions Insurance.

Injuries Insurance
No. of Pensions in 1000s at the end of

Year	Total	Injured Persons	Widows	Orphans	Year	Total	Injured Persons	Widows	Orphans
Industrial Injuries Insurance Institutes					Agricultural Industrial Injuries Institutes				
1950	376,6	265,5	74,8	34,7	1950	193,3	163,9	20,2	9,0
1955	515,1	384,4	92,8	36,3	1955	233,4	203,9	21,0	8,3
1960	598,5	457,1	105,5	34,7	1960	233,1	204,7	21,2	7,1
1965	684,7	520,8	119,2	43,3	1965	239,0	209,0	21,7	8,2
1966	692,9	526,9	121,3	43,6	1966	337,0	206,6	21,8	8,5
1967	698,5	531,8	122,4	43,2	1967	233,3	203,5	21,4	8,3
1968	698,6	531,2	122,9	43,5	1968	230,3	200,9	21,2	8,2
1969	696,5	528,2	123,5	43,8	1969	229,9	201,0	20,9	8,0
Municipal Injuries Insurance Associations					Executive Authorities				
1950	10,4	7,4	1,7	1,2	1950	56,0	34,8	12,9	7,9
1955	13,3	10,3	1,9	1,1	1955	67,9	46,4	14,1	7,0
1960	15,4	12,4	2,1	0,9	1960	68,9	50,3	13,8	4,6
1965	17,8	14,2	2,4	1,2	1965	69,4	51,5	14,1	3,7
1966	18,3	14,6	2,4	1,3	1966	68,0	50,4	13,9	3,5
1967	18,7	14,9	2,4	1,3	1967	67,0	50,2	13,1	3,6
1968	19,0	15,2	2,4	1,3	1968	67,4	50,4	13,6	3,3
1969	19,6	15,7	2,5	1,4	1969	66,4	49,6	13,3	3,0

Injuries Insurance — Total

Year	Total	Injured Persons	Widows	Orphans	Parents
1950	636,3	471,6	109,6	52,7	2,4
1955	829,7	645,0	129,9	52,6	2,2
1960	916,0	724,4	142,7	47,2	1,6
1965	1 010,9	795,5	157,4	56,4	1,7
1966	1 016,2	793,6	159,3	56,9	1,4
1967	1 017,5	800,4	159,4	56,4	1,3
1968	1 015,3	797,7	160,2	56,3	1,2
1969	1 012,4	794,5	160,2	56,2	1,5

Commencement and suspension of pensions payments

A claim to pension arises at the termination of the period of unfitness for work, at the latest, as a general rule, at the commencement of the 79th week following the accident. Injured persons not unfit for work receive the pension from the day of the accident. Benefits are not normally payable to aliens resident abroad, unless otherwise laid down in an international agreement. If the accident has occurred outside the Federal territory, payment of the pension is suspended so long as the beneficiary is normally resident abroad. For certain defined groups of persons an exception may be made, but even in these cases benefits in kind may not be granted.

Children's allowances

Children's allowances are payable if the injured person in is receipt of a pension of at least 50 % of the full pension, or of more than one injuries pension taking account of a total reduction of earning capacity of 50 %. Entitled children are: legitimate children, step children, children declared legitimate, adopted children, illegitimate children of a male insured person if paternity has been established or maintenance allowance is payable, illegitimate children, of an injured person, foster children if the relation existed prior to the accident, grand children and brothers and sisters, if they had been resident in the household of the injured person prior to the accident, or had been wholly or mainly maintained by him. The allowance for each child amounts up to its 18th year to 10 % of the pension, for the second child to at least 25 DM per month, for the third child 50 DM, for the fourth child 60 DM per month, and for every further child 70 DM per month. The amount for the third child is to be increased to 60 DM per months with effect from 1.9.1970.

Allowances are payable at the latest up to the 25th year in respect of a child in full time attendance in an educational establishment or in vocational training, or if the child is engaged in a voluntary 'social year', or if, after reaching the age of 18, it is incapable of earning its own livelihood as a consequence of physical or mental infirmity, for the duration of the condition. If education or vocational training are interrupted or delayed by compulsory military service, the period for which allowances are paid after the age of 25 is extended correspondingly.

Commutation of pensions

In certain cases an injured person may receive a capital sum in lieu of a pension. If, under consideration of the particular circumstances of an individual case, a pension is payable only for a limited period, the injured person may be granted a settlement to the amount of the probable cost of such pension. Other relevant possibilities depend largely on the degree of reduced earning capacity arising out of the accident or the industrial disease. A condition is that the condition must have reached a certain stage of permanence. For instance, an injured person may, on application, receive an amount equal to the capital value of his pension if reduced earning capacity is assessed at less than 30 %. In such cases entitlement to pension terminates in principle for his whole life time. If the reduction is more than 30 %, a settlement may be effected for the purpose of purchasing land, for the financial consolidation of existing property, and for various other purposes, mainly for house building. Such settlements, covering a maximum of 10 years, can take into account up to one half of the injuries pensions, less children' allowances. The amount of the settlement is nine times the annual amount of the pension on which it is based. At the end of the ten year period the claim to the commuted portion of the pension is revived. A settlement under similar conditions, though covering only a period of five years, may be made in the case of an injured person for the purpose of establishing or consolidating his means of livelihood, though only if this is held to be in the interests of the beneficiary. A settlement on the basis of the capital value of the pension is also possible in the case of a beneficiary who ceases to be resident in Germany, or who is normally resident abroad.

Supplementary pensions benefits

If the continued employment of an insured person in an enterprise entails the danger of the occurrence, reoccurrence, or an aggravation of an industrial disease, the insured person should be advised no longer to follow this, for him, hazardous occupation. In order to compensate him for possible reduced earnings, or for other financial loss, he is awarded transitional benefit. This may consist of a single payment up to the amount of a full years pension, or of monthly amounts to a total in a year of a full year's pension, payable for a maximum period of 5 years. This transitional benefit is payable in addition to an injuries pension.

Cash Benefits for Survivors

Death benefits

In the event of the death of insured persons following an industrial accident or disease, his survivors receive death benefit to the amount of one twelfth of his annual earnings, - at least 400 DM. In the first place this amount is intended to cover the cost of interment, and it is paid to the person responsible for the funeral arrangements. Any surplus is divided in certain proportions agongst the dependants who had lived in the household of the deceased. If death has occurred as a result of a fatal accident in a place other than the place of residence, the insurance will meet the costs of transport to the place of burial.

Survivors's pensions

Survivors' pensions are payable from the day of death to the spouse, the former spouse, the children and relatives in the ascending line, of an insured person dying as a result of an industrial accident or disease, from the day of death. This applies in cases in which the insured person is missing.

Widows' pensions amount to 30 % of the annual earnings of the deceased husband, and are payable until her death or re-marriage. This amount is increased to 40 % annually if the widow has reached her 45th year, and if she has the care of at least one child entitled to an orphans pension, or if, as a result of illness or other infirmity, her own earning capacity has decreased by one half for a period of more than three months. The widower of a female insured person receives a pension to the same amount as a widow, until death or re-marriage, if his wife, who has died as a result of an industrial accident or desease, had been wholly or mainly responsible for the maintenance of the family, and for as long as she would have been so responsible. Former wives of deceased insured persons receive a pension on application, if they had been entitled to a maintenance allowance at the time of death, or if the insured person had voluntarily made such allowance during the year preceding his death.

Orphans' pensions are payable in respect of every child of an insured person who has died as a result of an industrial accident or disease, whereby the regulations governing children's allowances are applicable mutatis mutandis, although in the case of foster children, grand children, and brothers and sisters, the time of death, and not of the accident, is decisive for the fullfillment of the conditions of award. Orphans' pensions amount annually to 20 %, in the case of full orphans to 30 % of the annual earnings.

If the deceased has surviving relatives in the ascending line whom he had mainly maintained from his earnings, they receive a pension of 20 % of his annual earnings for one parent (30 % for both parents), for so long as they would have been able to claim support from him had be not suffered the accident; parents have preference over grandparents. Total pensions payable to all survivours may not exceed 80 % of the annual earnings of the deceased.

If the death of a seriously injured person is not a result of the industrial accident or disease, the widow - under certain conditions also the widower and orphans - receive a single grant of 40 % of annual earnings. In particular hardship cases the payment of a regular allowance is also possible.

Commutation of widows' pensions

Widows and widowers may commute their pensions in order to purchase land, to build a house, or for similar purposes. The full amount of the widows' or widowers' pension may be taken into account in fixing the amount of the settlement, the amount and duration of which are in conformity with the regulations applicable to injured persons. If a widow re-marries she is paid a sum amounting to five times her annual pension.

Adjustment of Cash Payments

Benefits under Accident Insurance were formerly readjusted by means of specific legislative acts, in order to enable beneficiaries to share in economic development. The reform of Accident Insurance in 1963 adopted for the adjustment of pensions to wages movements the system of pensions adjustments already operative in social pensions' insurance, with due consideration to the peculiarities of accident insurance. Accident pensions and attendance allowances are re-adjusted when changes occur in the average gross wage and salary bill. In this manner the amount of increase is determined on the basis of the remuneration of a larger circle of persons than in the case of social pensions insurance; this arrangement takes due consideration of the groups of persons insured under Accident Insurance.

Pensions Adjustments

with effect from	%	1963 = 100
1.1.1964	9,0	109,0
1.1.1965	6,1	115,6
1.1.1966	8,9	125,9
1.1.1967	9,0	137,2
1.1.1968	7,2	147,1
1.1.1969	3,3	152,0
1.1.1970	6,1	161,3
1.1.1971	9,3	176,3

Finance

Contributions

The financing of Injuries Insurance is met mainly from contributions paid by employers alone. These contributions are so assessed as to cover the expenditure of the previous year. In order to meet current expenditure, the Industrial Injuries Insurance Institutes, as a general rule, collect advance payments based on the amount of the levy due for the preceding year.

In industrial undertakings, and in the mercantile marine, contributions are based mainly on earnings, though graduated in the 'danger classes' in which the individual enterprises are classified, and according to the number and seriousness of the accidents sustained in them - 'the incidence of risk'.

This consideration of the accident quota in the enterprises in the assessment of contributions is based on recognition of the fact that accidents are not an inescapable fate, but that they are all too often the result of inadequate safety precautions in the enterprises. The employer who has successfully operated safety measures in his business is rewarded in the form of reduced contributions. In the case of the Industrial Injuries Insurance Institutes, excluding mining, the average levy amounts to 1,5 % of earnings, in mining to 9,6 %. In agriculture the institutes fix contributions according to the labour requirements of the farms, the standard value of the land, or some other criteria laid down in the institutes' statutes. The Federal Government, the Lands, municipalities carrying their own insurance, nunicipal accident insurance associations, the fire brigades accident insurance funds, and the Federal Institute for Labour, finance their accident insurance from their own budget.

Adjustment of Expenditure

The Industrial Injuries Insurance Institutes may reach agreement amoungst themselves to meet resultant expenditure wholly, or in part. If the relation between the wages bill and the amount of pensions payable becomes so unfavourable that contributions in a particular branch would reach an unjustifiable level, a financial adjustment is made between the industrial Funds, including the Seaman's Fund. At the moment a part of the expenditure in mining insurance is being met by the remaining industrial institutes.

Income and Expenditure in mill. DM

Year	Income	Expenditure Total	Pensions	thereof Curative Treatment	Accident Prevention
1938	264	381	241	64	12
1950	656	599	425	82	13
1955	1 103	1 065	682	202	25
1960	1 871	1 789	1 196	323	37
1965	3 535	3 302	1 872	443	70
1966	3 817	3 652	2 010	490	74
1967	4 035	3 798	2 180	484	77
1968	—	4 061	2 307	465	87
1969	—	4 403	2 421	501	98

Organisation

Accident Insurance covering some 5 million establishments is administered by 36 Industrial Injuries Insurance Institutes, including the Mercantile Marine Institute, by 19 Agricultural Institutes, 12 Municipal Accident Insurance Associations, 6 Fire Brigade Accident Insurance Funds, 6 minicipalities registered as insurance carriers, the Federal Institute for Labour, 11 Federal Lands, and the Federal Government itself. In 1969 the industrial and agricultural institutes and the municipal associations employed some 13.000 persons. Most of the industrial institutes, with the exception of most Building Industry Institutes and the Sugar Industry Institute - as well as the relevant departments of the Federal Railways and the Federal Ministry of Transport - Department Waterways -, maintain district offices. Each institute administers accident insurance in the branches of trade and industry allocated to it. Employers are compelled to inform their workers as to which institute and which district branch their undertaking belongs. The Industrial Injuries Insurance Institutes, the Minicipal Accident Insurance Associations, and the Fire Brigade Accident Insurance Funds, are corporations in public law with the right of self-administration (see sector). All are subject to government supervision. In so far as the Federal Government and the Federal Lands are carriers of accident insurance, administration is in the hands of special executive authorities. The carriers of accident insurance are organised in the National Association of Agricultural Injuries Insurance Institutes, and the Federal Working Community of Municipal Accident Insurance Carriers.

Accident Insurance

Industrial Injuries Insurance Institutes (= BG)
(Gewerbliche Berufsgenossenschaften = BG)

Mining BG	in Bochum
Quarying BG	in Hannover
BG of the Ceramic and Glas Industry	in Würzburg
BG of Gas and Waterworks	in Düsseldorf
Founding and Rolling Mills BG	in Essen
Machine Construction and Metal Fittings Ind. BG	in Düsseldorf
Paper Manufacturing Industry BG	in Mayence
BG Printing and Paper Processing	in Wiesbaden
Leather Industry BG	in Mayence
Textile and Clothing BG	in Augsburg
BG Food, Drink, and Catering Trades	in Mannheim
Butcheries BG	in Mayence
Sugar BG	in Hildesheim
Building BG	in Hamburg
Building BG	in Hannover
Building BG	in Wuppertal
Building BG	in Frankfurt
South German Iron and Steel BG	in Mayence
South German Precious and Semi-Precious Metals BG	in Stuttgart
BG Precision Mechanics and Electrotechniques	in Cologne
BG Chemical Industry	in Heidelberg
North German Wood Working BG	in Bielefeld
South German Wood Working BG	in Munich
South Western Building BG	in Karlsruhe
Württemberg Bau BG	in Stuttgart
Bavarian Building BG	in Munich
Wholesale Trade and Warehousing BG	in Mannheim
BG for Retail Trade	in Bonn
Administration BG	in Hamburg
BG for Street Cars, Underground Railways and Railways	in Hamburg
BG for Vehicle Maintenance	in Hamburg
Mercantile Marine BG	in Hamburg
Inland Waterways BG	in Duisburg
BG for Health and Welfare Services	in Hamburg

Agricultural Industrial Injuries Institutes

Schleswig Holstein BG	in Kiel
Hannover BG	in Hannover
BG Oldenburg-Bremen	in Oldenburg
Brunswick BG	in Brunswick
Westphalian BG	in Münster
Lippe BG	in Detmold
Rhine BG	in Düsseldorf
Hessen-Nassau BG	in Kassel
Land and Forestry BG for the Government District of Darmstadt	in Darmstadt
BG Rhine-Hessen-Palatinate	in Speyer
BG Saarland	in Saarbrücken
Baden BG	in Karlsruhe
BG Württemberg	in Stuttgart
BG Upper Bavaria	in Munich
BG Lower Bavaria (Upper Palatinate)	in Landshut
BG Upper and Middle Franconia	in Bayreuth
BG Lower Franconia	in Würzburg
BG Swabia	in Augsburg
Horticultural BG	in Kassel

Municipal Accident Insurance Associations

Schleswig Holstein	in Kiel
Hannover	in Hannover
Oldenburg	in Oldenburg
Brunswick	in Brunswick
Westphalia/Lippe	in Münster
Rhine Province	in Düsseldorf
Hessen	in Francfort
Rhineland Palatinate	in Andernach
Baden Municipalities and Municipal Associations	in Karlsruhe
Würrtemberg	in Stuttgart
Bavaria	in Munich

Federal Executive Authorities

Federal Railways Executive Authority	in Frankfort
Federal Post Executive Authority	in Stuttgart

The Federal Minister of Transport —
Department Waterways   in Bonn
Federal Executive Authority for Acci-
dent Insurance   in Wilhelmshaven

Executive Authorities of the Federal Lands

Executive Authority Schleswig Holstein
                                  in Kiel
Municipal Associations as Executive
Authority for Lower Saxony in Hannover
Self-Insurance of the Land Bremen
                                  in Bremen
Hesse Executive Authority   in Frankfort
Land Executive Authority Rhineland
Palatinate   in Andernach
Self-Insurance of the Free and Hansa
City of Hamburg   in Hamburg
State Executive Authority for the
Saarland   in Saarbrücken
Executive Authority Württemberg-Baden
for the Government District North
Württemberg-Baden and South Württem-
berg
Baden/Hohenzollern   in Stuttgart
Executive Authority of the Land Würt-
temberg and Baden for the Government
District North Baden and South Baden
                                in Karlsruhe

State Executive Authority   in Munich
Self-Insurance, Berlin   in Berlin

Executive Authorities of the Municipalities

The Fire Brigade Accident Fund Schles-
wig Holstein   in Kiel
Hamburger Fire Fund   in Hamburg
Fire Accident Fund, Hannover
                                in Hannover
Fire Brigade Accident Insurance Fund
Oldenburg   in Oldenburg
Fire Brigade Accident Rhineland
                                in Düsseldorf
Fire Brigade Accident Fund Westphalia-
Lippe   in Münster

Fire Brigade Accident Funds

Self-Insurance of the City of Düsseldorf
Self-Insurance of the City of Dortmund
Municipal Accident Insurance of the City
of Cologne
Self-Insurance of the City of Frankfort
Municipal Accident Insurance of the
Capital City of Munich

Federal Institute for Labour in Nürnberg

Legislative basis

Third Book of the Reichs Insurance Ordinance dated 19.7.1911 (BGBl. III 820-1), last
amended by the Law dated 10.7.1970 (BGBl. IS.1037). Non-Contributors and Aliens
Pensions Reform Law dated 25.2.1960 (BGBl. III - 824 -3), last amended by the Law
dated 25.6.1969 (BGBl. I.S. 645)
Seventh Industrial Diseases Ordinance dated 20.6.1968 (BGBl. IS 721)
Accident Prevention Report 1967 (BTDr. VI/183) dated 12.12.1969.

Security of the Family

Introduction

A whole range of public social services affects the position of families directly and indirectly. In particular, all those measures conduce to the security of families by which the disposable income of families is increased by allowances for spouses and children. This takes place primarily in the form of children's and family allowances (e.g. increase in provincial differentials in the public services in respect of spouses and children), but also in the form of special benefits similar to children' allowances payable to recipients of social benefits (e.g. children's allowances in Statutory Pensions Insurance, in Statutory Industrial Injuries Insurance, and similar provisions in War Pensions and Related Services, as well as in Unemployment Assistance and Equalisation of Burdens). But the social security of the family is further indirectly guaranteed by benefits for survivors, by taxation measures, by the furtherance of capital formation, by the grant of rent allowances, by the inclusion of family members in statutory health insurance, and by measures for education and training.

Children's Allowances

Children's allowances are intended in the first instance to increase the disposable family income. Their purpose is to reduce the financial burden of the family with children, and so to balance out, at least in part, the financial advantages enjoyed by unmarried persons and families without children.

Children's allowances have not always been payable. Additions to wages and salaries in respect of children were paid between the two world wars only in a small number of branches, voluntarily, or on the basis of collective agreements. In 1935, the payment of allowances for the fifth and further children was commenced, later for the third and fourth child. In 1945 they were discontinued.

General payment of children's allowances commenced in 1954, pursuant to the 'Law on the Grant of Children's Allowances and the Establishment of Family Adjustment Funds' (KGG). The law, which came into force on January 1st. 1955, gave all employees, self-employed persons, and employed family members with three or more children, a claim to children's allowances. The original administrative authorities were the Family Adjustment Funds established within the Industrial Injuries Insurance Institutes. The funds were raised from the contributions of the employers and of other self-employed persons. On the basis of the Children's Allowances Extension Law, all other persons with three or more children were included with effect from February 1, 1956 (with the exception of members of the public services and social insurance pensioners).

In 1961, the Children's Allowances Regulations were extended by the Children's Allowances Fund Law, on the basis of which the payments of children's allowances were introduced in respect of the second child for persons whose annual income was not in excess of 7.2oo DM, and the payment of these allowances from the Federal budget was entrusted to the newly established Children's Allowances Fund.

The above regulations were co-ordinated in the Federal Children's Allowances Law of April 14, 1964; it was laid down that all children's allowances should be payable from the

Federal budget. Administration was transferred to the Federal Ministry of Labour. Allowances were, in part, substantially increased. Further improvements, in particular an increase for the second child, and an increase of the income ceiling for payment in respect of the second child, are in the course of preparation.

Figures under Children's Allowances Legislation (1969)

	1st Child	2nd Child	3rd and further children
Total number of entitled children in mills.	9,28	5,26	3,12
Of these of persons employed in the economy	5,77	2,71	3,06
Persons in the public services	1,68	0,95	0,57
Recipients of social benefits	1,07	0,47	0,26
Expenditure in mill. DM	2120	1970	2132
of this pursuant to Children's Allowances Regulations	–	813	55
in the public services	1510	922	615
Recipients of social benefits	610	235	135

Conditions and Amounts

Persons with two or more children receive children's allowances in respect of them, in so far as no other similar allowances are payable in the form of additions to wages or to pensions (e.g. in the case of employees in the public services or of recipients of social benefits). In cases in which there are no further children, allowances are payable in respect of the second child only if the income of the entitled person, and his wife, or her husband, does not exceed 7.800 DM per annum, (650 DM per month). This limit is imposed because of the reckonability of the number of children for income tax purposes, which remains without effect if the entitled person has more than two children. The ceiling is to be raised w.e.f. 1.9.1970 to 13.250 DM.

Amount of Children's Allowances
in DM per month

from	for the 2nd Child	3rd Child	4th Child	5th and further children
1. 1.55	–	25	25	25
1.10.57	–	30	30	30
1. 3.59	–	40	40	40
1. 4.61	25	40	40	40
1. 7.64	25	50	60	70
1. 9.70	25	60	60	70

Entitled children are legitimate children, children declared legitimate, adopted and illegitimate children, step children (resident in the household of the recipient), foster children (if the recipient has taken them into his household and contributes not inconsiderably to their maintenance), grand children, brothers, and sisters (if the recipient has taken them into his household, or if he contributes not inconsiderably to their maintenance). These children remain entitled in principle only up to the age of 18. Older children, remain — with certain other exceptions — entitled up to the age of 25 if they are engaged in full time education or vocational training. This limit may be extended for the period of compulsory military training, if as a result of such training, education or vocational training has been interrupted or delayed. Children who are incapable of earning their own livelihood as a consequence of physical or mental infirmity may remain entitled beyond the 25th year of age.

Children whose home or normal place of residence is not in the German Empire within the borders as at 31.12.37 cannot be considered. Exemption regulations are operative for the benefit of nationals of Members States of the EEC, or of states with which the Federal Republic of Germany has concluded reciprocal social security treaties.

At the end of 1969, some 2.1 mill. families were in receipt of children's allowances in respect of approximately 5 mill. children, pursuant to the Federal Children's Allowances Law.

In March/April 1970 children's allowances were payable to 4.979 families with 10 and more children; included in this number were 2.994 families with 10 children, 1236 families with 11 children, 486 families with 12 children, and 263 families with 13 and more children.

Number of Families entitled to Children's Allowances in 1970*

Number of children	Number of families in 1.000s	in % of the total number
2	300	14,7
3	1 030	50,6
4	407	20,0
5 and more	297	14,7

* estimated numbers

Finance

The expenditure for children's allowances, including administrative costs, is borne by the Federal Government.

Expenditure for Children's Allowances
in mill. DM

1955	1960	1965[1]	1966[1]	1970	1968	1969	1970[2]
446	906	2 752	2 930	2 654	2 596	2 675	2 671

1) including a training grant payable from 1.4.1965 to 30.6.1967
2) estimated figures

Organisation

The implementation of the Federal Children's Allowances Law is the responsibility of the Federal Institute for Labour, under the technical supervision of the Federal Minister of Labour and Social Order. Applications for payment are dealt with by the Employment Exchanges, but payment is made centrally by the Federal Institute itself.

Payment of Children's Allowances in the Public Services

Members of the public services (established officials, judges, non-manual workers, manual workers, regular soldiers, conscripts) with children receive, in addition to their emoluments, a children's allowance of 50 DM per month for every unmarried child. Children's allowances are also payable to pensioned civil servants and their survivors. These allowances are payable to established officials on the basis of legislation, to non-manual and manual workers on the basis of collective agreements. The definition of entitled children, is, with minor exceptions, the same as that pursuant to the Federal Children's Allowances Law.

Children's allowances are payable up to the age of 18, in the case of full time education or training or of a voluntary social year up to the age of 27. In the case of delays in education or training for which the persons affected are not responsible, beyond the 27th year, the allowance is payable for a period corresponding to such delays. For permanently incapacitated children there is no upper age limit, if the incapacitation occurred before the age of 27.

In contrast to allowances under the Federal Children's Allowances Law, this form of allowance is liable to income tax, in the case of manual and non-manual workers it is also liable for social insurance contributions.

The funds are provided, in the same way as wages and salaries, from the budgets of the employing authorities; expenditure in 1970 will amount to 1.6 milliard DM.

In addition, members of the public services, with the exception of manual workers, married and with children, receive a higher local differential. The differential is increased in respect of the first child by 40 DM, for the second up to the fifth child by 47 DM for each child, for each further child by 58 DM. Manual workers in the public services receive, on the basis of collective agreements, an additional social allowance, to the amount, since January 1, 1970, of 40 DM for the first child, 47 DM for each child from the second to the fifth, and 58 DM for each further child. District differentials and additional social allowances are liable to income tax, in the case of manual and non-manual workers to social insurance contributions. The children's allowances portions of the district differentials are payable to pensioned established officials only as to the same percentage as that of their pensions is to their pensionable salaries (maximum of 75 %); widows and orphans receive only the percentage corresponding to their percentage of the pension.

Additional Children's Allowances outside the Public Services

In numerous branches of the economy manual and non-manual workers receive household and additional children's allowance on the basis of collective or works agreements, irrespective of any claim they may have to statutory allowances. In the Banking and Insurance Industries amounts are approximately the same as in the public services, in industry they are lower.

Children's Allowances additional to Social Benefits

Special additional children's allowances are also payable to recipients of social benefits.

Pensioners of the administrations of Pensions Insurance receive an annual allowance for each child to the amount of one tenth of the General Basis of Computation.

Persons in receipt of a pension from Accident Insurance of 50 % or more in respect of reduced standard of employment receive an additional monthly allowance for each child to the amount of one tenth of the pension, to a minimum of 25 DM for the second child, 50 DM for the third child, 60 DM for the fourth child, and 70 DM for each further child.

War pensioners with a reduced standard of employment of 50 % and more receive for each child an additional allowance of 50 DM per month.

An unemployed person receives for each child entered on his PAYE-card a family allowance of 12 DM per week (52 DM per month).

Pursuant to the Equalisation of Burdens Law, additional children's allowances to the amount of 70 DM are payable.

In the case of war pensions and benefits payable under Equalisation of Burdens, the additional children's allowances are reduced by the amounts payable on the basis of other regulations.

The definition of entitled children in the meaning of this provision is substantially the same as that under the Federal Children's Allowances Law. The conditions under which allowances are payable are also largely identical with those under the Federal Children's Allowances Law.

Amounts of Children's Allowances

Branch	DM per month		Remarks
Fed. Children's allowances	1st child	NIL	In respect of the 2nd child
	2nd child	25.00	there is an upper income limit (7.800 DM)
	3rd child	50.00	if there are no further children
	4th child	60.00	
	from 5th child	70.00	
Pensions Insurance	ArV +		current pension
	AnV each child	81.50	New pensions from 1970
	each child	82.40	
	KnRV each child	86.00	current pensions
		86.90	new pensions from 1970
Accident Insurance	100 % of pensions to a maximum of	200.00	The maximum amount payable is based on maximum annual earnings. If the statutes of the Fund permit of higher amounts the children's allowance is correspondingly higher.
	From the 2nd child onwards the rates payable under the Fed. Children's Allowances are also payable		
Unemployment Insurance	each child	52.00	This amount is based on a weekly payment of 12 DM
War Pensions	each child	50.00	
Equalisation of Burdens	each child	70.00	
Socail Aid	up to 7 years	67.00	Average stabdard rates
	7th up to 14th	99.00	for the Federal Territory
	14th to 18th	119.00	in 1970
	18 and over	108.00	
Public Services	1st child	90.00	Payable in the case of established officials, non-manual and manual workers. The children's allowance amounts to 50 DM. The balance is a local differential, or (in the case of manual workers) a social supplement.
	2nd to 5th child	97.00	
	from 6th child onwards	108.00	

Tax-free Allowances for Children

For income tax purposes, tax payers receive tax-free allowances for children, for the first child 1.200 DM annually, for the second 1.680 DM, and for each further child 1.800 DM. These allowances lead, in so far as income tax is payable, to a reduction of the burden of taxation. This reduction amounts in the proportional zone of taxation rates — that is to say in the case of married couples with an income of up to 16.000 DM per annum — for the first child to 19 DM, for the second 26.60 DM, and for every further child 28.50 DM per month. In the progressive zone of taxation rates (a taxable income of between 8.000 DM — in the case of married couples of between 16.000 DM — and 110.000 DM) tax rebates are between 19 and 53 % of the applicable tax-free amount for children. In the upper proportional zone of the taxation rates (taxable incomes from 110.000 DM onwards, rate of taxation 53 %) monthly tax rebates are: for the first child 53 DM, for the second 74.20 DM, and for every further child 79.50 DM.

In the case of employees liable to wages tax, taxable earnings, gradated according to the size of the family, commence in the first instance with the annual earnings shown in the following table.

Tax free Allowances

1950 in DM	% of average gross annual earnings	Family Status		1970 in DM	% of average gross annual earnings
1531	48		single	3 450	26
1681	53		no child	5 160	40
2081	66		1 child	6 360	49
2331	74				
		married with	2 children	8 040	62
3031	96		3 children	9 840	75
3731	118		4 children	11 640	89
4731	150		5 children	13 440	103

Since, in taking into account the number of children in assessing income tax and wages tax in the case of persons with low incomes, the effect is not fully operative, or not operative at all, children's allowances are payable in respect of the second child. In the case of children accomodated away from home for educational or training purpose an additional exempt amount of 100 DM per month may be granted on application. Tax free rebates for children resulted in 1966 in a reduced tax revenue of about 4.000 mill. DM. This amount will increase w.e.f. 1.9.1970 to 4.300 mill. DM.

Other Services for the Security of the Family

In addition to benefits designed to increase the disposable income of the family, further social measures contribute to the security of the family.

Benefits for Family Accomodation and Owner-Occupier Homes

In view of the still inadequate housing available, especially in the case of large families in urban agglomerations, special measures for the promotion of house building have been undertaken.

The general measures in social housing in the form of *building loans from public funds* have been to the special benefit of persons whose family income, gradated according to the size of the family, did not exceed defined limits. In this connection the building of family homes was given preference over owner-occupier flats and rented accomodation. Within this order of precedence, housing for large families was accorded preferential promotion. In 1966 funds provided by the Federal and Land Governments amounted to approximately 3.2 milliard DM in the form of low interest loans, 70 mill. DM in the form of grants to pay interest and for incidental expenses. *Interest Free Additional Family Loans* are available for persons with two or more children building family homes and owner-occupier flats, in the case of two children to an amount of 2.000 DM for a family home, or 1.500 DM for an owner-occupier flat, plus 3.000 DM (family home), or 1.500 DM (owner-occupier flat) for every other child.

Exercise "Young Family"

There is, in addition, the exercise "Young Family" for married couples under the age of 35 who have been married for less than 5 years, and who have at least one child, on the basis of which loans are granted by Credit Institutes at 6 % for a maximum period of seven years, and to amounts of up to 4.000 DM to supplement their own resources (Total expenditure in 1966: 42.4 mill. DM).

Capital Formation in the Hands of Families

The promotion of a widely distributed formation of capital or property in the hands of families is the object of house building premiums, payable as to one half each from Federal and Land budgets, to meet payments to building societies, and for similar purposes, up to a maximum amount of 4.000 DM per annum, whereby, in view of the reduced ability to save with the growth of the size of the family, the amount of the premium increases from 25 % for recipients without children to 35 % for those with more than 5 children. Total expenditure amounted in 1966 to 975 mill. DM, to which must be added reduced taxation revenue to an amount of 790 mill. DM, for building society payments in the framework of the Special Expenditure Regulations.

Apart from these provision, saving premiums are payable for payments to a savings contract, as well as for expenditure for the pruchase of shares, whereby the premium rate increases in relation to the size of the family from 20 to 30 %, in addition to which the maximum premium payable also increases with the number of children to 480 DM. A particular benefit to *young* marriages is to be found in the provision whereby the period for which savings must be left untouched, 6 to 7 years, is reduced by 2 years without prejudice to the premium in the event of marriage. (Total expenditure in 1966: 458 mill. DM).

For earners of lower incomes there are additional premiums payable on the basis of the Law for House Building Premiums as well as on the Savings Premium Law. The additional premiums amount to 30 % of the house building premiums in the case of the Law for House Building Premiums and to 40 % of the savings premiums in the case of the Savings Premium Law.

Particular importance attaches to the Promotion of Capital Formation in the Hands of the Workers. This scheme was placed on a new basis by the Third Law for the Promotion of Capital Formation in the Hands of the Workers — "the 624 DM Law" —. The amount attracting concessions was increased to 624 DM annually with effect from 1970. With effect from 1971, and in lieu of the exemption from wages tax and social insurance contributions previously in force, an Employee's Savings Supplement comes into force. It amounts to 30 per cent. (In the case of workers with more than two children 40 per cent.) of the amount effectively invested. These concessions are granted in respect of effectively invested payments laid down in collective agreements and for amounts invested from current earnings. If a worker choses, for example, an investment pursuant to the Savings Premiums Law, or the Home Building Premiums, he receives, in addition to the Workers' Savings Premium the Savings and House Building Premium — and if he is in the low income bracket — an Additional Premium. By virtue of the gradation of statutory concessions according to family status, the number of children and the amount of income, there results, in the case of effective investments according to these two Premium Laws, total statutory concessions amounting to between 50 and 85 per cent. of the amount saved.

Total expenditure

The payments here enumerated are not the only ones made for the benefit of families. Expenditure for the establishment of families, for marriage counsel, the promotion of family holiday homes, and convalescent homes for mothers, reduced fares for children on public transport, and expenditure for the educational system, are further sums which contribute to the financial and social security of family life. Total expenditure serving this end directly or indirectly amounted in the Federal Republic of Germany to 46 milliard DM in 1968.

Legislative Bases

Federal Children's Allowance Law of 14.4.1964 (BGBI. I. S. 265), last amended by the Law of 21.12.1967 (BGBI. I S. 1259).

Third Law for the Promotion of Capital Formation in the Hands of the Workers of June 27, 1970 (BGBI. I. S. 930).

Safeguards against and in the Event of Unemployment

Promotion of Vocational Training, Promotion of Labour, Unemployment Insurance

Introduction

Safeguards against the occurrence of unemployment consist of: a vocational training system as comprehensive as possible, implemented by promotion of
    vocational training
    vocational further training
    retraining
    vocational rehabilitation, as well as labour placing effected through
measures for the security of employment and the
    creation of new jobs, namely,
    short time working allowances
    promotion of all-the-year-round employment in the building industry, as well as
    measures for the creation of jobs, and
benefits payable to the unemployed, namely
    unemployment benefit
    unemployment allowances.

The measures for the security of employment and the creation of new jobs are supplemented by the promotion of entry into employment in Berlin, and re-settlement aid for redundant miners. In addition, the health, accident, and pensions insurance, contributions of the recipients of benefits are also covered in certain cases.

Socio-political measures designed to ensure a maximum level of employment have priority over the payment of unemployment benefit and assistance. For this reason a close institutional tie exists beween unemployment insurance on the one hand, and other forms of aid, whose object is to secure employment and to create new jobs (Promotion of Labour), on the other hand labour placing, vocational guidance, and the promotion of vocational training. Labour placing and vocational guidance are free public services, designed to balance out supply and demand in the labour market. Full details cannot be given within the scope of this survey, which will, however, deal with the general measures adopted by the Federal Institute for Labour for the prevention, elimination, and termination of unemployment, as well as measures for vocational education.

Provision for the unemployed developed in Germany after the first world war. A comprehensive legal regulation of the law as applied to labour placing and unemployment insurance has been in force since 1927. As a consequence of the fluctuations in unemployment, and of political conditions, unemployment insurance has undergone a great many changes. In 1956 the law as applied to unemployment insurance was adapted to modern requirements and concepts by a comprehensive Amendment and Consolidating Law. At the end of 1959 the Law on Measures to promote all-the-year-round employment in the building industry, and the introduction of inclement weather payments, led to a considerable improvement of the financial position of building trade workers in winter. In 1966 the upper limits for contributions and benefits were raised. In 1967 the relation between earnings and unemployment benefit and unemployment assistance was improved, family allowances were increased, and childrens's allowances were no longer taken into account in assessing family allowances.

In 1969 the Law on Labour Placing and Unemployment Insurance in force since 1927, was replaced by the Law on the Promotion of Labour. This law lays the foundations for a future flexible labour market and employment policy. It is based on a realisation of the fact that rapid technical developments, automation, and industrial changes, are resulting in ever higher demands being made on the workers. It serves the requirements of modern working and occupational life. The main objects of the new law are:

Security of full employment,
Security of optimum occupational opportunities by means of vocantional training and adaptation,
Protection against loss of social status as a consequence of unemployment or short time working.

In the foreground of policy, therefore, is forward looking and timely aid; in addition, improved precautions against unemployment and other exigencies are provided.

In unemployment insurance, the amount of benefits provided depends to a greater extent on the existing economic and employment position than is the case in other branches of social security. The development of unemployment in Germany in past years displays considerable divergencies. Since about 1957, up to 1966, and again since 1969, the quota of unemployment stood at 0.4 %. At that time 94.800 unemployed contrasted with about 891.700 unfilled vacancies.

Unfilled Vacancies and Unemployed in the Federal Republic of Germany (Position as at April 1970)

Year Unfilled Va	Unfilled Vacancies	Unemployed	Unemployment Quota
1950	123 029	2 074 220	12,2
1955	231 773	1 047 886	5,6
1960	468 396	225 051	1,1
1965	661 042	126 862	0,6
1966	595 654	121 288	0,6
1967	295 737	501 303	2,3
1968	443 254	330 851	1,6
1969	763 302	155 181	0,7
1970	846 431	120 550	0,6

Scope

The categories of persons entitled to make claims under vocational labour promotion, and unemployment insurance are more extensive than those under other forms of social security. They are determined by the purpose for which the benefits are granted. Benefits under unemployment insurance are, as a general rule, dependent on contributions paid. The categories entitled will be enumerated in the following sectors.

Compulsory Insurance

The categories of persons compulsorily insurable are largely the same as those insurable under health insurance. Compulsorily insurable, therefore, are, in the first place, employed employees, including home workers, and persons engaged in vocational training, as well as their employers.

Monthly Insurable Earnings and Contributions Ceilung in DM

Period	Insurable Contributions Ceiling for Manual and Non-Manual Workers
up to 31.5.49	300
from 1.6.49	375
from 1.9.52	500
from 1.3.57	750
from 1.7.65	750
from 1.1.67	1 300
from 1.7.69	1 700
from 1.1.70	1 800

The insurance ceiling for non-manual workers has been abolished since 1968. Workers are also insurable who are not insurable under Health Insurance solely for the reason that their regular annual earnings were in excess of the earnings ceiling under Health Insurance, or who, on the occasion of increases in their annual earnings have claimed exemption on the grounds that they have taken out an insurance policy with a private company.

Compulsorily insurable are all persons performing compulsory military service, or alternative civilian service, called up for more than 3 days, who were compulsorily insurable directly before performing their service, or who were exempted solely on the grounds of employment abroad, or who were unemployed.

In contrast to the preceding legal position, persons insured under the Miners Special Scheme are now also compulsorily insurable w.e.f. from 1.7.1969. They will be required to pay contributions only from 1. 1. 1972 onwards (with a transitional arrangement until 31. 12. 1974). Similarly, workers employed in agriculture under long term contracts of employment, apprentices, trainees and re-trainees, are now also insurable.

Contributors in Thousands
in March, from 1965 onwards in April

Year	Contributors	Insured Persons in KnV[1] exempted from Payment	Other exempted Persons	Sick Persons not paying Contributions
1951	9 550	–	1 817	430
1955	11 071	–	1 635	598
1960	14 628	671	1 815	861
1965	15 929	524	2 069	632
1966	16 720	488	1 787	659
1967	16 447	427	1 797	445
1968	16 469	380	1 789	511
1969	18 617	351	804	580
1970	19 081	348[1]	797	219

1) KnV Miners Special Scheme Insurance
2) Persons insured under the Miners Special are exempted from payment of contributions for the time being

Exemptions

The categories not liable to pay contributions are mainly persons in subsidiary occupations, civil servants and xpensioners, as well as those engaged in training and education.

Exempt from payment are also workers aged 63, whose claim to an unemployability pension from statutory pensions insurance has been admitted, or who, by reason of a reduced standard of employment, are no longer permanently available for placing. Exempt also are workers who are attending an elementary or a higher school, persons performing only a negligible amount of work, casual workers – the latter with the exception of dockers – homeworkers who are also middlemen and who earn the bulk of their income in this capacity. Finally, foreigners engaged in vocational and further training are exempt under certain conditions.

Benefits for the Promotion of Vocational Training

Occupational demands made on gainfully employed persons are constantly changing as a consequence of rapid technical and scientific progress. In particular, automation is rendering many occupations redundant. New occupations are constantly emerging. Within the framework of an investigation conducted in 1964 (Microcensus), the extent and importance of occupational changes was more closely examined on the basis of certain selected occupations. It emerged, that of 6.9 mill. employed persons included in this investigation, 49 % were no longer following the occupation for which they had originally been trained. In order to ensure adaptability to the constant changes and new occupational demands, a comprehensive form of vocational training is clearly necessary, before and throughout the whole of the working life, and this has been made possible by the Federal Institute for Labour.

The Federal Institute can promote vocational training by means of individual training, further training, and retraining. There is, in fact, a legal entitlement to individual measures. Such individual measures can be supplemented in practice by institutional assistance, which enables the Institute to ensure an andequate supply of training establishments meeting the needs of an up-to-date form of vocational training.

The Federal Institute for Labour also has a duty to assist physically, mentally, or psychically handicapped persons in entering or re-entering employment in order to facilitate the integration of these persons into employment and society (occupational rehabilitation). The Institute is authorised to take suitable measures for entry into employment of those seeking work.

According to a statistical investigation about 41.000 men and 8.300 women were taking part in vocational training courses in May 1969. Pronounced interest was displayed in the courses for technical occupations (13.000), for metal manufacturing occupations (9.500), for office and administrative occupations (9.000). In almost 37.000 cases the Federal Institute for Labour met the full costs. In 2.500 cases the Institute shared the costs with other authorities, whereas in 10.000 cases other authorities themselves met the full costs. Half the workers involved were taking part in courses lasting more than a year.

Individual Promotion of Vocational Education

The individual promotion of vocational education includes vocational training, further training and retraining. Vocational training embraces the acquisition of the knowledge and skills necessary to follow an occupation. Further training is designed to complete, to expand, to retrain, or to improve existing knowledge and skills. Occupational re-training is designed to provide the new knowledge and skills necessary to permit the pursuit of a new occupation.

The promotion of participation in measures of vocational education extends to full time instruction, part time instruction (whilst still in employment), and correspondence courses. Grants are made only on condition that the training establishment comes up to expectations in the matter of the duration of courses, the curriculum, training methods, training, and the practical experience of the trainers.

Benefits for individual promotion of vocational training may be granted only on condition that the applicant is a suitable person, and that the asstistance given is expedient in consideration of the position and probable future development of the labour market, and of the applicant's own occupational wishes. Assistance granted by the Federal Institute for Labour is subordinate to measures undertaken by other bodies in public law, insofar such bodies are under a legal obligation to undertake such measures.

Promotion of Vocational Training

For the promotion of vocational training, the Federal Institute is authorised to award grants and loans to young persons and to adults for suitable training in individual firms or in supra- undertakings establishments, as well as for participation in basic educational and vocational courses, advanced courses, and other measures designed to prepare them for their future occupation.

The extent of such assistance is laid down in regulations issued by the Federal Institute for Labour, detailing the conditions, type and amounts. Assistance is granted only if the applicant is himself unable to provide the necessary means, and if those responsible for his maintenance cannot normally and reasonably be expected to do so.
Assistance may be granted to all Germans. Under certain conditions aliens may also be entitled.

Promotion of Further Training

The Federal Institute for Labour further promotes participation in measures designed to ascertain, to maintain, and to improve existing knowledge and skills, or to adapt them to technical developments, or to facilitate advance in the chosen occupation. A condition is a previously completed vocational training, or satisfactory occupational experience. As a general rule, measures are regarded as being suitable for promotion if they are aimed at facilitating occupational advance, the adaptation of existing knowledge and skills to new occupational requirements, the entry or re-entry of women jobseekers into employment, the taking of a final occupational examination, the training or further training of trainers, as well as the re-integration of older workers into employment.

Participation in occupational further training measures shall not normally be sanctioned if they last more than two years. This restriction does not apply to part time training taken whilst still in employment.

Every person who has followed an insurable occupation, or who intends to follow such an occupation, has a claim to further training assistance. Their skills and previous industrial experience must, however, justify the assumption that they will benefit from further training.

Promotion of Vocational Re-Training

In addition, the Federal Institute promotes participation in measures of vocational re-training of persons seeking employment. Re-training measures are measures which serve the purpose of facilitating a change over to some other suitable form of employment, and, in particular, which ensure or improve occupational mobility.

All persons seeking employment are entitled to participate. Any measure whose purpose is the re-training of persons seeking employment may be promoted. These are, more especially, measures designed to avert or to overcome a shortage of skilled workers, or to prevent or to terminate qualitative and quantitative underemployment. If it is possible by means of re-training to avert unemployment in the case of an applicant in employment, such training should be commenced at the earliest possible moment. The type and extent of the promotion of vocational re-training is the same as that in the case of vocational further training. Re-training should normally be financed only if it does not last more than two years.

Occupational Rehabilitation

In order to enable physically, mentally or psychically handicapped persons to enter or to re-enter employment, the Federal Institute for Labour has the duty to take all suitable measures necessary to maintain, improve, or restore their ability to work. The measures suitable for the occupational integration of handicapped persons closely resemble those adopted in the case of the individual and institutional promotion of vocational training. As measures of individual assistance must be regarded in particular labour and vocational guidance for handicapped persons, services for the vocational training of handicapped persons desirous of taking up an occupation, services designed to maintain, restore, or improve existing skills, services designed for training for an alternative occupation, aid in obtaining employment, or an apprenticeship or training engagement.

Persons entitled to participate include all physically, mentally, or psychically handicapped persons. During vocational rehabilitation these persons receive maintenance allowances on the same scale as in the case of individual vocational promotion measures.

The Federal Institute for Labour has a duty to co-operate closely with other responsible bodies in questions of the labour and vocational promotion of handicapped persons, and to give guidance at the earliest possible moment on the measures suitable in their cases. The Institute is empowered to pay training supplements to employers for the training of handicapped persons if it is not possible to arrange for their training in some other manner. The erection, extension, and equipment of workshops particularly suited to the special needs of handicapped persons may be promoted by the award of loans and grants.

The placing departments and specialist services of the Federal Institute for Labour were utilised for occupational integration by 100.400 handicapped persons in 1968. A further 67.000 individual cases were satisfactorily disposed of — over 20 % more than in 1967.

Cash Benefits during Vocational further Training, Re-Training, and Rehabilitation

The type and extent of assistance granted during vocational further training, re-training, and rehabilitation is laid down in detail in law. Those taking part in full time instruction receive a maintenance allowance, as do those attending courses in addition to following their normal occupation, though only if instruction takes up at least a third of their normal hours of work.

Maintenance allowances consist of a basic amount and family supplements. The basic amount depends on hourly earnings over a defined period prior to the commencement of the course, and on normal weekly hours of work. Maintenance allowance amounts during the first six months to 130 % of unemployment benefit, thereafter to 140 %. This amounts to 81.25 % or 87.5 % of the net earnings of a single person. Together with family supplements, maintenance allowances can, in future, amount to 95 % of the net earnings of a manual worker with two children. In addition, from the end of the first year of instruction, erarnings on which allowances are assessed are increased by 4 % half yearly, so that, in the case of protracted courses of instruction, the level of previous net erarnings can be reached. Earnings, and the corresponding basic allowances, can be seen in the following table, the basis of which is a uniform rate of earnings. This is the nearest DM amount divisible by 5 rounded off to the basis of computation.

Example for the Grant of a Basic Amount in DM per Week

Customary Wage	Basic Amount during the first 26 weeks of payment	for the further duration of payment	Maximum Amount
50	36,00	38,40	42,00
100	66,60	71,40	84,60
150	93,60	100,80	126,60
200	121,80	130,80	159,60
250	148,80	160,20	193,20
300	174,60	188,40	226,80
350	198,60	214,20	261,00
400	220,80	237,60	295,20

The family supplement amounts to 14.40 DM per week.

Income which the recipient of a maintenance allowance receives from self-employment, family employment, or as wages, is taken into account only insofar as it, after deduction of tax, social insurance contributions, contributions to the Federal Institute für Labour, and necessary and unavoidable expenses, does not exceed 50 DM per week.

In addition, other costs arising are refunded wholly or in part by the Federal Institute. These include fees, the costs of teaching materials, fares, working clothes, as well as the costs of board and lodging if the trainee has to live away from home.

In addition the Federal Institute may award grants to employers in respect of workers who are unable to work up to the required standard until after a settling-in period. The payment of such supplements is not limited to workers who have undergone a vocational training, further training, or re-training course. The supplement for the whole settling-in period may not exceed 60 % of agreed wage rates, or of the local rate normally payable for the job. It is not payable for more than one year.

Health, accident and pensions insurance of the recipients of maintenance allowances is dealt with in a special sector at the end of the chapter.

Institutional Promotion of Vocational Training

In the framework of the institutional furtherance of vocational training, institutions, in particular training workshops, serving the purpose of training, further training, or re-training, may be promoted by the award of loans or grants for the purpose of building, extending, and equiping the institutions. In exceptional cases promotion may extend to the maintenance of the institution. Promotion by the Federal Institute can be granted only if the organisors of the institution themselves make a reasonable contribution from their own resources. Any institution serving the purpose of professional training in special schools, or serving in the main the purpose of an association or of an undertaking, or working for gain, may not be assisted, except in special circumstances.

Promotion of Entry into Employment

In order to assist job seekers to enter into employment, the Federal Institute for Labour is authorised to make grants to meet the costs of applying for the job, for travel costs and costs of removal, and may grant separation allowances in the case of running a separate household, allowances for working gear, transitional allowances, and similar assistance, which may prove necessary to facilitate the entry into employment. In lieu of such benefits loans may be granted. The benefits may be granted only to persons unable to meet the expenses from their own resources.

Loans and grants up to a maximum of 60 % of agreed rates, or of customary local rates, may be made to employers for a period of up to two years, to facilitate the occupational integration of job seekers who are difficult placing propositions under normal labour market conditions. Further, the Federal Institute is authorised, under certain conditions, to promote the establishment of workers' and young persons' hostels by awarding loans or grants.

Tax Concessions for Training, Further Training, and Re-training

Under the First Taxation Amendment Law of 1968, expenditure incurred by a tax payer for his vocational training, for a change of occupation (re-training), or for his further training in an occupation he is no longer following (e.g. a housewife training to return to her former occupation) may, with effect from 1969, be deducted as to DM 900 per calendar year from taxable income, as special expenditure. If he is compelled to live away from home, the amount is increased to DM 1.200. The costs of vocational further training in the normal occupation were already deductible to the full extent as necessary and unavoidable costs on the basis of existing law.

Services for the Security and Creation of Employment

Supplementary to an economic policy designed to secure full employment, a structural policy oriented on social policy for the security and creation of employment contributes, to the avoidance of unemployment and of short-time working. For this reason, the Federal Institute for Labour is required to invest that part of its reserves not essential for sucuring its ability to pay benefits in such a manner that structural and labour market policy interests are promoted, and that, in particular, the investments contribute to an improvement of the structure of employment in certain areas and in certain branches of the economy. Measures designed to secure placing in permanent employment are to be given priority. In this connection the Federal Institute is required - in order to create new employment - to devote special attention to measures for the establishment, extension, modernisation, and rationalisation of industrial production undertakings in recognised distressed areas, and districts scheduled under the Regional Action Programme. For the improvement of the employment structure the Federal Institute for Labour provided a total of 6,2 milliiard DM between 1952 and 1969.

The following benefits are also provided to safeguard jobs and create new jobs:

Short-time working allowances to safeguard jobs in the event of a temporary shortage of work in the firm;

Inclement weather payments, productive promotion of winter building, and other measures designed to ensure continuity of building employment during inclement weather, with the object of ensuring all-the-year-round employment in the industry, as well as measures for the creation of new jobs, in particular for older workers.

In order to cope with industrial changes in individual branches (mining, iron and steel production), social grants are made. There are special incentives for entry into employment in Berlin.

Short time working benefits

The payment of short time working benefits to workers who, as a consequence of industrial change or for similar causes, are in receipt only of reduced earnings, or of no earnings at all, is one of the benefits which serve to preserve employment. For this reason short time working benefits in the event of temporary stoppages are payable only if it can reasonably be anticipated that payment will secure the workers' jobs, and will guard the employer against the loss of his experienced workers. Payment may be made in respect of any firm regularly employing at least one worker. Excepted are firms which have no regular working hours, firms in inland waters fishing, including pisciculture, seagoing and inland waterways employment, travelling showmen, theatre, cinema, and concert undertakings.

In contrast to previous practice, short time working benefits are now payable in agriculture and forestry. Home workers wholly or mainly dependent on their earnings in that capacity are also entitled to claim.

Benefits are payable only in respect of firms in which the temporary stoppage is due to industrial conditions, including internal structural alterations, or to some unavoidable circumstance. The stoppage must be reported to the local Employment Exchange. Payment is conditional on the circumstance that for at least four weeks one third of the staff, that thereafter for at least four weeks one tenth of the staff, lose more than 10 % of their working time. Payment is not made if the stoppage is customary in the branch, in the firm, or is seasonal; or arises from internal organisational causes. Payment is made to homeworkers in respect of any calendar month in which their earnings fall more than 20 % below customary earnings owing to lack of work.

Payment can be made in respect of any one firm only for a maximum period of six months; the Federal Minister of Labour and Social Order is empowered, by means of a legal regulation, to extend this period to twelve months in the event of exceptional conditions in the labour market. This regulation can be limited to firms in defined branches of the economy.

Every worker has a claim to the payment of short time working benefit, who, subsequent to the commencement of the stoppage in a firm in which short time benefit is payable, continues to follow insurable employment without notice of termination having been given, or who, for urgent reasons, takes up such employment, and who, in consequence of the loss of working time is in receipt only of reduced earnings, or of no earnings. Workers who, on reaching the age of 63, are no longer required to pay contributions, are also entitled. If certain conditions are satisfied, workers under notice may also receive benefit. Casual domestic workers have no claim to benefit.

Benefit is assessed according to the number of hours lost, the amount according to the hourly wage the worker would have received but for the short time working. Short-time working benefit is paid in respect of the whole amount of lost earnings. The requirement pursuant to the previous legal regulations requiring the worker to bear a share of the loss himself is no longer in force. Family allowances are payable in addition to benefit. Short time working benefit for homeworkers amounts to one half of the difference between average earnings in the six months preceding the short time working, and the earnings in any particular month in which short time is worked. In addition, family allowances to the amount of 5 % of lost earnings are payable. Benefits payable may not exceed 65 % of lost earnings. Short time working benefit is also payable if a firm closes down temporarily. The special compensation formerly payable is thereby rendered superfluous. In 1969 the Federal Institute for Labour paid out 4 mill DM in short time working benefits.

Number of Short Time Workers and Firms Working Short Time in the Federal Territory
Annual Average Figures

| Year | Short Time Workers thereof | | women | Firms Working Short |
	total	men		Time
1951	93 444	41 579	51 865	2 430
1955	24 675	10 030	14 645	868
1960	3 305	1 515	1 790	118
1965	1 105	611	494	32
1966	15 816	8 838	6 978	259
1967	142 694	89 310	53 384	2 323
1968	10 388	6 588	3 800	399
1969	1 322	–	–	55

Promotion of all-the-year-round Employment in the Building Industry

For the promotion of building operations during inclement weather, i.e. of continuous all-the-year-round employment in the building industry, the following benefits are payable:

Inclement Weather Payments

In order to secure the jobs of building trade workers during the winter, and to enable employers to retain their experienced staffs, loss of earnings otherwise sustained by building trade operatives in the inclement weather period (November to March) are compensated for by the payment of inclement weather payments. Inclement weather payments are made in respect of building contracting firms if, during the inclement weather period, workers cannot be dismissed without notice because of weather conditions, and if, in the case of a stoppage of work, and without prejudice to any claim to annual holidays, there is entitlement to a wages supplement at least for the period between December 25th and January 1st. Payment is in principle conditional on the fact that the loss of work arises solely from impossible weather conditions, that a full day has been lost, and that the loss is reported to the Employment Exchange without delay.

Every building trade operative has a claim to inclement weather payment who, at the onset of the break, is in employment, is not under notice to finish, is in insurable employment in a job affected by climatic conditions, and who loses at least one full day's work. Expenditure for inclement weather payments amounted in 1969 to almost 834 mill DM. In the inclement weather period 1969/1970 about 1,3 milliard DM was paid in respect of 51 mill lost days.

The amount payable is dependent on the hourly earnings which would have been payable if there had been no break, and on the number of hours the worker would have worked on the particular day. The amount payable is laid down in official tables; the rates payable are increased in respect of family supplements by 0,30 DM per hour lost. Rates are increased by a standing-by allowance to compensate recipients for outlay arising. Inclement weather payments amount to between 62,5 % and 80 % of net earnings.

Inclement Weather Payments
Days lost, and Amounts Paid Out in the Federal Territory

Years[1]	Lost Days Thousand	Amount of Expenditure in Mill DM
1960/61	10 803	131
1961/62	26 829	399
1962/63	52 634	858
1963/64	31 311	534
1964/65	27 064	492
1965/66	24 728	468
1966/67	13 296	343
1967/68	23 398	624
1968/69	34 649	823
1969/70[2]	51 000	1 300

1) Period covered — 1.11. to 31.3.
2) Estimated figures

Promotion of Productive Winter Building

The promotion of winter building is a service provided from the Unemployment Insurance Fund, the object of which is to promote all-the-year-round employment in the building industry more effectively than previously.

Since 1.1.1970, building contractors may receive payments towards the additional costs of building in winter for work carried out in January and February. All work performed by building contractors on building sites on which both the site and the workers are adequately protected against the weather entitles to such payments. This applies if the building work can also be carried out during the scheduled period by the use of protective gear.

In future, payments will be made in respect of all types of building. The legal restriction limiting payments to publicly subsidised, social, and tax favoured building has been cancelled. Payments are, however, conditional on a minimum of 800 hours work being performed during the scheduled period.

Amounts payable depend on the number of hours worked by the insured workers during the scheduled period, and on the rates payable in different cases. Rates amount to 1,50 DM for outside building and 0,60 DM for excavation work, according to the nature of the work, and to 1,20 DM in other cases. In the event of exceptional increases in the cost of winter building, rates payable may be amended by a legal regulation.

By the end of January 1970 about 4.500 application for payments for productive winter building had been received by the Employment Exchanges in the Federal territory. Expenditure in 1969 amounted to nearly 65 mill. DM.

Other Services for Contractors and Workers in the Building Industry.

In addition to inclement weather payments and productive winter building payments, other disbursements may be made to contractors and workers in the industry. The Federal Institute for Labour is empowered to make grants, loans and interest allowances in respect of the purchase or hire of machines and apparatus designed to enable building to continue during winter weather. This arrangement enables even small contractors to buy the necessary gear. Further, workers may receive an allowance for journeys home from the building site, and for the purchase of the additional clothing and fotwear necessary in winter, as well as separation allowances if the job is beyond daily travelling distance. These payments may be made only if it is not customary and reasonable that they are met by the employer himself, and if the worker himself has no means, or insufficient means, to meet them.

Measures for the provision of employment

In the case of long term unemployed, especially older workers for whom no suitable jobs can be found, the Federal Institute for Labour is empowered to subsidise the creation of jobs.

Projects which are in the public interest can be promoted by the award of money grants and additional loans to the employers. A condition is that the work would otherwise not be carried out, or not to the same extent, or only at some later period. Priority is given to projects conducive to fulfilling the conditions prerequisite for providing permanent jobs for the unemployed, in particular those designed to counter the effects of industrial change and technical developments, to further, to make possible, or to complement, measures for structural improvements, or to provide jobs for the chronically unemployed.

In addition to juristic persons in public law, private contractors and organisations may receive subsidies if they conduce to a revival of the labour market in an economic or socio-politically desirable manner. Payments are made only in respect of previously underemployed workers placed by an Employment Exchange. In view of the peculiarities of the contract of employment in these cases, the conditions for giving notice of termination differ from those customary though otherwise legal conditions of employment are applicable.

For the purpose of providing employment for older workers, 50 % of agreed rates of pay, or of locally customary rates, may be refunded by the Federal Institute for Labour to employers engaging additional labour, insofar as the situation of, and developments in, the labour market seem to render such payments advisable in order to reduce unemployment amongst older workers. In addition, the Institute may make loans or grants to employers for the erection, extension, and equipment of their undertakings, or parts thereof, for the employment of older workers.

The Federal Government, in conjunction with the Federal Lands, the Churches, and a number of private undertakings, has founded the Society for the Improvement of Employment Structure Ltd. in Essen; which, basing itself on certain foreign models, has set itself the task of providing jobs under suitable conditions of employment for older workers. Relevant institutions have already been established in Essen and Dortmund.

Promotion of entry into employment in Berlin

The geographical position and the unfavourable age composition of the population of Berlin make it necessary to increase the inflow of labour from the Federal territory into Berlin, for which purpose special finiancial incentives are provided.

Pursuant to the Berlin Aid Law of 19.8.1964 (BGBl. IS.6741.10.1968 (BGBl. IS.1049), later amended 23.6.1970 (BGBl. IS 8
Pursuant to the Berlin Aid Law of 19.8.1964 (BGBl. IS. 674) in the version of 1.10.1968 (BGBl. IS. 1049), later amended 23.6.1970 (BGBl. IS 826), workers in Berlin are granted tax rebates and supplements to their wages and salaries. With effect from 1.1.1971, an 8 % addition to earnings in lieu of existing tax rebates is payable, and a monthly children's allowance of 22 DM with effect from 1.1.1970.

In order to maintain and consolidate the efficiency of Berlin indurstry, and pursuant to the Guide Lines of the Federal Government on the Promotion of Entry into Employment in Berlin of 31.1.1962 (Federal Gazette 1964 No. 26), last amended on 18.2.1970 (Federal Gazette No. 33), workers proceeding from other Federal Lands to take up employment in Berlin receive transitional payments, and travelling and removal expenses, including the costs of visits home; all costs are borne by the Federal Government. These benefits are payable to persons taking up employment in Berlin for a period of at least one year.

In the period between September 1st 1961 and March 31st 1970 some 185.000 workers have taken up employment in Berlin, and have taken advantage of these concessions. During the same period government expenditure under this heading amounted to 75,6 mill DM.

Adjustment Aid for Miners

The structural changes taking place in the supply of energy, and the consequential adjustments of the mining industry to the changed situation in the energy market, as well as the concentration of production to the most economical pits, have led since 1957 to a very large number of pit closures. The number of workers employed in hard coal mining fell from 599.000 (1958) to 254.000 (end of December 1969). Since the position in hard coal mining has, in the meanwhile, considerably improved, the employment position has also changed,so that the measures here described have declined somewhat in importance.

Over and above a number of economic measures adopted for the benefit of coal mining , for example a tax on fuel oil, generous social aid was provided for miners compelled to leave the pits and seek work elsewhere. In addition to the Miners' Special Scheme Adjustment Benefits, payable to older miners from the Miners' Special Scheme Pensions Insurance Fund, (see relevant sector) the following assistance allowances are payable in the case of a change of employment:

an adjustment payment in the case of reduced earnings in some other branch of industries of up to 80 % to 95 % of former net earnings in mining for a transitional period of up to 18 months;

fares to the new job as to one half; if they are in excess of 20 DM monthly in full, for a period of up to one year;

a separation allowance if the new job is beyond daily travelling distance - at the rate of 10 DM per diem for a transitional period of up to 3 years, in addition, the costs of a

visit home monthly; necessary in consequence of the change of the place of employment, in addition, in some cases, a refurnishing allowance of up to 1.500 DM.

In the way of assistance for occupational promotion, benefits are payable pursuant to
the Labour Promotion Law (see 'Vocational Promotion'); in addition, a retraining
allowance of between 60 and 120 DM monthly is payable, according to family status.
In the event of temporary unemployment, miners receive transitional payments of up
to 90 % of their former monthly net earnings to increase their unemployment benefit
for a period of 12 months, in some circumstances for a longer period, up to a total
income of 600 DM per month.

Transitional Grants. Miners over 50 years of age and pensioners receive a settlement
grant of 4.000 DM, if they are entitled to a Miners' Special Scheme Compensation
Benefit of 2.000 DM.

Miners in the North-Rhine Westphalian hard coal mining areas and the Hessen brown coal
areas receive, in addition to the above mentioned benefits, further supplementary payments from Land Funds, alternatively the periods for which benefits are payable are
increased up to 24 months.

Benefits are payable to redundant miners if they have been employed in the pit for six
months before the process of closure commences. Benefits payable to workers in iron ore
mining, in the iron and steel producing industry, and in bituminous coal mining, are
similar to those payable in hard coal mining.

Benefits payable to workers in iron ore mining, in the iron and steel industry and in
bituminous coal mining correspond to those payable to workers in hard coal mining: they
have been published in the Guide Lines of the Federal Ministry of Labour of 13.2.70
(Fed.Gazette 1970 No. 34), for iron ore mining and the iron and steel industry on
14.4.70 (Fed. Gazette No. 69) and for bituminous coal mining on 26.7.1966 (Fed.
Gazette 1966 No. 140).

From 1959 to the end of 1969 about 174 mill. DM was expended in benefits and grants.
Expenditure is borne as to one half by the Federal Government, as to one half by the
Commission of the European Community.

Benefits for the Unemployed

In addition to labour market policy measures for the security and creation of jobs
designed to avert unemployment, benefits are payable in the event of unemployment,
namely unemployment benefit and unemployment assistance. Health, Accident, and
Pensions Insurance of the recipients of unemployment benefit and unemployment assistance are dealt with in a special section at the end of this chapter.

Unemployment Benefit — Statutory Conditions —

An unemployed person has a claim to unemployment benefit if he is available for work,
has satisfied the contributions conditions, has registered with an Employment Exchange,
and has made a claim for benefit. Beyond the age of 65 there is no claim to benefit.

A worker is unemployed if he is temporarily not in a job. Home workers are also workers within this meaning. Any one employed for not more than 20 hours per week is regarded as unemployed. A worker is not regarded as unemployed if he works for more than 20 hours a week in the family business, or as a self-employed person, or in more than one occupation for more than 20 hours per week.

Every unemployed person is available for placing who is willing and able to follow an occupation - without regard to the possible duration thereof - under the conditions generally customary in the labour market. An unemployed person not incapable of following an occupation is available for placing even if, in consequence of a reduced standard of employment, he is able to work only a limited number of hours. An umemployed person is not regarded as available for placing if he is unable, or is not allowed, to work more than 20 hours per week because of his reduced standard of employment, and who is regarded as incapable of following his normal occupation under the provisions of statutory pensions insurance, or who is in fact or in law restricted. Whether he is incapable of following his normal occupation pursuant to the regulations of statutory pensions insurance is a decision which rests solely with the authorities of the relevant insurance fund; until a ruling is given an unemployed person is not so regarded.

The contributions conditions are satisfied if the unemployed person has followed an insurable occupation for 26 weeks, or for six months, in the three years preceding registration as an unemployed person. Periods for which no remuneration has been paid do not qualify. Qualifying periods are also periods during which the unemployed person was performing conscript service, or alternative civilian service, or after reaching the age of 63, as are also periods of employment in the former Reichs territory, and, in the case of deportees, periods of employment outside the former Reichs territory, if the unemployed person is able to produce proof of his status as a deportee. Moreover, periods of employment abroad may be equated with periods of employment at home.

A Claim to Unemployment Benefit is allowable

following insurable employment for .... weeks	for .... days
26	78
39	120
52	156
78	234
104	312

If, after satisfaction of a previous qualifying period, less than three years have elapsed, a claim for unemployment benefit is allowable at least for the period allowable before satisfaction of the new qualifying period. The duration of the claim for unemployment benefit depends on the period of insurable employment in the three years preceding the registration as unemployed.

The period of claim to unemployment benefit is reduced by the number of days for which benefit has been paid, for the number of days for which benefit has been refused, or for days on which the unemployed person has, without good reason, failed to claim benefit whilst still unemployed.

The claim to benefit rests if the unemployed person is in receipt of earnings, or has a claim thereto, or if he (or she) is entitled to maintenance allowance, sick pay, household allowance, injury pay under statutory injuries insurance, income adjustment payments under the Federal Pensions Law, maternity benefits, transitional payment under statutory pensions insurance, special payments under the Protection of Motherhood Law, unemployability pension, or premature retirement pension under statutory pensions insurance. If the unemployed person has left voluntarily, or has been discharged for industrial misconduct, and is therefore deliberately, or as a result of gross negligence, himself responsible for his unemployment, or if, despite his attention having been called to the possible legal consequences, he refuses employment offered to him by an Employment Exchange, or if, without good and sufficient cause, he refuses to take part in measures of vocational training, advanced training, or re-training, or if he walks out on such training measures without good cause, he is disallowed benefit for a period of two to four weeks, according to the circumstances of the case. He loses all claims to benefit if, after a four weeks disallowance period, he again gives grounds for a further four weeks disallowance period.

If an unemployed person, despite his attention having been called to the possible legal consequences, fails without good and sufficient cause to report to the Employment Exchange when so requested, his benefit is disallowed for six days. Benefit may also be disallowed, wholly or in part, if, by his conduct, the unemployed person, deliberately or by gross negligence, obstructs enquiries as to whether the conditions for the payment of benefit have been satisfied in his case, or who fails to report in the prescribed manner.

The payment of unemployment benefit may not result in intervention in industrial disputes. Special regulations lay down the conditions under which benefit may, exceptionally, be paid to persons unemployed in consequence of an industrial dispute in which they are not directly involved.

The waiting days formerly imposed have been abolished, since such waiting days are unjustifiable in the case of social benefits whose function is that of a substitute for earnings.

Rates of Benefit

Unemployment benefit is made up of a basic amount plus family allowances.
The basic amount is assessed on the average hourly earnings and the agreed weekly hours of work in a defined period of at least twenty days prior to registering as unemployed. The basic amount is so assessed that a single unemployed person receives an average of about 62.5 % of his previous earnings, less statutory deductions; this amounts to between 42 and 60 % of his previous gross earnings. Earnings, and the corresponding basic amounts, are laid down in a table. The assessment of the basic amounts depends on fixed scales. The scales are based on the rounded off DM amount divisible by 5 of the amount of earnings. The maximum amount on which benefit is assessed may not exceed 60 DM per day, 415.39 DM per week, or 1.800 DM per month. The basic amount is adapted to the circumstances of the claimant by the payment of family allowances.

The maximum amount on which benefit is assessed, currently 1.800 DM, is at any one time the same as the maximum amount on which contributions are payable in manual and non-manual workers' pensions insurance. In this manner the maximum amount of benefit payable is kept "dynamic". – i.e. automatically adjustable.

Family allowances amount to 12 DM per week for each dependent. They are payable in respect of a wife (or husband) not living separated, for every child in respect of which a tax rebate is allowed or would be allowed on application, for illegitimate children if paternity has been established or a maintenance allowance is payable, and in respect of whom tax rebate is allowable, or would be allowable if the child were legitimate.

Childrens' allowances cease at the age of 18, unless the child is in full time vocational training, is performing a social year, or is physically or mentally incapable of earning its own livelihood. The total benefit payable may not exceed a fixed amount, namely 80 % of the net earnings of a married claimant with 2 children.

Any income of which an unemployed person is in receipt at the same time as benefit is payable, either from self-employment or paid employment, is taken into account as to one half, insofar as the amount, after deduction of taxes, social insurance contributions, and necessary and unavoidable expenses, exceeds 15 DM per week. Claims to benefit must be made personally. Whenever so requested during the period benefit is payable, the unemployed person must report to the Employment Exchange.

Examples of Basic Rates Payable
in DM per Week

Standard Wage	Basic Rate	Maximum Rate
50	27,60	35,40
100	51,00	70,80
150	72,00	106,20
200	93,60	134,40
250	114,60	162,60
300	134,40	191,40
350	153,00	219,60
400	169,80	248,40

Recipients of Basic Rates of Benefit in 1000s as an Annual Average

Year	Unemployment Benefit			Unemployment Assistance		
	Total	Men	Women	Total	Men	Women
1950	541	390	151	916	658	258
1955	454	287	167	436	271	164
1960	175	117	58	51	38	13
1965	97	73	24	12	10	2
1966	97	73	24	10	9	1
1967	320	236	84	36	32	4
1968	192	137	55	53	47	6
1969	105	72	33	28	25	3

Unemployment Assistance

Unemployment assistance is payable instead of unemployment benefit if there is no claim to benefit, either because benefit has been exhausted, or because other conditions have not been satisfied. Rates are lower than benefit rates.

Regulations governing unemployment assistance are analogous to those under unemployment insurance, insofar as they do not run counter to the special conditions applicable to assistance. Assistance is payable to a claimant who has satisfied the general conditions for the payment of benefit only if he is not entitled to benefit for the reason that he has not satisfied the qualifying period, if he is in need, or if, in the year preceding his registering as unemployed and making a claim, he has been in receipt of benefit, or has been in paid employment for at least ten weeks. Various special regulations take account of special cases. An unemployed person is regarded as being in need if he is unable to maintain himself without the receipt of assistance, and if any income of which he is in receipt is less than assistance rates. He is not regarded as being in need if his means, those of a spouse, or his parents, or his own children living in his household, do not justify the grant of assistance. Amounts of income of which a spouse, the parents, or the children are in receipt, but which are not taken into account, were considerably increased pursuant to the Labour Promotion Law. Certain emoluments are not taken into account at all in assessing the amount of assistance payable. The conditions applicable to the assessment of basic rates of benefit, to family allowances, and to subsidiary occupations, are applicable mutatis mutandis to unemployment assistance; rates payable are, however, lower than benefit rates.

Examples of Basic Rates Payable in DM per Week

Standard	Basic Rate	Maximum Rate
50	23,40	35,40
100	42,60	70,80
150	60,60	106,20
200	78,60	134,40
250	96,00	162,60
300	112,80	191,40
350	128,40	219,60
400	142,80	248,40

In connection with the assessment of assistance rates, however, it must be noted that assistance rates payable immediately after the exhaustion of benefit are assessed on the basis of the same previous earnings as were benefit rates. In all other cases the basis to be taken for assessment is the amount of earnings the unemployed person can earn in the future.

Health, Accident, and Pensions Insurance for Recipients of Benefits

The insured person's membership under statutory health insurance remains uninterrupted during periods in which he is in receipt of short time working benefit, or inclement weather pay. In the case of unfitness for work during the receipt of short time working benefit, or inclement weather pay, sick pay is assessed on the basis of the last regular earnings. Contributions payable in respect of these categories are assessed on the basis of the earnings taken for the assessment of the short time working benefit, or inclement weather pay, and on the number of agreed hours of work which the claimant would have worked on the days in question. The employer pays that portion of the contribution payable in respect of the difference between earnings and short time working benefits, or inclement weather pay. On application 75 % of this amount may be refunded.

All persons are insured against accidents who are under an obligation to resort to the Employment Exchange when so requested if, in fulfilling this obligation, they report to the place designated or, on the instructions of an office of the Labour Administration, to some other place. Persons taking part in measures for their vocational further training or re-training, or in communal tasks, are also covered.

During the receipt of short time working benefits the contract of employment requiring the payment of pensions insurance contributions remains in force. Contributions are payable on the basis taken for assessing benefit, and in respect of the number of regular hours the recipient would have worked on the days in question.

The portion of the contribution payable in respect of the difference between normal earnings and short time working pay is payable by the employer, to whom 75 % of his costs are repayable on application. In the matter of consideration of the periods of unemployment and the receipt of inclement weather pay for the purposes of Pensions Insurance see the Section "Pensions Insurance of Employees".

Finance

The funds required by the Federal Institue for Labour for carrying out its work are raised from the contributions of insurable workers and their employers. Exceptions are insured persons whose regular remuneration does not exceed 180 DM per month, or who are engaged in a voluntary social year. In these cases the employer pays the full contribution.

Employees and employers each pay a maximum 1 % of the basis of contributions computation. The basis for computation in the case of employees is the actual or notional basis for the assessment of contributions to statutory pensions insurance, presently 0,65 % of earnings up to a maximum of 1.800 DM per month. For employers, the basis of assessment is the grand total of the basis of the assessment of the contributions of all insured workers in their employ. Special regulations apply in the case of conscripts and persons performing alternative civilian service (i.e. conscientious objectors).

Contribution Rates

Period	in %
up to 31. 5. 49	6,5
from 1. 6. 49	4,0
from 1. 4. 55	3,0
from 1. 3. 57	2,0
from 1. 8. 61	0,0
from 1. 4. 62	1,4
from 1. 1. 64	1,3

Income and Expenditure of the Federal Institute for Labour in Mill. DM

Year	Income	Total	Expenditure thereof Unemploy- Benefit	Unemploy- Assistance	Inclement Weather Pay	Short time working benefit and other unemployment benefits	Measures for the creation of employment	Promotion of entry into employment of vocational training, and rehabilitation, maintenance allowances	Promotion of professional advance in the framework of vocational advanced training	Promotion of qualifications in the framework of vocational advanced training	Measures for the promotion of all-the-year-round employment in the building industry
1950	1 450	880	585	–	–	20	51	13	–	–	–
1955	1 806	1 406	899	–	–	15	97	34	–	–	–
1960*)	1 584	617	221	–	26	3	9	40	–	–	–
1965	2 046	1 582	391	–	537	1	5	77	–	–	65
1966	2 261	1 557	401	–	425	9	3	83	–	–	72
1967	2 595	3 171	1 642	110	350	207	10	102	50	2	72
1968	2 764	2 987	1 179	172	615	28	18	178	55	4	71
1969	2 999	2 889	674	82	834	4	13	397	46	6	65

*) 9 months

The Federal Government is empowered, according to the financial position of the Federal Institute for Labour, to reduce contributions temporaily. It has frequently made use of these powers; between 1. 8. 1961 and 31. 3. 1962 the payment of contributions was suspended; for the period between 1. 4. 1962 and 31. 12. 1963, contributions were reduced to 1.4 % and from 1. 1. 64 to 1.3 %. Contributions in respect of persons performing compulsory military service are borne by the Federal Government. As a general rule contributions are collected by the Sick Funds together with health and pensions insurance contributions.

The costs of unemployment assistance are borne by the Federal Government. However, no refund will be made to the Federal Institute for Labour in respect of assistance allowances paid to claimants immediately after the exhaustions of Statutory benefit. This regulation will apply up to 31. 12. 1975.

Total disbursements for unemployment assistance reached a record level in 1951 at 1.233 mill DM; they fell in 1966 to 32 mill DM. The main item was cash payments, amounting in 1951 to 1.120 mill DM, in 1966 to 27 mill DM, in 1969 to 33 mill DM.

The Federal Government is under an obligation to make contributions towards the cost of unemployment insurance to the Federal Institute for Labour. This obligation must be met only when the reserves of the Institute have been reduced.

Cash and Investment Assets of the Federal Institute for Labour

Position at the End of 1969 in Mill. DM

Cash holdings and current a/c	51.4
Deposits in banks and savings banks	1.731.6
Treasury bills, interest free exchequer bills and other bills	500.0
Other share holdings and debt book demands	1.443.9
of these	
Debt book demands on the Federal Government	351.8
Loans and interest bearing bills against the Federal Railways and Post	.22.3
Debenture bonds	159.3

Communal Loans.	162.5
Other Share holdings	432.5
Loans	2694.0
to the	
Federal Government	20.0
Railway and Post	500.0
Lands	248.3
Municipalities	5.0
Public Undertakings	13.7
Credit Institutes	1519.8
Other loans	387.0
Building sites and buildings	240.3
Total	6549.9

Any deviations are due to rounding off.

Organisation

Measures arising from the Labour Promotion Law are the responsibility of the Federal Institute for Labour, which is organised in a Head Office, 9 Regional Offices, and 146 Employment Exchanges. In order to cope with general administration, the Central Office for Labour Placing in Frankfort, the Institute for Labour and Occupational Research in Erlangen, and a Central Office for Personnel Administration and Finance in Nürnberg, have been established, Total personnel at the end of 1969 numbered about 32.250.

The Federal Institute for Labour is a self-governing body, (see the Section ,,Self-Administration''); its organs are the Administrative Council and the Executive Committee of the Institute, as well as the administrative committees in the Employment Exchanges and the Regional Offices.

The Federal Institute for Labour has been entrusted with various other responsibilities, including the payment of childrens' allowances, and, in part, those arising from the Severely Injured Persons' Law. (Collection of refunds in cases in which the obligation to work has not been fullfilled). Administrative costs arising from the payment of children's allowances are refunded by the Fed. Government (1969 = 58.5 mill. DM).

Head Office of the Federal Institute for Labour in Nürnberg

RO Baden-Württemberg
  in Stuttgart
RO North Bavaria
  in Nürnberg
RO South Bavaria
  in Munich
RO Berlin
  in Berlin
RO Hesse
  in Frankfort

RO Lower Saxony/Bremen
  in Hannover
RO North-Rhine-Westphalia
  in Düsseldorf
RO Rhineland-Palatinate/Saarland
  in Saarbrücken
RO Schleswig-Holstein/Hamburg
  in Kiel
RO = Regional Office

Legislative bases

Labour Promotion Law of 25. 6. 1969 (BGBl. I S. 582) last amended by the Law of 22. 12. 1969 (BGBl. I S. 2360).

Promotion of Vocational Training

Introduction

Before 1939 only very limited facilities for occupational promotion were available. Assistance for vocational promotion could be obtained only through the medium of unemployment insurance, public assistance, and war pensions and related services. The second world war and its aftermath led to interruptions, delays, and prolongations of the vocational training of juveniles. In order to make good the losses arising, laws providing for the promotion of vocational training were enacted which, in the widest sense, were concerned with the repercussions of the war. These relevant measures are gradually coming to an end. Supplementary to the measures within the framework of the laws dealing with the aftermath of the war, new forms of training assistance have emerged. In the framework of the Federal Children's Allowances Law, training grants were awarded from the end of April 1965 up to the end of June 1967. The promotion of studies in the framework of the Honnef and Rhöndorf models also serves the purpose of fostering industrial training. In addition, further measures have been taken on the basis of Federal Land legislation, and relevant services made available. All this has led to a great number of legal regulations, which have rendered the legal position of the promotion of training extremely complicated and difficult to oversee.

Previous attempts at a reform in this field failed for the reason that Federal Government legislation was not applicable. It was not until 1969 that competence in this field was conceded to the Federal Government.

The promotion of vocational education, in particular of occupational training, was provisionally re-regulated in 1969 under the Law on the Promotion of Labour (cf. "Safeguards against Unemployment"). In the same year the Law on the Promotion of Vocational Training made it possible to establish a uniform Federal system in the field of the promotion of vocational training in the schools. The promotion of university study, as provided in the Honnef and Rhöndorf models is to be revised in subsequent uniform legislative regulations.

Vocational training in apprenticeship and trainee trades was placed on a new basis by the Vocational Training Law of 1969. Apprenticeship and trainee relations are no longer to be relegated to the sphere of social security. Only those grants are provided which are necessary to cover the immediate costs of training and living costs. Such grants will enable juveniles to complete the training for which they have an aptitude, but of which they are themselves unable to bear the costs. In this manner inequalitites of opportunity are being levelled out.

In addition to the grants under the Law on the Promotion of Vocational Training, other grants are awarded under special legislative regulations. Particular groups of persons are entitled under the

Federal Pensions Law
Equalisation of Burdens Law
General legislation dealing with the aftermath of the war
Federal Evacuees Law
Returnees Law
Prisoners' Aid Law
Federal Compensation Law

Further grants are made by the
Federal Institute for Labour
by Social Aid from the Honnef Model
from the Rhöndorf Model
by special Study Foundations
(e.g. the Study Foundation of the German People, the Protestant Study Foundation of the German People, the Protestant Study Scheme Villigst, the Catholic Cusanus Scheme, the Friedrich Ebert Foundation, the Co-Determination Foundation of the DGB, the German Academic Exchange Service, the Foundation Volkswagenwerk, the Victor Gollancz-Foundation).
Training Grants are awarded in general
for attendance in schools of general education
(secondary and higher schools),
for training in an apprenticeship or trainee trade,
for attendance in vocational trade schools and
specialist schools, as well as for university study.

The money for the measures of promotion is provided as a rule from the budgets of the different authorities responsible for the promotion of training. The following table shows details:

Training Grants

Authority	Numbers of Persons in 1000s							Expenditure in Mio DMs						
	1955	1960	1961	1962	1963	1964	1965	1955	1960	1961	1962	1963	1964	1965
War Pensions and related Services	–	13.5	113.1	97.7	101.4	90.1	87,8	58.3	102.8	133,2	153,0	184.7	166.0	163.7
Socail Aid	–	8.9	6.8	5.5	16.0	18.7	21,8	22.3	16.5	20,8	21,4	14,8	19.7	23.7
Equalisation of Burdens	140.7	64.0	20.1	25.4	20.2	14.0	–	96.0	41.0	45,0	41,0	42.0	33.0	25.0
Returnees Law	1.1	0.3	0.2	–	–	–	–	0.9	0.3	0.3	0.3	0.2	0,1	0.1
Federal Institute for Labour	6.9	30.6	44.9	51.5	62.5	66,2	65.4	3.3	12.2	23,4	27.9	36.9	36.2	35.7
Honnef Model	1.5	32.3	32.0	36.0	35.0	41,0	46.0	1,7	45,1	70.1	75.8	72.5	87.7	111.0
Study Foundations	1.2	3.0	3.3	3.4	3.4	3.4	3.4	6.8	3.7	4.8	5.0	5.0	5,5	5.4
Federal Youth Plans	–	15.2	15.8	12,5	8.1	6.9	5.5	–	1,7	2.9	2,9	3,0	3,0	3,0

The latest legislative reform has not affected the promotion of training for certain categories of persons in receipt of benefits and services in compensation for losses suffered as a result of the war and its aftermath, (the promotion of categories), since it may safely be assumed that the numbers of such persons are continuously decreasing. This does not apply in the case of regulations under the Federal Pensions Law. It was, however, not considered appropriate to incorporate this special regulation in the Law on the Promotion of Vocational Training, since benefits under the Federal Pensions Law are, as a rule, higher than those under the Vocational Training Law. In 1969 some 80.000 educational and training grants were being paid under War Pensions and Related Services.

The Law on the Promotion of Vocational Training came into force on 1. 7. 1970. The following paragraphs give details on the Law on the Promotion of Vocational Training, its scope and benefits.

Scope

The following categories receive training grants:
Pupils in Secondary Schools from Class 11 onwards, and of Higher Technical Schools,

Pupils in Vocational Further Training Schools, Evening Schools, Evening Secondary Schools and Colleges,
Pupils in Vocational Technical Schools, in so far as a final examination in a Secondary School, or comparable qualifications, are a condition of entrance,
Pupils in Technical Colleges,
Works Students required to undergo practical training as a condition of attendance at any of the above educational institutes.

In the case of secondary school pupils from class 11 onwards there are presently some 275.000, in the case of Higher Technical Schools some 50.000 persons. Pupils in Vocational Further Training Schools number about 12.000, with approximately the same numbers in evening schools, evening secondary schools und colleges. 70.000 pupils of the above mentioned types are in attendance in vocational technical colleges. In other technical colleges there are about 90.000 pupils. Of this total of 509.000 persons, probably about one half will be able to receive financial assistance on the basis of the Vocational Training Promotion Law. The families of the remaining pupils are in receipt of incomes which, in the view of the legislator, are sufficiently high to enable them to meet the costs of their children's training and education.

Benefits

There is a legal entitlement to promotion of training conforming to inclination, aptitude, and performance, if the applicant himself is not in a position to finance it. Training is approved in principle only in the Federal Republic of Germany; under certain circumstances grants may be made for training abroad.

Conditions

Personal qualifications required are German nationality, aptitude, and age. Exceptions to the limitation to German nationality are possible on the basis of international agreements and supra-national legal regulations. Exceptional talent is not called for. Grants are awarded if the performance of the trainee justifies the belief that he can successfully complete his training. This is assumed so long as the trainee regularly attends the place of training, or continues as a works student. Grants are not made if the trainee has reached the age of 30 at the beginning of the final phase of his training. Exceptions are made in the case of trainees who have acquired the necessary educational qualifications in a vocational further training school, an evening school, an evening secondary school or college (the second educational track), or if special circumstances justify such exception.

Grants are made in so far as the trainee himself, the spouse, or the parents cannot reasonably be expected, on the basis of their assets and income, to meet the costs of maintenance and training (the so-called 'family dependent furtherance').

The following monthly income limits apply to parents and spouses:

for the parents themselves	700 DM
for a single parent and the spouse of the trainee	500 DM
for every child undergoing training pursuant to this Law, or some corresponding regulations	50 DM
for unprovided children under 15	160 DM
for unprovided children over 15 and others entitled to maintenance	240 DM.

Income of the parents or spouse of the trainee in excess of these limits is disregarded as to 25 %. The percentage is increased by 5 % for every unprovided child. In addition there is a hardship clause.

In the case of attendance in evening secondary schools and colleges, the income of the parents is not to be taken into account at all (the 'family independent furtherance'), but only that of the trainee himself or of the spouse.

If the trainee has an income of his own, an amount of 50 DM per month is disregarded in the case of pupils in schools of general education, higher technical schools and occupational technical schools, in other cases 100 DM per month. If the trainee is married, 300 DM in respect of the spouse, and 150 DM for each child is not taken into account.

Amounts

In the framework of the Promotion of Training, rates are fixed according to need, payable as a lump sum to cover costs of living and costs of training.
Lump sum rates are as follows:
for pupils in continuation schools of general education, higher technical schools and occupational technical schools, 150 DM per month;
for pupils in technical colleges and in the training institutes of the 'second educational track', 300 DM per month.

The above rates are payable if the pupil is living with his family. If he has to be accommodated elsewhere the rate is 320 DM per month in the case of pupils in secondary schools, higher technical schools, and occupational technical schools, or 350 DM in the case of specialist schools, schools of further vocational training, evening institutes evening secondary schools and colleges. When accommodated in a boarding establishment the actual costs are payable up to an amount of 320 DM or 350 DM per month, plus 20 DM pocket money per month; Accommodation in a boarding or similar establishment must, however, be essential for the purposes of the course.

Necessary costs of travelling to the nearest training establishment are refunded in the case of pupils living with their families, less a reasonable personal contribution.

In order to cover extraordinary expenditure arising directly from training, in particular above-average training and boarding establishment charges, grants in excess of the above amounts may be made if necessary to avoid hardship.

Procedure

The Law is implemented by the Federal Lands. In every urban and rural governmental district there is an Office for the Promotion of Vocational Training.

The Federal Minister for Youth, Family and Health will have the assistance of an Advisory Council which will make proposals for the implementation of the Law, in particular for the progressive development of the system of vocational training promotion, having due regard to new forms of training, e.g., correspondence courses.

This Council will also make proposals on the adjustment of allowance rates, if this should be nexessary to keep them in line with rising incomes and changes in the costs of living. The Federal Government, for its part, has a duty to revise rates every two years, and, if necessary, to propose amendments to the Law.

A new provision is an obligation on the part of the Office for Vocational Training to make advance payments. If the trainee is able to prove that his parents are not providing the amount for his maintenance provided for in the Law, and if his continued training is thereby endangered, allowances will be paid, after the parents have been questioned, without such amount being taken into account.

On the other hand, the Office can transfer in writing the claim for maintenance which the child has in common law against its parents to the Federal Authority, and can take proceedings against them in the courts on behalf on the Federal authorities. By means of the obligation on the part of Training Promotion to make advance payments a better guarantee than hitherto is provided that disputes between parents and children do not endanger the training.

Finance

The costs of vocational training are borne by the Federal Government, costs of administration are borne by the Lands.

In view of the projected allowances and upper income limits, the implementation of the Law will cost about 400 mill. DM per year in 1970 and 1971. Financial provision has been made in the long term Federal budgeting. Since an increasing number of pupils must be anticipated in the coming years, Federal budgeting has provided for expenditure of 500 mill. DM annually from 1972 onwards.

Legislative bases

Vocational Training Promotion Law of 19.9.1969 (BGB.I. S. 1719).

War Pensions and Related Services

Introduction

Provision for war injured and their widows and orphans in the form of cash payments became legally guaranteed only after, following the introduction of universal conscription, wars became struggles between whole nations, and the numbers affected increased enormously. In the Franco-German war of 1870/71, German losses were 49.000 dead, of a total loss of about 200.000. In the first world war (1914/18) German losses were 1,9 mill., of a total of almost 10 million dead; 4,2 mill. Germans were wounded. In the second world war 4 mill. German soldiers died, and 2,8 million civilians died as a result of bombing, political persecution, or in the course of flight or expulsion.

During the course of the first world war preparations already began for social provision for war victims, which assumed legal form in the Reichs Pension Law of 12.5.1920, a law which remained in force until 1945. Following divergent laws enacted In the Lands, the Federal Pensions Law of 1.10.1950 again established uniform legislation for the whole Federal territory. In the subsequent years a whole series of laws introduced improvements. The amending Law of 1960 inaugurated compensation for reduced standard of employment, and severely injured persons' supplements for unemployables, and so made possible far-reaching consideration for individual occupational and financial losses, and for serious damage to health. The subsequent amending laws brought even further improvements, in particular the 2nd Amending Law the extension of compensation for occupational losses for all severely injured persons, and the introduction of compensation for losses for all widows; the 3rd Amending Law the adjustment of pension rates.

Pursuant to the First Adjustment Law 1970 the pensions of pensioners, orphans, and parents were increased by 16 % w.e.f. 1.1.1970, those of widows by 25,3 %. The Second Adjustment Law of the summer of 1970 will increase cash payments by an average of 5,5 %.

In the case of serving soldiers of the Federal Army, conscientious objectors performing alternative civilian duties, of the former German army, of the former German Protection Police, members of the Civilian Defence Corps, political prisoners from East Germany, and their survivors, as well as of dependents of prisoners of war, special laws under the Federal Pensions Law, are applied mutatis mutandis. In this manner provision for soldiers of the Federal Army is linked to that of soldiers of the first and second world wars.

Function of War Pensions and Related Services

The function of War Pensions and Related Services is to provide compensation in respect of injuries sustained, by means of curative treatment, special gymnastics, medical treatment, help from War Victims Welfare, and cash payments. In the case of survivors, the object is to mitigate as far as possible the financial consequences arising from the death of the breadwinner.

Scope

Germans are entitled to pensions and related services if their home or customary place of residence is in the Federal territory, or in the German Eastern territories at present under alien administration, or abroad. War victims of other nationalities are entitled if their home or customary place of residence is in the Federal territory, and if the injury is in causal connection with service in the framework of the German Armed Forces, or with military service for a German organisation, or if the injury has occurred in Germany, or in territories occupied by the German Armed Forces, directly as a result of war action. These persons may receive benefits abroad with special sanction. Supplementary regulations may be issued.

War victims who have a claim to provision from some other State on the same grounds receive no benefits under the Federal Pensions Law, unless otherwise specifically provided under bi-lateral agreements.

The number of entitled persons rose from 4,1 mill.(1950) to 4,4 mill(1952), since when it has continuously declined. In 1969 the number was 2,6 mill., i.e. 64,5 % of the 1950 number; the main reasons was the decrease in the number of orphans' pensions from 1,4 mill. in 1950 to 55.000 in 1969.

In addition to persons entitled under the Federal Pensions Law, there were in 1968 a total of about 12.500 persons who had a claim to benefit under that law for the reason that other laws had declared the Federal Pensions Law to be applicable in their cases. Benefits were payable in 1968 to 5.412 persons (3.212 injured persons, 1.848 widows, 305 orphans, and 46 parents) on the basis of the Prisoners Aid Law, and to 6.177 persons (4.685 injured persons, 514 widows, 858 orphans, 10 parents) on the basis of the Soldiers Pension Law. The remaining persons are conscientious objectors injured in the course of alternative civilian service (7) dependants of prisoners of war (a total of 300), and reparations cases abroad (a total of 582).

Claims to Pensions

Injury to health, or death, entitling to pension and related services, must be a direct result of war action, imprisonment as a prisoner of war, internment abroad, or internment in the German eastern territories not under German administration on the grounds of German nationality or membership of an ethnic German group. The injuries may also be the result of an accident sustained by the injured person on the way to or from curative treatment arising out of the injuries, to or from spa treatment, special group gymnastics, or measures to promote working and occupational ability, or when summoned for examination as to condition, or in the course of any such actions, or as a result of military or similar service; or with a general deterioration of health due to penal or compulsory measures, if these have taken place under circumstances which can be regarded as a flagrant injustice.

The probability of a causal connection as a consequence of injuries sustained suffices for acknowledgment of the deterioration of health. If such probability is not acknowledged for the reason that there is medical uncertainty as to the cause, a pension may still be awarded in the same way as on the grounds of injury. Deliberately self-inflicted injuries do not give rise to a claim. If hardships result as a consequence of the strict application of current regulations, hardship grants can be paid.

Injuries and losses recognised as a direct result of the war are those which are in connection with one of the two world wars, with hostilities, the effects of weapons of war of all kinds, military or civil authority measures arising out of hostilities, flight from immediately threatening danger to life and limb arising out of war action, also occurrences resulting in injuries arising from the military occupation of German territory, or of former German territory, of from compulsory resettlement or deportation; post war injuries arising from the war, which have brought similar dangers in their wake, caused in connection with both world wars by members of the armies of occupation. Not recognised for this purpose as direct consequences of the wars are the conditions to which all sectors of the population were exposed for protracted periods. This includes the black out, shortage of food and medicines, unsatisfactory accommodation, and the resultant dangers of infection.

Military service is every form of service pursuant to German Military Law, i.e. voluntary or compulsory service as a soldier, as a civilian official attached to the Armed Forces, or leader of a special unit, in the Volkssturm, in the military police, and in anti-aircraft batteries on the home front. In the case of German expellees, service in the Armed Forces of the country or origin pursuant to the regulations there valid rendered prior to 9.5.1945 ranks equally with service in the German Armed Forces. In the case of German nationals, service in the Armed Forces of one of the States allied to the German Reich during one of the world wars, or in the Czecholosovakian or Austrian Armed Forces, counts as service in German Armed Forces, if the claimant had his home or permanent residence within the borders of the German Reich as at 31.12.1937.

Recognised as service of a military nature in the widest sense is every form of service rendered by civilians for the fighting troops, e.g. the Labour Service, the services of female auxiliaries; the voluntary nursing services attached to the Armed Forces during the war, as well as service under the Emergency Services Regulations, in pre-military training camps, and in anti-aircraft units during the war.

Scope of Pensions and Related Services

Pensions and Related Services include: curative treatment, special gymnastics for injured persons, medical treatment, war victims welfare, pensions, constant attendance allowance, burial money on the death of the injured person, death benefit, survivors' pensions, burial money on the death of a survivor.

Curative Treatment and Gymnastics for the Disabled

Curative treatment and measures disgned to restore health and to ensure occupational re-integration occupy the foremost place in the framework of the services. The beneficiary is entitled, for the purpose of regaining and retraining his physical strength, to take part in gymnastics for the disabled; to this end Disabled Persons' Sports Clubs may be established.

Curative treatment

Curative treatment for injured persons is approved in respect of physical disorders consequent on an injury, or of the acknowledged effects of an injury, in order to overcome or improve the reduced standard of employment, or the unemployability, occasioned by the injury, and in order to avert a deterioration of the condition, or to relieve physical complaints.

Curative treatment may also be approved in the case of seriously injured persons, even though their physical disorder is not the result of the injury, or of the recognised consequences of the injury, unless they are entitled to other statutory provision. Under certain conditions, curative treatment for the whole extent of the physical disorder may be approved, even though only the deterioration of the condition is acknowledged as an outcome of the injury.

Curative treatment includes medical and dental treatment, hospitalisation, sanatorium treatment, home nursing, the provision of medicines, dressings, and other necessary articles, the provision of dentures and orthopaedic aids.

The nature and extent of curative treatment co-incide largely with that provided by Social Health Insurance for its members. The injured person here has a free choice of doctors; in certain cases he can claim second class accommodation in a hospital. The number of spa cures approved averages 63.000 annually. Curative treatment is carried out on behalf of the War Pensions and Related Services by the National Health Funds; the costs are met as to a certain amount.

Constant improvements in line with the general progress of medicine are being effected in medical treatment, whether as in patient, out-patient, or sanatorium treatment, as well as in the supply of medicines, dressings, and other medical requirements. These include a number of special institutes for paraplegics and for kidney and liver complaints.

Therapeutic gymnastics are also a part of the benefits provided, since such exercises are a suitable means of strengthening the will to recovery and the willingness to work on the part of the sufferers. There are some 1.100 Injured Persons Sports Groups in existence, with 58.000 members. In 1968 more than 36.000 took part in the exercises.

Orthopaedic Treatment

In order to mitigate the effects of the injury, artificial limbs and other orthopaedic aids are supplied. Blind persons are supplied on request with a guide dog, for whose upkeep a sum of DM 70 per month is payable, from 1.1.1971 DM 74. If no guide dog is kept, the blind persons may receive the same amount for the services of a human guide.

If the effects of the injury occasion exceptional expenditure for clothing, and wear and tear of underclothing, a lump sum of between 9 and 58 DM monthly is payable (from 1.1.1971 between 9 and 61 DM). Higher amounts are possible.

Orthopaedic appliances were supplied in 1950 for 619.000 injured persons, in 1968 the number was 450.000, including 5.770 blind persons, 18 with fourfold amputations, 37.000 with one arm amputated, and 115.000 with one leg amputated. Expenditure for orthopaedic care increased from 43 mill. DM (1950) to 106 mill. DM (1968).

Compensation for loss of income

The injured person has a claim to compensation for loss of income if, on account of a physical disorder which is acknowledged to the be effect of his injury, or of a recognised consequence of such injury, he is incapable of employment in the meaning of social health insurance regulations, is an inpatient in hospital, or if a period of convalescence has been sanctioned. Compensation is payable so long as the conditions are satisfied; this is no longer the case if the unfitness for work develops into a condition which, in all probability, cannot be corrected in the next 78 weeks (permanent condition), or when an unemployability pension or a retirement pension has been awarded under social pensions insurance. Compensation amounts to 100 % for the first six weeks and 90 % from the seventh week onwards, of the net income of which the beneficiary had been in receipt. In the case of hospital in-patients 65 % of the net income is payable. The amount increases in respect of dependants by 10 % per person (living in the household), for others by 5 % to a maximum of 90 %.

If the necessary treatment of the effects of an injury result in a considerable loss to the means of livelihood, an allowance to a maximum of 70 DM per diem may be paid.

War Victims' Welfare

War Victims' Welfare makes itself responsible for war injured persons and their survivors, and helps to overcome or to mitigate the effects of the injury, or the loss of the bread-winner, to the best of its ability, and in accordance with the circumstances of the particular case. Its efforts are directed to enabling the beneficiaries to gain and retain a reasonable status in life; they consist of personal help, and of payments in cash and in kind.

Injured persons are given every form of assistance designed to maintain, restore, or improve their occupational efficiency, and to enable them to hold their own at their place of work in competition with uninjured persons; in particular, vocational advanced training, retraining, training, education, placing in suitable employment and security of that employment, and loans for the establishment and security of an independent livelihood. This type of assistance is also available for widows.

Educational grants are awarded to the injured person for his children, to orphans, to ensure their physical, mental and moral development, as well as suitable vocational training.

Injured persons and their survivors are also entitled to convalescent tratment and assistance in the matter of living accommodation. Special care and treatment is devoted to persons exceptionally hard hit as a consequence of their injury — blind persons, persons without hands, paraplegics, brain injured persons, persons in receipt of constant attendance allowances, and other injured persons, if, as a consequence of tuberculosis or facial disfigurement their earning capacity is reduced by at least 50 %.

In 1969 expenditure on War Victims' Welfare amounted to 465 mill. DM. Educational grants were made in respect of 75.000 children and orphans, at a cost of 175 mill. DM.

Medical Treatment for Dependants

Severely injured persons are entitled to medical treatment for their dependants, recipients of constant attendance allowance for their attendants. A condition is that the dependants are not entitled to treatment from some other statutory source, that they are resident in the household of the injured person, and that they are wholly or mainly maintained by him.

Types of Pension

Of particular importance to war victims is the provision made for them in the form of regular cash payments.

The *Basic Pensions* payable to injured persons, widows, and orphans, without regard to their financial position, primarily serve the purpose of compensating for the imponderable additional expense and burdens occasioned by the physical disability, the loss of the husband, or of at least one parent. In the case of widows and orphans, these pensions have also, to a certain extent, the function of a substitute maintenance allowance.

The *Most Severely Injured Supplement,* to which persons with exceptional impairment to health are entitled, complements the basic pension in practice.

The *Adjustment Pension* is designed to secure the livelihood of severely injured persons, their widows and orphans — if they satisfy certain conditions. In accordance with the purpose of this allowance the amount payable is dependent on the income available.

The *Husband or Wife, and Children's Supplements* again complement in practice the adjustments pensions in respect of the family status.

Business Losses Pensions for injured persons and their widows are payments intended to compensate for financial loss sustained in causal connection with the injury or with death, in so far as these are not compensated in the case of the injured person by payment of the Basic Pension, and in the case of widows by the payment of the Basic and the Adjustment Pension.

Partens' Pensions serve, in consideration of the loss of support consequent on the death of the cildren, to secure the livelihood of the parents. Payment and amount again depend on available income.

Constant Attendance Allowance is intended to meet the expenses arising from the helplessness of the injured person.

The type and amount of the pension payable to an injured person is assessed on the basis of his reduced earning powers. This is adjudged in accordance with the degree of physical impairment in the general world of labour; mental side effects and suffering are also taken into consideration. The same conditions are applicable to injured juveniles. The reduction of earning powers is rated higher if the injured person, due to the nature of the effects of his injury, and before the occurence of the injury, had suffered particular loss in respect of the occupation he was exercising, had commenced, or at which he can prove he was aiming, unless labour and occupational promotion measures which he can reasonably be expected to undertake offer a suitable alternative. For substantial external physical injuries fixed percentages are payable, e.g. loss of an eye 30 %, complete deafness 70 %, loss of an arm or an leg 70 to 80 %.

Basic Pensions for Injured Persons

An injured person has a claim to a Basic Pension so long as his earning powers are reduced by 25 % or more as a result of the injury. Unemployabilitiy is assumend if reduced earnings are rated at more than 90 %; this is always so in the case of blind persons.

Amount of Basic Pensions
in DM per month

ab	Reduced Earnings Powers in %							
	30	40	50	60	70	80	90	100
1.10.50	15	20	25	35	45	55	65	75
1. 1.55	18	24	31	43	56	69	83	97
1. 4.56	25	33	40	50	67	85	100	120
1. 5.57	30	38	48	60	80	100	120	140
1. 6.60	35	45	65	80	105	150	180	200
1. 1.64	45	60	80	105	140	170	210	240
1. 1.67	53	70	95	120	165	200	240	270
1. 1.70	61	81	110	139	191	232	278	313
1. 1.71	64	85	116	147	202	245	293	330

Cash Benefits for Severely Injured Persons

Severely injured persons receive cash allowances in addition to the Basic Pension. Nearly half of all recipients of Basic Pensions are severely injured persons, that is to say, their earning powers are reduced by 50 % and more. At the age of 65 the Basic Pension is increased by 12 DM per month, w.e.f. 1.1.1971, by 13 DM since, it is assumed that the effects of the injury are more difficult to bear in old age. In 1970 about 102.000 such supplements are payable.

Severely Injured Persons' Supplements are payable in cases of unemployability if compensation is to be paid in respect of particularly serious damage to health; allocation to the seperate grades of this supplement takes place in accordance with a points system laid down in a legal regulation. A claim arises when the assessment reaches at least 130 points, or a claim to constant attendance allowance at least in grade III is allowable.

Recipients of Pensions
1000s at the End of the Year

Year	Reduced Earning Powers in %								Total
	30	40	50	60	70	80	90	100	
1950	568	216	359	85	190	54	7	66	1 546
1955	577	230	300	89	157	65	10	74	1 503
1960	542	218	279	88	141	69	13	69	1 419
1965	507	205	260	87	124	71	18	66	1 337
1968	482	192	228	87	108	70	26	64	1 257
1969	472	190	223	87	105	70	26	64	1 237

Severely Injured Persons Supplement
in DM per month

from	Grade I	II	III	IV	V	VI
1.6.60	20	40	60	–	–	–
1.1.64	20	40	60	80	100	–
1.1.67	30	60	90	120	150	–
1.1.70	37	74	111	148	185	222
1.1.71	39	78	117	156	195	234

Adjustment Pensions

Adjustment Pensions are intended as a compensation to severely injured persons, who, because of their state of health, their age (man: 65, Woman: 50), or for some other reason for which they are not personally responsible, are unable to follow an occupation they could otherwise reasonably be expected to follow, or could do so only to a limited extent, or only at the expense of above average strain. Corresponding to the purpose of this pension, its amount is dependent on available income. The pension is reduced by the amount of the income taken into account, and ceases to be payable when, after deduction of the exempted amounts, available income reaches at least the same amount as the full pension. Recipients of constant attendance allowance of at least Grade III receive the full Adjustment Pension, the remainder at least one half thereof. Severely injured persons under 18 receive an Adjustment Pension to a maximum of one half.

Full Amount of Adjustments Pensions for Injured Persons
in DM per month

from	Reduced earning capacity in percentage. 50	60	70	80	90	100
1.10.50	40	40	50	60	75	90
1. 8.53	48	48	60	72	90	108
1. 1.55	52	55	65	78	98	120
1. 4.56	70	75	95	115	135	160
1. 6.60	100	100	120	150	180	200
1. 1.64	110	110	140	170	210	240
1. 1.67	120	120	165	200	240	270
1. 1.70	139	139	191	232	278	313
1. 1.71	147	147	202	245	293	330

The full Adjustment Pension is reduced by the amount of income taken into account. A distinction is made between income from current employment and other sources of income. The first type is income from employment, agriculture and forestry, trade, self-employment, sick pay, household allowances, transitional payments, income balance payments, unemployment benefit, compensation for loss of earnings, inclement weather pay, and similar payments. The income limit at which an unemployable injured person ceases to have a claim to Adjustment Pension is fixed in the case of current employment at one twelfth of the General Basis of Computation in Manual Workers' Insurance (1970 = 859 DM) per month), and in the case of other sources of income at one twentieth (1970 = 520 DM per month). To a certain extent income is not taken into account. This exempt amount is also assessed on the basis of the General Basis of Computation. In the case of income from current employment it amounts to 1.5 % (1970 = 155 DM per month), in the case of other sources of employment o.65 % of the General Basis of Computation (1970 = 67 DM per month).

It will be seen that the exempt amount and the income limit change in line with the changes in the General Basis of Computation in Manual Workers' Insurance. By virtue of this arrangement, war victims benefit from the annual re-adjustment of pensions in the social pensions insurance scheme without the need for special legislation, and the administration is spared the tremendous task of re-assessment. Details are laid down in a legal regulation.

Husband and Wife Supplement

Married severely injured persons have a claim to a supplement for husband or wife additional to the claim to Adjustment Pension; this claim takes account of the family status. The full amount is 35 DM per month, from 1. 1. 1971, 37 DM, and is dependent on other income, Recipients of constant attendance allowance always receive the full amount.

Children's Allowances

Children's allowances are payable in respect of every child of a severely injured person, to the amount of 50 DM per month. Whereas recipients of constant attendance allowances receive children's allowances to the full amount, in other cases equal or similar allowances payable from other sources are taken into account, as is, to a certain extent, the income of the injured person. At the end of 1969, 57.690 severely injured persons were in receipt of children's allowances.

Children within this meaning are: legitimate children, children declared legitimate, adopted children, step children resident in the household of the injured person, foster children if the relation existed before acknowledgement of the effects of the injury, and illegitimate children, though those of male persons only if paternity has been legally established, or if a maintenance allowance is payable.

Children's Allowances
in DM per month

from	1st and 2nd child	3rd and further children
1.10.50	10	15*)
1. 8.53	20	20
1. 1.55	20	25
1. 5.57	25	30
1. 3.59	25	40
1. 1.64	40	40
1. 7.64	50	50

*) This amount was payable in respect of all children in the case of reduced employability of 70 % and above.

Allowances are payable up to the 18th year, and further, at the latest, to the 27th year, in the case of children in full time education or vocational training, or those performing a voluntary social year. Allowances are also payable in respect of children who on reaching the age of 21 are by reason of physical or mental infirmity incapable of earning their own livelihood; they continue to be payable as long as the condition persists. In the event of an interruption or delay of vocational or educational training arising from compulsory military service, the allowance is payable beyond the 27th year for the period of such service. This also applies in the case of voluntary service, if the period is reckonable against the period of compulsory service in the Armed Forces, on active police duties, or as a development country helper — to a maximum of three years. It also applies in cases in which educational or vocational training have been delayed for reasons for which neither the pensioner nor the child is responsible, for the duration of such delay.

Compensation for Loss of Earning Capacity

A severely injured person whose earning capacity in his trade or occupation has been reduced by reason of his injury receives compensation to the amount of four tenths of the loss sustained, to a maximum of 580 DM monthly, from 1. 1. 1971 612 DM. The basis of computation for such compensation is the loss assessed in each individual case. A comparison is made of actual income and the income of which the injured person would probably be in receipt if the injury had not been sustained. The yardstick applied is the actual average earnings and the incomes obtained in the comparable salary and income groups in the public services. The procedure is governed by legal regulations.

It is anticipated that about 115.000 severely injured persons (about 21 % of the total) will receive this form of compensation in 1970.

Constant Attendance Allowance

For so long as the injured person, as a consequence of his injury, is so helpless that he requires constant attendance for his regularly recurring everyday needs, a constant attendance allowance at the rate of Grade I is payable.

If the condition is so serious that the pensioner is permanently confined to bed, or requires exceptional nursing service, the allowance may be raised according to the expenditure arising in the particular case, to the rates under Grades II. III. IV or V. Blind Persons receive an allowance at least under Grade III, unemployable brain injured persons at least under Grade I. In any case in which expenditure for outside help exceeds the allowance, a reasonable increase may be sanctioned. Recipients of a constant attendance allowance at least under Grade III continue to receive the allowance even when undergoing hospital, sanatorium or spa treatment, lasting more than one month, in all other cases payment is suspended. In the case of necessary hospital treatment the pension payments are reckoned against the costs arising; the pensioner continues to receive 58 DM per month, and his dependants an amount at least equal to the survivors' pension to which they would be entitled if the injured person had died as a result of his injuries. In 1968 constant attendance allowance was payable to more than 39.000 seriously injured persons.

Amount of Constant Attendance Allowance
in DM per month

from	Grade I	II	III	IV	V
1.10.50	50	75	100	125	150
1. 8.53	60	90	125	150	175
1. 1.55	60	90	125	150	200
1. 4.56	75	110	150	175	225
1. 5.57	75	110	150	175	275
1. 6.60	100	150	200	240	350
1. 1.64	100	170	240	310	400
1. 1.67	115	195	275	355	460
1. 1.70	133	226	319	412	534
1. 1.71	140	238	337	435	563

Cash Benefits to Survivors

Widows receive uniform allowances. In the case of orphans a distinction is made between half and full orphans. Parents do not receive a basic pension, but an amount based on Adjustment Pension rates.

Burial Allowance

On the death of a pensionable injured person, if death is a result of his injury, a burial allowance of 750 DM is payable, in other cases 375 DM. Death is accepted as a consequence of his injuries and in respect of which the pension was payable. A burial allowance up to 750 DM is also payable in the case of a non-pensioners dying as a result of injuries. Any allowance payable on the basis of some other statutory provision is taken into account.

Burial Allowance
in DM

| from | Injured persons | | Survivors | |
	Death is result of the injury	is not a	widow with child	other cases
1.10.50	240	120	240	120
1. 4.56	300	150	300	150
1. 6.60	500	bis 250	500	250
1. 1.64	750	bis 375	750	375

If an injured person dies in the course of hospital treatment, or as a result of his injuries, away from his permanent place of residence, the costs of transport to the former residence are refunded. If death occurs abroad, a contribution to costs only is payable.

On the death of a pensionable survivor, an allowance of 750 DM is payable in the case of a widow with at least one pensionable child surviving, otherwise 375 DM.

Death Benefits

The survivors of a deceased pensioner receive death benefits to the amount of three times the pension payable in the month of his death, plus constant attendance allowance, however at the maximum in Grade II. This benefit is payable in addition to survivors' pensions.

Widows' pensions

If the pensioner has died from his injuries, or from the effects of his injuries, the widow or widower has a claim to a widows' (widower's) pension. Death is in all cases regarded as a consequence of the injuries if the pensioner dies of an ailment recognised as a pensionable ailment, and in respect of which the pension was paid. A pension is payable to a widower if his deceased wife who has died as a result of her injuries had wholly or mainly maintained him, or if he was incapable of work, or if his income was inadequate.

The widow and the widower have no claim to pension if the marriage took place only after the occurrence of the injury, and had not lasted at least one year, and if the marriage took place only for the purpose of becoming entitled to a pension.

Every widow receives a basic pension of 188 DM per month. Adjustment Pension to a maximum 188 DM is payable in the case of widows, who as a result of illness or other

Amounts of Basic and Full Adjustment Pensions for Widows
in DM per month

from	Basic Pension	Adjustment Pension
1.10.50	40	30 oder 50
1. 8.53	20 oder 40	60
1. 1.55	24 oder 48	70
1. 4.56	30 oder 55	95
1. 5.57	70	95
1. 6.60	100	100/150
1. 1.64	120	120
1. 1.67	150	150
1. 1.70	188	188
1. 1.71	198	198

ailment has lost, not merely temporarily, at least one half of her earning capacity, or is 45 of age and has the care of at least one pensionable child. This is also the case if the child had been in receipt of an orphans pension until reaching the age limit, or until marriage.

A widow with three or more children in receipt of orphan's pensions or allowances, receives for the third and every further child an allowance of 50 DM per month. Other equal or similar amounts payable in respect of the child are taken into account.

Compensation for Occupational Losses in the Case of Widows' Pensions

Under certain conditions the widow receives a Compensation for Loss if her income is less than half the income of which her husband would have been in receipt if he had not suffered the injury. The Compensation for Loss corresponds to the Compensation for Business Losses for the pensioner; it amounts to four tenths of the differential amount between one half of the standard average income and the gross income of the widow, to a maximum amount of 290 DM per month (w.e.f. 1.1.1971 - 360 DM per month). In addition, the widows of pensioners who at the time of their death had a claim to an Unemployability Pension and a constant attendance allowance in Grade III receive particularly favourable treatment in respect of reckonable average income. The compensation for loss in the case of these widows is calculated on the basis of a minimum income corresponding to the end salary of a Chief Executive Officer (Oberregierungsrat), plus provincial differentiation in Grade II of District A under the Federal Civil Servants Salary Law (Bundesbesoldungsgesetz).

Recipients of Survivors Pensions
in 1000s at the End of the Year

Year	Widows	Half Orphans	Full Orphans	Single Parents	Married Parents	Total
1950	935	1 319	36	126	97	2 513
1955	1 169	1 083	48	194	146	2 640
1960	1 164	395	22	159	94	1 834
1965	1 157	91	7	145	69	1 469
1968	1 134	57	6	145	61	1 403
1969	1 128	49	5	144	57	1 383

Pension to a former wife

In the case of the divorce, dissolution, or annulment of a marriage, the former wife is in the same position as the widow if the deceased, at the time of his death, was under an obligation to pay a maintenance allowance, or, in the year preceding his death, had paid such allowance. If the marriage had been divorced, dissolved, or annulled because of the mental illness of the deceased, the former wife receives a pension without regard to these conditions if the illness had been in causal connection with the injury, and the pensioner had died as a result of the injury.

Re-Marriage Settlement - Restitution of Pension

In the event of re-marriage the widow receives a settlement in lieu of pension to the amount of 9.400 DM, i.e. fifty times the amount of the Basic Pension. This applies even in the case that at the time of the re-marriage there was no claim to a pension for the reason that no application had been made.

If the new marriage is dissolved or annulled, the widow not being pronounced the guilty party, or the party mainly guilty, the claim for a widow's pension is revived. This applies if the widow, prior to her re-marriage, had not been in receipt of a pension, although her former husband had died from the effects of his injuries. If the marriage has been dissolved or annulled within 50 months of the re-marriage, the amount of the settlement paid is taken into account as to one fiftieth of the sum for each month of the period.

Settlement in the Case of Re-Marriage

from	DM
1.10.50	1 200
1. 4.56	1 980
1. 5.57	2 520
1. 6.60	5 000
1. 1.64	6 000
1. 1.67	7 500
1. 1.70	9 400
1. 1.71	9 900

Orphans' Pension

If the death results from injuries, or the effects of injuries, the orphans' receive orphans' pension. Orphans in this meaning are: legitimate children, step children resident in the household of the deceased, foster children whom the deceased had maintanined without remuneration at the time of his death at least for a period preceding his injury, or the official recognition of the effects of his injury, or for at least a year, illegitimate children, though those of male pensioners only if paternity has been credibly established.

The number of orphans' pensions has decreased to one twentieth during the last twenty years, since the orphans have gradually passed the age limit with the passing years since the war.

Amount of Basic and Full Adjustment Pension for Orphans
in DM per month

from	Basic Pension Half Orphan	Full Orphan	Adjustment Pension Half Orphan	Full Orphan
1.10.50	10	15	21	45
1. 8.53	10	15	26	50
1. 1.55	12	18	36	60
1. 4.56	15	25	50	75
1. 5.57	20	30	50	75
1. 6.60	30	60	60	90
1. 1.64	35	70	70	100
1. 1.67	45	85	80	110
1. 1.70	52	99	93	128
1. 1.71	55	104	98	135

Orphans' Pensions are payable up to the age of 18, or to the date of marriage. Pensions are payable up to the age of 27 to an unmarried orphan in full time education or vocational training, or during a voluntary service; the pension continues to be payable beyond the 27th year for a period corresponding to the period of service. If there is a claim to more than one pension pursuant to the Federal Pensions Law, or pursuant to any laws which declare the Pensions Law to be applicable, only one pension is payable.

The Basic Pension for a half orphan is 52 DM per month, for a full orphan 99 DM, the full Adjustment Pension 93 DM for a half orphan, and 128 DM for a full orphan. The full Adjustment Pension is decreased by the amount of reckonable income. These regulations apply to injured persons mutatis mutandis.

Parents' Pensions

If death results from an injury, or the effects of an injury, the parens may receive a Parents' Pension. Natural parents are treated in the same way as adopted parents, if they had adopted the deceased, step parents and foster parents if they had maintained the deceased without remuneration, grand parents if the deceased had contributed to their support, or might have done so. Further conditions are: unemployability within the meaning of Manual Workers' Pension Insurance, and that the mother has reached the age of 50, or the father the age of 65. The full Parents' Pension amounts in the case of one surviving parent to 157 DM per month, two surviving parents to 232 DM per month. The regulations for injured persons are applicable for the reckonability of income, though the exempt amount is reckoned at the rate of 0,65 %.

Amount of Full Parents Pension

from	One Parents	Two Parents
1.10.50	50	70
1. 8.53	60	84
1. 1.55	70	100
1. 4.56	75	110
1. 5.57	90	130
1. 6.60	100	150
1. 1.64	115	170
1. 1.67	135	200
1. 1.70	157	232
1. 1.71	166	245

If several children have died from the effects of injuries, the Parent's Pension is increased in respect of each child by 35 DM per month in the case of one surviving parent, and by 46 DM per month where there are two surviving parents. If the child was the only child, or the last surviving child, or if all, or at least three children have died from the effects of their injuries, the Parents' Pension is increased by 104 DM in respect of one parent, and by 145 DM in respect of two parents.

Allowances

If a pensioner who, at the time of his death, was in receipt of an Unemployability Pension, or of constant attendance allowance, did not die from the effects of his injuries, the widow and orphans receive an allowance. This allowance can be paid if the pensioner, at the time of his death, was in receipt of pension based on a reduced standard of employment of at least 70 %. The allowances are payable as to two thirds, in the case of the widows and orphans of recipients of constant attendance allowances to the full amount, of the standard widows' and orphans' pensions. In the case of re-marriage, the regulations on the payment of a settlement are applicable mutatis mutandis. Widowers receive an allowance on the same conditions as those applicable to widows.

Adjustment of Pensions

Current war pensions are to be brought into line annually with wages and salary movements to the same percentage as the General Basis of Computation in Non—Manual Workers' Pensions Insurance (for details see sector 'Non;Manual Workers' Pensions Insurance'). It is anticipated that benefits will be increased by 5,5 % i.e. from 1.1.1971. The increased rates are shown in the text of this chapter.

Double Pensions and Suspension of Pensions

If a war pension is payable at the same time as a widow's or orphans' pension, then only the more favourable Adjustment Pension is payable in addition to the basic pension. If a war pension or a widow's pension is payable at the same time as a parents' pension, the adjustment pension is taken into account in fixing the parents' pension. The same procedure is followed in the case of allowances. If a Business Losses Pension coincides with a Losses Compensation Pension for widows, the first of the two is taken into account as income.

If pensions and other benefits from War Pensions and Related Services coincide with similar benefits under social Industrial Injuries Insurance, or with a Civil Service Pension, payment of war pension is suspended if the claims derive from the same cause, to the amount of the payments from Injuries Insurance, or the amount of the difference between a normal Civil Service pension and payments under Civil Service accident regulations. Claims to curative treatment also rest if, for the same reason, a claim for similar services exists under Civil Service regulations.

Commutation of Pensions

Commutation is a capitalisation of the pension covering a limited period. It is payable, at official discretion, only for a specified purpose for the purchase or consolidation of landed property. The Basic Pension only may be commuted. The amount payable is nine times the annual Basic Pension.

Personal conditions for approval are: The applicant must be under 55 years of age, the claim to pension must be recognised and must be expected to continue for at least 10 years, and there must be a guarantee that the money will be put to a useful purpose.

Maximum Amounts of Commutation of Pension
in DM

| Pensioners with a Reduced Standard of Employmnet in %s of | | | | | | | | |
30	40	50	60	70	80	90	100	Widows
6588	8748	11880	15012	20628	25056	30024	33804	20304

Between 1950 and 1968 375.000 commutations of pensions were approved at a cost of 2,1 milliard DM. In 1968 the average amount approved was about 8.500 DM.

The Capitalisation Law - KOV - passed at the beginning of 1970 is designed to secure the financial basis of the capitalisation of Basic Pensions. For the time being commutation of pensions is to be replaced by capitalisation, with the help of the capital market, and with the assistance of the Equalisation of Burdens Bank. The necessary funds are to be raised outside the Federal budget; interest and the administrative charges of the Equalisation of Burdens Bank will continue to be borne by the Federai Government.

Commencement, Amendment, and Termination of War Pensions and Related Services

Payment of pensions, and of increased pensions, commences with the month in which the conditions are satisfied, though at the earliest in the month in which application is made. Officially fixed higher benefits commence in the month in which the reasons therefore become known in the offices of the War Pension Services. If the improved benefits are payable because of a change in the family status, or on reaching the age of 65, they begin in the month the event occurs. In general a reduction or cancelation of payments takes effect at the end of the month following notification. If the cancelation is due to some positive event (death or marriage), payment ceases at the end of the month in which the conditions are no longer satisfied.

A special ruling obtains in the fixing of Adjustment Pensions. As a rule these pensions are assessed and paid for a period of 12 months. At the end of this period, a final assessment is made. Special regulations govern procedure.

Survivors pensions begin at the earliest in the month following death. For the rest the regulations applying to pensions are valid matatis mutandis.

If there is a substantial change in the conditions governing the assessment of pensions, the claim is revised correspondingly.

If a pensioner refuses to comply with measures required by the administrative authority, or refuses to give necessary information about his family, his assets, or his income, the pension may be withheld wholly or in part for the duration of such refusal.

War Pensions and Related Services for War Victims resident abroad

Germans who have their homes or customary places of residence in States with which the Federal Republic of Germany has diplomatic relations are treated in the same way as pensioners at home. At the end of 1969, nearly 108.000 pensioners were receiving pensions and other services abroad.

Curative treatment in respect of their injuries is also assured for pensioners living abroad. They can obtain a refund of proven, necessary, and reasonable costs arising from curative treatment undertaken on their own initiative in the country of residence, up to the amount of twice the cost of similar treatment in the Federal Republic. In especially justified cases, a higher amount may be sanctioned, wholly or in part. The costs of medicines, dressings, and other medical necessities, can be refunded as to the full amount. For the rest no allowance is payable in respect of specific cases of illness not the effect of the injury, for therapeutic gymnastics, or capitalisation of pension; in cases of need a grant is payable. Therapeutic gymnastics are not conducted abroad.

In the case of other war victims not resident in the Federal Republic or resident in a State with which the Federal Republic does not maintain diplomatic relations, the claim to pension rests. The Federal Minister of Labour and Social Order may sanction a pension to a reasonable amount. Such sanction has normally been given, though for war victims in the German Eastern territories temporarily under foreign administration, in most East and South European, and some other States, only in part.

Finance

The costs of War Pensions and Related Services are borne by the Federal Government, whereas the personnel and other administrative costs are borne by the Federal Lands. By reason of payments made by other form of social insurance taken into account in the assessment of war pensions there is probably a saving of 1,2 milliard DM in this field.

Expenditure on War Pensions and Related Services
— Federal Budget — in mill. DM

Year	Total	including War Pensions	Widows Pensions	Orphans Pensions	Parents Pensions	Curative Treatment
1950	2 338	745	1 093		75	183
1955	3 444	956	1 567		179	222
1960*)	3 518	1 070	1 279	151	129	193
1965	5 195	1 935	2 338	75	237	387
1968	5 984	2 255	2 721	77	231	539
1969	5 919	2 220	2 688	66	210	542

*) 9 months

Organisation

The care of war victims is in the hands of Pension Offices established pursuant to the Federal Law and subject to the official supervision of the Ministers of Labour and the Senators for Labour in the Federal Lands. In the Federal territory there are 11 Land Pensions Offices, 55 Pensions Office, 27 Orthopaedic Pensions Offices, 11 Pensions Medical Inspection Offices, 1 Sick Book Registry, 1 Testing and Procurement Office for Medicines and Appliances, 7 Pensions Hospitals, 1 Pensions Sanatorium, 11 Pensions Convalescent Homes, and the Sanatorium Valbella in Davos/ Switzerland. There are three training institutes for the training and advanced training of personnel.

Land Pension Offices (LVAmt)

LVAmt Baden-Württemberg	in Stuttgart
LVAmt Bavaria	in Munich
LVAmt Berlin	in Berlin
LVAmt Bremen	in Bremen
LVAmt Hamburg	in Hamburg
LVAmt Hesse	in Frankfort
LVAmt Lower Saxony	in Hannover
LVAmt North Rhine-Westphalia	in Münster
LVAmt Rhineland-Palatinate	in Coblence
LVAmt Saarland	in Saarbrücken
LVAmt Schleswig-Holstein	in Neumünster

Employed personnel amounts to 17.000 established officials, salaried employees, and manual workers; 850 medical doctors are employed full time.

The main burden of administration falls on the Pensions Offices. They are under the supervision of the Land Pensions Offices. The Land Pensions Offices are independently active only in certain specific pensions matters; for example, they reach decisions on the

213

commutation of pensions, on the approval of spa and sanatorium treatment, on the refusal of orthopaedic appliances (approval is the responsibility of the Orthopaedic Pensions Offices), and other measures in the field of curative treatment.

Curative and medical treatment is carried through mainly by the statutory Sick Funds on their own responsibility. War Victims Welfare is in the hands of the organisation of the same name.

Legislative bases

Federal Pensions Law of 20.12.1950, in the version of 20.1.1967 (BGBI. I S. 141), last amended by the Law of 10.7.1970 (BGBI. I. Page 1029).

Law on Maintenance Aid for the Dependants of Prisoners of War of 13.6.1950, in the version of 18.1.1964 (BGBI. I S.218)

Prisoners' Aid Law of 6.8.1955, in the version of 29.9.1969 (BGBI. IS.1793) amended by Law of 10.7.1970 (BGBI. I. Page 1029)

Soldiers' Pension Law of 26.7.1957, in the version of 20.2.1967 (BGBI. I S 201), last amended by the Law of 10.7.1970 (BGBI. I. Page 1029)

Ordinance on War Victims Welfare of 30.5.1961, in the version of 27.8.1965 (BGB.I S. 1031)

Pensions Capitalisations Law - KOV - 27.4.1970 (BGBI. I. Page 413).

Equalisation of Burdens

Introduction

Following the 1870/71 War, the civilian population received compensation for the material losses suffered; in June 1871 a law to this effect was enacted. After the first world war statutory regulations to compensate for war losses led only to partial compensation. As a consequence of the Treaty of Versailles of 28.6.1919, a number of laws were enacted between 1923 and 1928 providing compensation for Germans suffering loss of property in the ceded territories. Some 10,4,milliard marks were paid out in respect of 390.000 cases of expropriation. In the course of the second world war, similar regulations were issued covering material losses, the purchase of replacements, the ascertainment of the amounts involved, and maintenance allowances. In 1945 these regulations were suspended. In August 1949 the Law on the Alleviation of Urgent Social Need (the Immediate Aid Law) came into force in the Combined Economic territory. This Law, as the forerunner of the Equalisation of Burdens Law, provided in the first place aid to meet living costs — maintenance allowances — at a cost of nearly 6 milliard DM. In 1952 legal regulations were issued to deal with the assessment of losses suffered as a result of deportation, and of war losses, (Assessment Law), designed as preparatory regulations for the Equalisation of Burdens Law. In the same year there followed laws governing the currency losses arising from the loss of deportees' savings accounts, and the Law for the Alleviation of Hardships arising from Currency Reform. Since that time all these laws have been extended and improved, though the basic legislative structure has remained unaltered. In the course of the following years the Equalisation of Burdens legislation has been improved as a result of 22 amendments; more than 50 legal regulations have laid down obligations and entitlements in detail. Pursuant to the draft of the 23rd Amending Law on Equalisation of Burdens submitted by the Federal Government in June 1970, the income and assets limitations so far imposed on refugees and migrants from East Germany are to be abolished. As a consequence of the second world war, of almost 17 mill. Germans living in territories east of the Oder-Neisse line, and other territories from which deportations took place, some 14. mill. had been deported by 1950, of whom 7,7 mill. have reached the Federal Republic of Germany; about 4,4 mill. remained in the first instance in the then Soviet Occupied Zone and other reception areas; 2,1 mill. died, or are missing. About 2,6 mill. remained in, or were prevented from leaving, their homelands. In 1969 nearly 12,2 mill. deportees were counted in the Federal territory. As a consequence of these deportations, a loss of property amounting to about 100 milliard DM was sustained. In the Federal territory itself, mainly as a result of air bombardment, 3,4 million persons suffered material losses totalling 36 milliard marks. Prior to currency reform in 1948, savings accounts, life insurances, mortgages, and shares, to a total value of 100 milliard DM were affected. On these grounds 368.000 persons have entered claims to payments under the Equalisation of Burdens Law.

Functions of the Equalisation of Burdens

The object of Equalisation of Burdens is to provide compensation on the basis of social justice, and with due consideration for the national economic position, for injuries and losses sustained as a result of deportations and of damages occurring during and after the war, and of the reform of the monetary system resulting from the Currency Reform of

1948. Payments and services are awarded under the specific provison that the award and the acceptance thereof do not imply renunciation on the part of the deportees, or of others suffering losses and damages, to a claim to restitution of the abandoned property. Included in the Equalisation of Burdens regulations are the losses sustained in East Germany as a result of the war, and of the political conditions prevailing there since the end of the war.

It is intended that the Equalisation of Burdens shall have been completed at the latest in 30 years time, i.e. by 31.3.1979. By this time it is anticipated that the Equalisation of Burdens Levies will have been collected, and the Main Compensation Claims will have been met. Other expenditure and income will go on long beyond this point. For instance, reconstruction loans are to be amortized in 50 years; war injuries pensions are awarded for life. It is, therefore, not to be expected that the Equalisation of Burdens will be finally disposed of until the year 2015. According to present estimates the final cost of payments and services under the Equalisation of Burdens will be 110 milliard DM. Current annual expenditure is running at about 4 milliard DM.

Scope

The Equalisation of Burdens provides for compensation to persons who have suffered the loss of their property, or of their means of livelihood. The losses in question are war losses arising in the Federal Republic in the period between 26.8.1939 and 31.7.1945, damages consequent on the deportation of German Nationals from German territories east of the Oder-Neisse line, and from foreign territories, 'east damages', i.e. those sustained in the eastern territories of the German Empire within the frontiers of 1937, now under alien administration, but which are not deportee damages, losses of savings and deposit accounts resulting from the currency reform of 1948, and losses sustained by refugees from East Germany.

Benefits

Compensation benefits on the grounds of deportation losses, of war damages, 'east damages', savings accounts losses, and zone losses, are granted both with and without legal entitlement.

— Thousands at the End of the Year

Year	Total	Maintenance Allowance incl. self-employed supplement	less compensation pension	Compensation Pension total allowance	incl. maintenance	Maintenance Allowance and Compensation Pension together
1955	847	–	814	60	33	874
1960	684	62	505	289	179	794
1965	596	224	338	354	258	692
1968	502	245	254	326	248	580
1969	475	246	235	312	240	547

Benefits to which legal entitlement exists are: main compensation, war losses pensions, household effects compensation, compensation for losses of the savings accounts of refugees arising from currency reform, and for similar losses by other depositors. Main compensation is limited to a maximum amount of 50.000 DM in respect of losses in East Germany.

Benefits without legal entitlement are: re-settlement loans, i.e. investment loans for the industrial economy, the free professions, agriculture and house building, as well as — in the past — loans for the creation of employment, for aid in obtaining accommodation, advances from the hardship fund for the purchase of household effects, loans to set up in business, benefits on the basis of other measures of promotion, e.g. vocational training aid, building of hostels, acceptance of sureties, participation in public institutes, loans for building housing estates for refugees.

All these benefits and services serve the purpose of balancing out losses and damages suffered. Included in these social benefits in the meaning of those here enumerated are not only war damage pensions and maintenance allowances for political refugees from East Germany, which, in the case of old and unemployed beneficiaries represent their main and immediate social security. Their intention is, by making full provision for the beneficiaries, to absolve them from the need of applying for social aid, and from dependence on their relatives.

The war damages pension combines the principle of social security with the principle of compensation under the Equalisation of Burdens scheme. It is awarded in two forms, of which each individually, or both together are applicable, namely, as maintenance allowance, or as compensation pension. The purpose of maintenance allowances is primarily to meet the cost of living. These benefits are complemented by additional benefits provided under health insurance, and by death benefits. Compensation pensions are mainly compensation in the form of a pension.

Conditions for the Award of War Damages Pensions

The entitled person is the person directly affected, e.g., the deportee, the owner of a war damaged or bombed-out house, or the holder of a bankbook. Insofar as such persons have died before submission of a claim, the surviving spouse is entitled to claim. If a beneficiary dies whilst in receipt of war damages pension, the pension continues payable to the surviving spouse, if the widow is 45 years of age at the time of the death, or if the widower is 65 years of age, or is unemployable at the time of the death. After the death of the direct beneficiary, and of the spouse, a pension may continue to be payable to an unmarried daughter, if, instead of following an occupation, she had had the care of her parents, or of one parent, until death, whilst living in the family home, and if she would have been the heiress of the lost property.

War damages pensions are payable on condition that deportation damages, war damages, east damages, or loss of savings accounts, have been sustained.

In the case of deportation, war damages, and east damages, the most important are those arising from the loss of or the damage to business property, to agricultural or forestry holdings, to loss of land or to working capital, as well as to equipment and installations necessary for the pursuit of the normal occupation, or for scientific research. In the case of deportation and east damages, losses in respect of Reichsmark bank deposits and other monetary claims (e.g. mortgages) are also taken into account.

Savings account losses are only those arising from the loss of savings accounts and savings deposits in the Federal Republic following the currency reform of 1948, as a consequence of the fact that they were converted in the relation of 10 : 1, or less, or were not converted at all. The principal losses in this respect were those sustained in respect of bank and savings bank accounts and mortgages.

In the case of deportation, war damages, and east damages losses, it is the loss of the professional or other bases of livelihood which is the most frequent and especial element of the loss sustained. The essential loss suffered is here not so much the loss of assets as of current income. The basis on which such loss is assessed is the normal income of which the person sustaining the loss, and the spouse, were in receipt in the years 1937, 1938, and 1939. Such loss is taken into account if the average income in those years amounted to 35 RM per month.

Losses must be officially assessed. Loss of property is ascertained on the basis of the Ascertainment Law, (Feststellungsgesetz), savings accounts losses, and loss of the means of livelihood, on the basis of the Equalisation of Burdens Law (Lastenausgleichsgesetz). The basic amounts in the case of married couples (loss of property), and loss of income, are aggregated. The amount of losses sustained also affects the war damages pension to a defined extent.

Personal Conditions

War damages pensions are awarded as a general rule only to claimants born before 1.1.1890 (in the case of women 1.1.1895). Application for payment may be made only up to 31.12.1970. Exceptions are made in the case of persons entering the Federal Republic at a later date, in respect of whom the period for which application may be made is extended for 2 years beyond the date of entry. The limitation to the above dates of birth precludes the possibility of further persons 'growing into entitlement' year by year. Of persons born after 31.12.1894 (women), it is assumed that, despite any losses they have sustained, they will themselves have been in a position to make provision for their old age. Concessions are made in the case of former self-employed persons.

A war damages pension is awarded to an unemployable person not satisfying the age conditions, who is unable to maintain himself from his own income and assets, and of whom this cannot reasonably be expected. A person is regarded as unemployable who, pursuant to the Equalisation of Burdens Law, is, by his own efforts and by use of his own skills and qualifications, unable to earn half the amount which a physically and mentally healthy person customarily earns in the same district. An unemployable woman is treated in the same way in this respect as an unemployable man — without regard to her age — if, on the date of her application she has the care of at least 3 children living in her household. The position of equality in this respect ends if the woman no longer has the care of at least one child, unless she is over 45 years of age, or is unemployable.

Assessment of War Damage Pensions

The two types of war damage pension, maintenance allowance and compensation pension, are assessed on different bases.

Maintenance allowances are paid as a fixed sum, varying according to the size of the family, compensation pensions as a percentage of certain amounts lost. In both cases maximum amounts of income are applicable which, in the case of maintenance allowances, are considerably lower than in the case of compensation pensions.

The principle that war damage pensions are payable only if the claimant is unable to maintain himself from his own resources, or cannot reasonably be expected to do so (subsidiary ranking of war damage pensions) is thereby, and on the basis of other regulations, variously implemented and is considerably less in the case of war damage pensions. The following paragraphs set out the two types of war damage pensions separately.

Maintenance Allowances

Amounts

Maintenance allowances have been payable since 1.4.1949. Expenditure at the end of 1969 amounted to more than 20 milliard DM.

Amounts of Maintenance Allowances
in DM per month

					Supplementary Amounts	
from	Claimants	Spouses	Children	Full Orphans	Attendance Allowance*	Accommodation in Homes
1. 4. 49	70,00	30,00	20,00	35,00	–	–
1. 10. 51	85,00	37,50	27,50	45,00	–	–
1. 7. 54	100,00	50,00	35,00	55,00		
1. 4. 57	120,00	60,00	42,00	65,00		
1. 6. 59	140,00	70,00	47,00	72,00		
1. 6. 61	155,00	85,00	49,00	80,00		
1. 6. 63	175,00	105,00	60,00	90,00	50,00	20,00
1. 6. 65	190,00	120,00	65,00	100,00		
1. 6. 67	205,00	135,00	70,00	110,00		
1. 6. 70	235,00	155,00	80,00	130,00		

* Increased in Certain cases to 65 DM; with effect from 1.6.63 to 75 DM, from 1.6.67 to 90 DM

Maintenance allowance rates have been frequently increased; current rates are shown in the above table. For instance, a married couple with two entitled children receives 550 DM per month. In the event of attendance being necessary the amount is increased by 50 DM, in the case of accommodation in a home by 20 DM. If the person requiring attendance is not in receipt of an additional attendance allowance, the attendance supplement is increased to 90 DM. The average monthly maintenance allowance rose between 1959 and 1969 from 94 to 196 DM, i.e. by more than double.

The payment of maintenance allowance is dependent on a certain upper income limit, which may not be exceeded by the income of the family unit. The family unit includes the immediate claimant, the spouse, and entitled children. Income includes all amounts received by the family unit in cash or kind (commodities, free board and ledging) which, after deduction of all amounts pursuant to income tax law regulations to cover necessary and unavoidable expenses, must be taken into account. Certain forms of income are disregarded to the advantage of the claimant, e.g. legal and voluntary contributions from relatives, charitable gifts, as well as the basic pension and most severely injured persons' allowances under War Pensions and Related Services. In numerous cases other amounts are also disregarded, e.g. nearly all forms of pension, and finally other emoluments are taken into account only in part, namely from agriculture and forestry, from business activities, from self-employment and paid employment, as well as state gratifications, and voluntary payments made in respect of former employment or a former occupation. In addition to a maximum amount of income allowed, an overall limit is set. If the combined incomes of the family unit, including maintenance allowance, are greater than double the amount of the maximum amount of income allowed, the maintenance allowance is reduced by the amount of the excess. The grant is further dependent on a financial resources limit of 12.000 DM; in certain hardship cases this limit may be exceeded. In these cases, too, certain statutory payments, which are laid down in detail, are disregarded, namely certain payments under Equalisation of Burdens, and single compensation payments in respect of arrest and imprisonment. Finally, payment of maintenance allowances is in some cases limited in duration. If there has been no loss of the means of livelihood, the duration in the case of war damages, East damages, or savings accounts, depends on the basic amount of the loss suffered, insofar as it does not exceed 5.600 DM.

Maintenance allowances are reckoned in part against the main compensation claim; this was the case up to 1957 as to 50 %, to 1961 as to 40 %, to 1965 as to 20 %, and subsequently as to 10 %.

Special Regulations for former self-employed persons

In the case of former self-employed claimants, special regulations apply if their old age and survivor's insurance provisions have been completely lost, or seriously reduced, as a result of the loss of their means of livelihood; this applies equally to the conditions for the payment of maintenance allowance as to the assessment of its amount. Special consideration is given to self-employed persons who, on the basis of losses sustained, have a claim to main compensation to a minimum amount of 3.600 DM, and whose lost means of livelihood depended mainly on their own labours, or on claims arising therefrom, in particular on pensions provisions made from the proceeds of the business. Included also are persons who are able to prove that they have sustained a loss of at least 2.000 RM annually, formerly earned by self-employment. This is the case as a rule when the claimant did not follow any paid employment in addition to self-employment.

Amount of Self-Employed Persons Allowance from 1.6.1970

In the case of a finai amount of main compensation in DM	In the case of average annual income from gainful employ- ment in RM	Self-employed persons allowance in DM per month	Marriage allowance in DM per month
–	to 4 000	55	30
to 4 600	" 5 200	70	35
" 5 600	" 6 500	85	40
" 7 600	" 9 000	95	45
" 9 600	" 12 000	105	50
over 9 600	over 12 000	115	60

The special provisions to which reference is made apply also to claimants born in the years 1890 to 1905 (women 1895 to 1910), who have reached the age of 65 (women 60), or who have become unemployable by 31.12.1970. Maintenance allowances are increased by the amount of the self-employed pensions allowances; a further increase is possible in certain cases.

Health services and death benefits

A person entitled to maintenance allowances who is not entitled to health services pursuant to some other statutory regulation has a claim to such services for himself and his entitled dependents, including out-patient medical and dental treatment and the provision of dentures, medicines, dressings, and appliances, to the same extent as the recipient of Social Aid. In the event of a protracted period of hospital treatment, the beneficiary is expected to make a certain contribution to the charges. (Claimant 75 DM, spouse 55 DM, child or full orphan 35 DM). In the case of voluntary health insurance, the recipient of maintenance allowances may receive a refund of contributions paid to the amount of 30 DM per month for himself and any other person insured by him.

Recipients of maintenance allowances can also insure for death benefits on payment of 1 DM per month (0,50 DM for a spouse). Death benefit is 500 DM per person, which may not be taken into account in respect of other comparable payments which may be due.

Death Benefits

from	DM
1. 4. 52	240
1. 6. 59	300
1. 6. 65	500

Compensation Pensions

Compensation pensions are intended to compensate in the form of current monthly cash payments for the loss of large financial resources, or of a high income; in the case of a simultaneous claim to main compensation, it also represents payment of main compensation in the form of a pension. This form of pension has been payable since 1953, at a cost, up to the end of 1969, of nearly 4 milliard DM.

Conditions and Amount

Compensation pensions are payable only if the income of the family unit does not exceed a certain upper limit; if the conditions for the claim are satisfied, this limit is raised by the amount of any care and attendance allowance, and of any self-employed persons' allowance payable.

Compensation pensions are also subject to an overall upper limit. If the pension, plus maintenance allowances, plus other income (after deduction of tax free amounts and other concessions) exceeds the simple income limit, the pension is reduced by the excess amount. If the pension, plus maintenance allowances, plus allowances, plus other income (including certain emoluments not allowable under the tax free amounts regulations) exceeds one and a half times the upper income limit, it is also reduced by the excess amount.

The amount of pension payable in respect of loss of financial resources and assets depends on the amount of the loss. Based on the amount of the ascertained loss expressed in Reichsmark, a basic amount in DM is assessed according to a fixed table — the basic amount of the War Losses Pension. This can be identical with the main compensation, but can also vary from it, in particular, if allowance is made for losses in respect of which main compensation makes no provision.

The amount of compensation pension paid out is assessed on the basis of a percentage of the basic amount of war losses pension payable; it amounts annually to at least 4 % of the basic amount. If the claimant is over 65 years of age on receiving the first payment of the pension, a further old age allowance of 1 % becomes payable annually. For the rest the following minimum percentage rates are payable:

8 % if the basic amount is not payable mainly on account of savings account losses,
7 % for war injured and accidents pensioners with a reduced standard of employment of 80 % and more,
8 % for recipients of constant attendance allowances under war pensions and related services, and for persons not in receipt of such allowances, but who are infirm

If the beneficiary claims maintenance allowances as well as a compensation pension in respect of savings account losses, and if at the same time, the beneficiary is claiming maintenance allowances, the blocked amount is increased by 30 %. If the beneficiary is claiming only compensation pension (or if he can do so because of exceeding the upper income limit), certain minimum basic amounts must be reached (see table). In the case of compensation pensions payable in respect of the loss of the means of livelihood, the amount payable depends on the amount of the income lost.

Minimum Basic Amounts of Savings Accounts Losses

Age on First Payment	Minimum Amount in DM
80 Jahre	3 000
75 Jahre	3 700
70 Jahre	4 400
65 Jahre	5 100
under 65 Jahren	5 800

Special Regulations for Former Self-Employed Persons

Compensation pension in respect of persons who have suffered the loss of their professional, occupational, or other basis of livelihood, is payable at fixed rates laid down in special regulations (see table). In this case it is not the loss of assets which is taken into account, but the loss of income earned in the years preceding the loss, generally speaking in the years 1937 to 1939. Family allowances, self-employed persons allowances, and constant attendance allowances are not payable. They are taken into account in assessing maximum incomes. The possession of assets is disregarded. If compensation pension only is payable there is no claim to health services or death benefit.

If the claimant has also lost the benefit of a contingent private pensions' insurance claim, the above rates are increased by 50 %; the upper age limit for claims is also more favourable. A claim to compensation pension exists if the claimant was born after 31.12.1889 (a woman after 31.12.1894), but before 1.1.1906 (a woman before 1.1.1911), or becomes unemployable at the latest by 31.12.1970.

General Regulations on War Damages Pensions

Benefits commence on the first day of the month following the receipt of the application, insofar as special regulations do not apply. They are suspended if, and for as long as, the conditions of award are not satisfied. If a war losses pension has been suspended without a break for five years after 31.12.1964, it is, as a general rule, regarded as permanently ended.

A war losses pension ceases to be payable on the death of the beneficiary, unless the surviving spouse, or an unmarried daugther, satisfies the conditions for continued payment. In the case of a maintenance allowance payable for life, the heirs receive payment for a further month (in some cases in addition to death benefit).

If the beneficiary has a claim to main compensation, all amounts so far paid currently are taken into account, in full or in part, immediately current payments finally cease.

Although the claim for main compensation has, in many cases, been fully met by payment of the war losses pension, the recipients of a maintenance allowance alone, or of a maintenance allowance plus a compensation pension, receive a minimum amount of the main compensation in cash.

For the rest, there are detailed statutory regulations on the satisfaction of claims to main compensation during the payment of current war losses pensions, as well as on the award of war losses pension on partial satisfaction of main compensation.

If refugees, war losses victims, and East losses victims, satisfy the conditions for the award of a war losses pension as well as for the grant of a loan to re-establish themselves in business, they have an option. If such a person has, in the first instance, attempted to re-establish himself in business with the aid of such a loan, and if he subsequently claims a war losses pension, then, in order to avert duplicated benefits, such pension may be awarded only if the amounts previously received are repaid as to a certain amount to the Equalisation Fund. Reconstruction loans for house building, and for the promotion of subsidiary agricultural employment, are not an obstacle to the simultaneous payment of war losses pensions.

The principle of the subsidiary status of war losses pensions does not hold in relation to benefits under social aid. Consequently, if a beneficiary is awarded a war losses pension retrospectively for a period during which he has been in receipt of social aid, the retrospective amounts must be refunded to the administration of social aid. In the same way, if the recipient of a current war losses pension is accommodated in an institution or home, the pension is payable to the Social Aid Fund. This regulation leaves unaffected the obligation on the part of the Social Aid Fund to provide relief in the case of need, despite the payment of a war losses pension.

Current Grants in Aid

In the case of certain groups of persons current grants in aid may be payable from the Hardship Fund of the Equalisation Fund, insofar as the loss substained has resulted in a loss of the means of livelihood. Entitled persons are those registered as political refugees from the German Democratic Republic (DDR), similar persons and refugees not satisfying the appointed day requirements, persons denied payment of a liquidation pension after the first world war on grounds of race, residents of the Land Berlin who have sustained war losses in East Berlin, and residents of the German Customs Union territory, (Kleines Walsertal and Gemeinde Jungholz/Tirol). These grants in aid are payable under conditions similar to those applying to maintenance aid (to a certain extent also to compensation pensions).

Finance

The Equalisation of Burdens is financed from the capital wealth levy, the mortgages gains levy, and the credit gains levy; the levy is raised as a general rule on 50 % of the unit value of residual property and assets as on 21.6.1948. Since, however, the proceeds of these levies do not suffice to meet all payments, it is necessary to meet a part of the expenditure from taxation. The Federal Government and the Federal Lands are under an obligation to contribute to expenditure from their own budgets. By the end of 1969 the Immediate Aid Fund and the Equalisation Fund had received the following sums:

Equalisation levies, including Immediate
Aid Levy and Conversion debts . . . . 40,4 Mrd. DM

Subsidies from Federal Government
and Federal Lands . . . . 20,1 Mrd. DM

Re-payments of Loans, and other
ordinary receipts . . . . 7,9 Mrd. DM

Proceeds from Securities Reform . . . . 0,4 Mrd. DM

Loans from the capital market . . . . 6,2 Mrd. DM
Total   75,0 Mrd. DM

Expenditure in respect of war losses pensions has risen continuously since 1965, although the number of recipients has declined. The payment of compensation in respect of household effects was largely concluded by the end of 1960, whereas expenditure in respect of main compensation first commenced to a considerable extent in 1959.

Expenditure from the Equalisation of Burdens Fund according to Types of Benefit
in mill. DM

Year	Total	Main Compensation	Household Effects Compensation	Currency Reform Compensation	Savings Acets. Compensation	Compensation Pensions	Integration Household Building	Grants Trade and Industry	Agriculture	Other Grants	Maintenance Allowances
1950	1 801	—	249	—	—	—	492	215	59	50	736
1955	3 906	—	1 026	40	138	59	1 104	260	280	108	798
1960*)	3 052	652	332	23	206	204	545	60	61	60	725
1965	4 160	1 141	61	10	198	343	261	8	42	26	1 422
1968	3 970	1 489	35	5	203	319	70	3	31	12	1 320
1969	4 091	1 576	32	5	209	300	79	3	28	10	1 276

*) 9 months

By 31.12.1969 72.3 milliard DM had been paid out from the Equalisation Fund. The distribution of this sum amongst the different groups of claimants, according to the nature of the benefit, is shown in the following table.

Expenditure from the Equalisation of Burdens Fund according to the different Groups of Claimants
in mill. DM

Type of Benefit		Total	Amount paid out up to 31.12.1969				
			Refugees	War losses Claimants	Savings Accounts Claimants	Refugees from East Germany	Other Claimants
Main Compensation		13 139	9 617	3 365	–		157
Household Effects		9 295	5 026	3 752	–	455	62
Compensation and similar Payments							
Equalisation of Currency		1 097	1 043		54	–	–
Old Savings Accounts							
Compensation		2 998	150	361	2 458	29	–
Compensation Pensions		3 989	2 858	321	805	–	5
Settlement Grants in Aid	House Building	12 456	8 230	3 748	–	427	50
	Industrial	2 473	1 406	657	–	332	78
	Economic Agricultural	2 188	1 896	132	–	154	6
Other Grants		1 265	911	143	14	190	7
Maintenance Allowances		20 269	15 559	1 368	3 327	–	16
Totals*		72 254	48 418	14 617	6 760	2 052	407

* Deviations possible, since benefit types are shown incompletely

Organisation

Equalisation of Burdens is administered by the Equalisation Authorities, at the head of which is the Federal Equalisation Office, under its President; pursuant to Article 120 a, inserted in the Basic Law for the purposes of the Equalisation of Burdens, the powers of the Federal Government have been delegated to this body to enable it to carry out its duties. The law serving the purpose of the implementation of the Equalisation of Burdens lays down, with the sanction of the Federal Council, that, in the field of equalisation benefits, they shall be administered in part by the Federal Government itself, in part by the Federal Lands on its behalf, and that the powers vested in the Federal Government and the supreme responsible Federal authorities by virtue of the Basic Law shall be delegated wholly or in part to the Federal Equalisation Office. In the exercise of these powers the Federal Equalisation Office does not require the sanction of the Federal Council. The Presidium of the Federal Equalisation Office administers the Equalisation Fund on its own responsibility, and decides on the distribution of the monies. The President has the support of a Control Committee and a Permanent Advisory Council. The Control Committee, elected from amongst the members of the Federal Parliament, and nominated by the Land Governments, supervises the administration of the Equalisation Fund; decrees issued by the President on the disposal of the funds require its sanction. The Permanent Council has an advisory function; it is comprised of representatives of the claimants and of experts.

Intermediate authorities are the Land Equalisation Offices, which constitute a department of a Ministry in each Land. They are subject to technical supervision by the President of the Federal Equalisation of Burdens Office. A further section of the administration is comprised of the Appeals Committees, which, as supra-regional offices, are generally a part of the Land Equalisation Offices. The Appeals Committees consist of a member of the Equalisation Administration as chairman, and two claimants as assessors.

At the lower level of administration are Equalisation Offices. In every rural district and municipality there is an Equalisation Office as part of general administration, wherever necessary branch offices; joint offices covering several districts are permissible. Increasing use is being made of this arrangement.

In order to ensure uniformity of administration representatives of the interests of the Equalisation Fund are nominated to the Equalisation Offices, the Appeals Committees, and the Administrative Courts; their function is to ensure that the funds are not disposed of illegally or improperly.

Legislative bases

Equalisation of Burdens Law of 14.8.1952 in the version of 1.10.1969 (BGBI. I. 1909) amended 18.7.1970 (BGBI. I. p. 1093). Ascertainment Law of 21.4.1952 in the version of 1.10.1969 (BGBI. I. p. 1885).

Currency Reform Adjustment Law of 27.3.1952, in the version of 1.12.1965 (BGBI. I. p. 2059), amended by the Law of 15.7.1968 (BGBI. I. p. 806).

Old Savings Accounts Law of 14.7.1953 (BGBI. III − 621 − 4), last amended by the Law of 18.5.1965 (BGBI. I. p. 419).

Aid for Refugees from the DDR

Introduction

Following the second world war 3.6 mill. people have fled from East Germany and East Berlin. Between 1949 and the end of 1969 nearly 3 mill. persons have made application under the Emergency Reception Procedure to be registered as persons who have fled from their homes as a result of the state of duress existing under the prevailing political conditions.

Registered political refugees from the DDR are granted assistance from the Hardship Fund of the Equalisation Fund: current assistance allowances (maintenance allowances) special current assistance allowances, allowances for the purchase of household effects as well as loans for starting up in business, or for obtaining accommodation. Since the other refugees were also nearly all destitute, they were in a state of distress rendering aid measures necessary. For this purpose more than 45 mill. DM was disbursed to 250.000 refugees up to 1969. These measures were based in the first instance on an agreement between the Federal Government and the Federal Lands (Guide Lines on Furnishing Aid); in 1965 legislative provision was made. For details see "Refugee Aid Law".

In respect of assets and possessions left behind in East Germany no special compensation was payable until 1969. In order, however, that such losses should not be overlooked, they were registered under the Security of Proof and Ascertainment Law of 22.5.1965, in the version of 1.10.1969 (BGBl. I. p. 1897), and proofs are deposited under a special procedure. All losses of property and wealth sustained in East Germany and East Berlin as a consequence of the second world war and its political and economic aftermath and as a result of National Socialist measures, that is, losses corresponding to those for which provision is made under the Equalisation of Burdens Law, have been registered. Pursuant to the 21st Amending Law to the Equalisation of Burdens Law of 18.8.1969 (BGBl. I. p. 1232) losses sustained, as ascertained on the basis of Security of Proof and Ascertainment Law, are included under main compensation under Equalisation of Burdens, to a limited extent, based on socio-political considerations.

Political prisoners from the DDR were already given a claim to cash payments and other forms of aid in 1953. The period of such imprisonment is taken into account in assessing pensions under statutory Pensions Insurance.

Refugees Aid Law

Scope

Pursuant to the Refugees Aid Law of 15.7.1965 (BGBl. I. p. 612), last amended by the Law of 15.7.1968 (BGBl. I. S. 806), all Germans are entitled to aid who, during or after the occupation of Germany left the then Soviet occupied Zone, and, from 1949 onwards the territory of the DDR, and entered the Federal Republic. Anyone entering after 26.8.1950 was required to pass through the Emergency Reception Centre, or a similar procedure. In order to avoid hardship, aid may be granted to persons who have lost their means of livelihood as a consequence of the fact that the zonal and sector boundaries have arbitrarily split communities. This applies particularly to West Berliners whose business and means of livelihood were situated in East Berlin.

In addition to persons who are debarred on the bases of other laws from the receipt of care and assistance (e. g. because of offences against humanity), such persons are debarred as fled because of criminal offences, or who, without good and sufficient reason, left Federal territory and have now returned from the DDR.

Benefits under the Refugees Aid Law are subsidiary to benefits under other laws, with the exception of Social Aid.

Benefits and Finance

Entitled persons under the Refugees Aid Law receive largely the same benefits as the registered refugees from the DDR from the Hardship Fund of the Equalisation of Burdens:

Current assistance grants, loans for starting a business and housebuilding, as well as — in lieu of Assistance for the purchase of household effects — Furnishing Grants. In so far as benefits under current allowances show minor differences they are to be brought into line by an amendment to the Refugees Aid Law.

Furnishing Grants, in contrast to assistance for the purchase of household effects, are subject to an income limit. They amount to 500 DM, plus 120 DM for the spouse, plus 60 DM for other members of the family. The basis taken is the income for the 24 months preceding the application. The income limits imposed are to be increased by one half by an amendment to the Refugees Aid Law.

The Law is administered by the Adjustment Administration (Ausgleichsverwaltung). The Federal Government bears 80 % of the costs, the Lands 20 %.

Help for Political Prisoners

Scope

Pursuant to the Prisoners' Aid Law of 6.8.1955, in the version of 29.9.1969 (BGBl. I. p. 1793), aid is granted to Germans who, after the occupation of their place of residence, or after 8.5.1945 in the territory of the then Soviet Zone of Occupation, in the DDR, in East Berlin, or in territories from which expulsions have taken place, and who were incarcerated for reasons for which, in accordance with free democratic concepts, they could not be held responsible. They must have had their homes, or their permanent place of residence in the Federal territory on 10.8.1955, or have taken up, or who take up, such permanent residence under certain conditions (e. g. as refugee from the DDR, or in the course of the re-union of families).

Benefits

When, in the early 50s, numerous political prisoners entered the Federal territory, there was no legislative basis on which care and assistance could be provided. In order to provide prompt aid for them recourse was had to already current regulations; former political prisoners were treated in the same way as former prisoners of war.

Financial aid granted (Integration grants) therefore corresponded to the rates payable as compensation to prisoners of war, that is to say, at the earliest w.e.f. 1.1.1947 30 RM, from 1.1.1949 60 DM, per month, and, from the 5th year of incarceration onwards, at the earliest w.e.f. 1.1.1951, 80 DM for every month of incarceration. After two, four, and six years of incarceration, integration aid is further increased by 20 DM per month for each month of imprisonment.

In addition, persons who were incarcerated solely because of their personal attitude after the occupation of their place of residence, or after 8.5.1945, receive a supplementary integration allowance of 250 DM for every complete quarter of imprisonment from the third year onwards, though at the earliest w.e.f. 1.1.1949. The Prisoners' Aid Law also provides for allowances in respect of injuries, and for the care of survivors, corresponding to those under the War Pensions and Related Services Law.

Dependents of political prisoners entitled to maintenance allowances are also entitled to other benefits corresponding to those provided under the regulations for the grant of maintenance allowance to the dependents of prisoners of war.

Further, former political prisoners receive the help and concessions provided for in the Returnees Law and other relevant legislation, e.g.: Discharge allowance, transitional allowances, unemployment benefit, sick pay, training allowances, precedence in the allocation of accommodation, vocational welfare, employment in the public services.

The Foundation for Former Political Prisoners, operating since 1969, can provide financial aid for persons particularly adversely affected by the results of their incarceration.

Finance and Organisation

To date integration aid has been paid out to an amount of 180 mill. DM. For the year 1970 the sum of 11.5 mill. DM has been provided. Amounts disbursed to injured persons and their survivors in 1969 were nearly 12. mill. DM. The costs are borne by the Federal Government.

Whereas the Pensions authorities are responsible for current payments (Injured persons and survivors welfare, maintenance allowances), the remaining benefits are the responsibility the Deportees and Refugees Offices.

Rent Allowances

Introduction

Primarily as a consequence of the two wars, available accommodation has been officially allocated (compulsorily administered), rents have been controlled (Price control), and notice could not be given except on special grounds (tenants' protection), for 40 years. As a result of the second world war 1.85 mill. dwelling units were completely destroyed, and a further 450.000 seriously damaged, i.e. some 22 % of existing living accommodation. Although work on the re-building of damaged and destroyed property was commenced shortly after the end of the war, the position in 1950 was still that, in face of a demand by 15.5 million applicants, only 10 mill. normal dwellings were available; there was, therefore, a deficit of 5.5 mill. As a consequence of government housing promotion, an average of 500.000 houses or flats have been built since the establishment of the Federal Republic of Germany in 1949; by 1969 app. 11 mill. had been built, some half of them in the framework of social housing projects, the total available in 1969, being 21 mill., so that the pre-war level had already been surpassed. In this situation the controls above referred to have gradually been relaxed, commencing with the year 1963, and most rents have been increased. The price index of the cost of living for rents increased from 1962 100 to 160.1 in February 1970, whilst the price index of the cost of house building rose from 1950 100 to 241 by the end of 1969. This is a result both of the improved quality of housing and of the higher building costs and the high price of land.

Governmental promotion of housing is implemented by the use of public funds (social housing), and by tax rebates. Whereas, within the framework of social housing, people in the lower income brackets in search of reasonable accommodation benefit only indirectly from the limitations imposed on the property owner in the matter of the allocation of accommodation, and the fixing of rent, rent allowances payable pursuant to the Rent Allowances Legislation provide direct help, designed to offer protection both to the tenant and the landlord, those not in a position to pay high rents, alternatively to meet the high costs arising, from the loss of the home, or from too heavy a financial burden.

In the enactment of the currently valid version of the Law, recourse was had to the experience gained with a similar law enacted in 1960 of which it must be said that advantage was not taken of the grants payable. In 1965. As a consequence, the Law was revised, simplified, and to the extent anticipated extended in its scope. The grants under the old Law were replaced by rent allowances, payable in respect not only of old and social housing, but also of housing built with the aid of tax rebates, and of privately built housing. The draft bill for the Second Rent Allowances Law prepared by the Federal Government provides for further improvements in grants.

Function

Taking account of the high cost of building and of sites, and the improved standard of housing, the purpose of the Law is to ensure that the rent payable by a tenant, or the charges falling on an owner, for suitable accommodation, shall be reasonable in relation to their income. Pursuant to the Rent Allowances Law, rent and financial aid are granted as a supplement to family income. This ensures a financial burden tolerable for each party.

There is a legal entitlement to the payment of rent allowances; the allowances are not, therefore, a benefit under social aid which the recipient might be required to refund if his financial position improved. The claim to rent allowances is not transferrable, and cannot be pledged nor distrained on.

Scope

Rent allowances are payable to a tenant who is entitled to accommodation under arrangements similar to a rent contract (for instance under a co-operative rent contract, or under a contract similar to a rent contract providing for accommodation for life), or to the owner of a house accommodating several families, occupying a flat in his own house.

An allowance to meet charges arising is payable to owner-occupiers of a house, to small holders, and in respect of agricultural land worked as a subsidiary occupation, to owner-occupiers of a flat, and to persons living in a dwelling on the basis of a permanent contract similar in nature to ownership. A lease holder is treated in the same way as the owner. Further, an allowance towards charges arising is payable to persons in respect of dwellings etc., occupied by them if they have a claim to transfer of title of a building, of a small holding, of agricultural land worked as a subsidiary occupation, or of transfer of property rights on a dwelling, or of permanent right of residence, if they are already bearing the charges.

Pursuant to a ruling of the Federal Constitutional Court of 14th November, 1969, recipients of social aid may not be debarred from the grant of rent allowances This ruling also applies to rrecipients of war pension's so that these persons are also entitled to rent allowances.

The number of households in receipt of rent allowances has increased rapidly since 1965. Of approximately 21 mill. households in the Federal Republic of Germany, the following were claiming allowances at the year end as shown.

Of these 89 % received rent allowances, and 11 % allowances to meet charges occurring.

The number of Recipient Housholds

Year		Number
	1964	163 000
	1965	395 000
	1966	606 000
	1967	691 000
	1968	811 000
Mid	1969	463 000

Benefits

Rent allowances are payable
  if the family income, with due consideration to the persons in the household, does not reach a defined maximum amount;
  if the rent payable, or charges arising, exceed the amounts the recipients may reasonably be expected to pay and, if there are no specific grounds for refusal.

Allowances are payable only on application. The entitled claimant is always the head of the household. The head of the household is that member of the family mainly responsible for the maintenance of the members of the family belonging to the household at the time the application is made.

Familiy Income

A claim to rent allowances is admissible only if the family income is not in excess of 9.000 DM annually. This amount is increased by 1.800 DM in respect of the second and every further member of the family belonging to the household; these are husband or wife, great grandparents, grandparents, parents, children, grandchildren, brothers and sisters, uncles, aunts, nieces, nephews, parents-in-law, children-in-law, sisters of the husband or wife, illegitimate children, foster children, adopted children, or children connected with the applicant by being declared legitimate, and foster parents. These members of the family may be temporarily absent from the household.

The family income is calculated on a basis different from that in other cases. It takes account of the total income of all members of the household, but also disregards many other sources of income. In computing the family income, the amount of the annual income of each member of the family belonging to the common household is reduced by the amount allowed under taxation laws for necessary business or occupational expenses, by the amounts payable in respect of children's allowances (monthly: 25 DM for the second, 50 DM for the third, 60 DM for the fourth, and 70 DM for the fifth and every further child), by a lump sum to the amount of 15 % in respect of taxes and insurance contributions payable, and in some cases by exempted amounts for special groups (refugees from the Soviet Zone and persons with small incomes). Reckonable as income in the meaning of the payment of rent allowances to recipients of social aid or war pensions are the continuing maintenance benefits payable as social aid or war pensions, and other payments to recipients of social aid, and of family members of his household, even if such payments are without influence on the grant of social aid.

Living Space

A further limitation to rent allowances lies in the living space considered necessary for a family. Rents or charges arising for living spaces of the following sizes only may be considered:

For a single person	40 qm
for two persons	50 qm
for three persons	65 qm
for four persons	80 qm
for every further family member	10 qm each;

Special regulations apply in particular cases. In the event of the death of a member of the family the claim to rent allowances remains unaffected for the following two years.

Amounts Reasonably to be borne by a Household

Rents or charges arising, are regared as bearable by the household if they do not exceed the percentages of the monthly family income shown in the following table:

Reasonable Rent or Charges in % of the Monthly Family Income

Scope	Monthly Family Income of up to									more than
	200 DM	300 DM	400 DM	500 DM	600 DM	700 DM	800 DM	900 DM	1000 DM	1000 DM
for a single person for a household with	14	16	18	20	21	22	22	–	–	–
2	12	14	16	18	20	21	21	22	–	–
3	12	13	15	17	19	20	20	21	22	22
4	12	12	14	16	17	18	19	20	21	21
5	11	11	13	15	16	17	18	19	20	20
6	10	10	12	13	14	15	16	17	18	19
7	9	9	10	11	12	13	14	16	17	18
8	7	7	8	9	10	11	12	13	14	16
9 or more family members	5	5	6	7	8	9	10	11	12	14

Reasonable Rent in % of family income	Maximum Rate of Allowance in % of Rent
5 – 13	90
14 – 15	70
16 – 17	55
18 – 19	45
20 – 22	35

However, rent allowances, even in the case of a percentage of the family income which the family can reasonably be expected to bear, may not exceed the following percentage of the actual rent:

The maximum amounts to which rents or charges arising may be considered are uniform throughout the Federal territory. The law distinguishes between allowances for old and new property. The following maximum amounts per square meter, are payable.

In municipalities	For Living Accommodation with Central Heating with bath	without bath	without Central Heating with bath	without bath
Of "A" Districts	2,40	2,20	2,20	2,00
Of "S" Districts with less than 100.000 population	2,60	2,40	2,40	2,20
Of "S" Districts with more than 100.000 population	2,80	2,60	2,60	2,40
In new housing the following maximum rates per square meter are payable				
Of "A" Districts	3,30	3,10	3,10	2,90
Of "S" Districts with less than 100.000 population	3,50	3,30	3,30	3,10
Of "S" District with more than 100.000 population	3,70	3,50	3,50	3,30

Grounds for Refusal

Even in cases in which, under the above enumerated conditions, rent allowances would be payable, they may be withheld by reason of certain grounds for refusal. The grounds are: taking into account the personal and financial position of the family, the amount they can reasonably be expected to pay the full rent, or the full charges arising;

the impossibility of their paying the rent, or meeting the charges, because of serious fault on their own part; if they can reasonably be expected to utilise other assets in their possession;

payment of rent allowance for a second house or flat; continued residence in condemned property, or in inadequate accommodation, if a move to more suitable accommodation is possible, and can reasonably be expected;

leaving existing accommodation without reasonable grounds to move into other accommodation clearly beyond the financial position of the family;

the possibility and reasonableness of a move into other accommodation more suited to the financial and personal position of the members of the family belonging to the household and

suitable accommodation and use of the accommodation by a person who is only temporarily absent from the family (e.g. — student as subtenants).

An allowance to meet charges arising is not payable if the amount of the charges per square metre of the accommodation taken into account exceeds the upper limit by more than 35 %, in special cases up to 40 %.

In so far as other payments similar to rent allowances are made from Federal, Land, or municipal funds for the purpose of the economic preservation of property, such payments are taken into account.

Amounts of Allowances

The average rent allowances payable per month and case have developed as follows:

Year	Rent Allowance	Average Amount per Case and Month broken down as follows Rent Allowance	Allowance for charges arising
	DM	DM	DM
1965	43,51	40,63	69,91
1966	45,57	42,11	73,17
1967	47,62	44,35	76,09
1968	49,75	46,59	78,89
1969 (half year)	50,96		

Finance

Rent allowances are paid out by the Federal Lands, and refunded as to one half by the Federal Government. Allowances are paid by authorities as laid down in Land laws, or by authorities appointed by the Lands, as a rule, twelve monthly.

Expenditure on rent allowances increased almost four times between 1965 and 1969.

Expenditure on Rent Allowances

Year	Mill. DM per annum
1961	12
1965	146
1966	397
1967	429
1968	512
1969	580
1970	960
1971	1336
1972	1550
1973	1686

from 1970 onwards estimated

Legislative bases

Rent Allowances Law of 23.6.1960, in the version of 1.4.1965 (BGBl. l. p 177).

Social Aid

Introduction

Within the framework of the overall system of social security in the Federal Republic of Germany there still remains, even today, a wide field in which social aid can be given only in the form of public welfare from public funds.

This closes the gaps left open by other systems of social security for the reason that this form of service is not proper to them, or because they do not cover certain categories of people, or because their benefits are inadequate in individual cases. Welfare service has not been, and is not, limited to certain categories of persons, identifiable by defined characteristics, or to persons entitled to some other form of benefit or aid; it is rendered entirely on the grounds of the need of the individual affected, when the need arises, and if he is unable to meet it from his own resources. Social aid is rendered regardless of whether the state of distress is or is not the fault of the individual claiming it.

Poor Law and welfare services were, at the beginning of the century, mainly the responsibility of local authorities and private charities. Since, at the time, the idea perdominated that the poor were more or less themselves to blame for their poverty, they were given barely enough for subsistence. Welfare was granted only by governmental action. It was only in the aftermath of the first world war, when it came to be acknowledged that social need could arise out of causes other than the fault of the individual, that Poor Law relief was replaced by public welfare. The Welfare Regulations, and the Imperial Guide Lines on the Conditions, Type, and Amounts of Public Welfare of the year 1924 were, at that time, as up to date as is social aid to-day, which was condified in 1962 in the Federal Social Aid Law. By virtue of this reform, the law as applied to public welfare has been brought into line with the modern concept of the constitutional and social state, as well as with changed social conditions. Two amending laws (1965 and 1969) took account of experience gained in the actual administration of the Social Aid Law, and introduced a number of improvements in benefits, as well as improving the measures for ensuring the integration of handicapped persons.

General

Social Aid is granted to meet the cost of living, or in special exigencies of life. It is intended to enable the recipient to lead a life consistent with the dignity of man. Its aim is to enable the recipient, as far as possible, and independent of such aid, to participate in the life of the community as an active and economic man; in this connection he is expected to help to the best of his own ability (help to help yourself).

Amongst the principles upon which the Social Aid Law continues to be based is the granting of aid according to the special circumstances of each individual case (the principle of individualisation), with social help as a secondary consideration. The first named principle is intended to ensure that the type, from, and extent of aid granted must depend on the special circumstances of each case. Aid is granted to each individual as required by his particular situation. Individual wishes as to the type of aid are to be considered as far as possible. Whereas in 1950 expenditure on cash benefits exceeded that for benefits in kind, the position has since been reversed. Although recipients accommodated in institutions number only about one third of the total, this is mainly because of the very large number of persons outside the institutes who receive only single payments.

The principle that social aid is only a secondary consideration means that aid is given only to those unable to help themselves, or to obtain help from other sources. Obligations on the part of third parties, in particular of those legally obliged to maintain the applicant, or other social insurance Funds, remain uneffected; the obligations of the administrators of Social Aid take second place to such obligations.

Recipients of Social Aid
At the end of the Year — in 1.000s

Year	Total	Recipients not in Insitutes	in Institutes
1950	1 628	1 293	335
1955	1 328	922	361
1960	1 108	792	316
1965	1 404	1 044	360
1967	1 531	1 117	446
1968	1 503	1 084	454

In the great majority of the different types of aid the applicant has a legal entitlement to the aid; he can make good his claim in the courts. This applies only to the basic entitlement to aid, since, in these cases, too, the administration decides at its official discretion as to the type and amount of aid granted.

Aid can take the form of personal aid, cash benefits or benefits in kind. It can be granted in or outside institutes, homes or similar establishments.

Application for the grant of Social Aid is not necessary; it comes into action immediately the authorities, or their agents, become aware that the conditions are fulfilled. The offices are under an obligation to take preventive action if a threatened state of distress for an individual can thereby be averted, or to grant follow-up aid if this appears necessary to ensure the success of aid previously granted.

Aliens receive as a rule the same benefits as German nationals. However, they have no legal entitlement to certain types of aid, such as vocational training aid, except in so far as international agreements specifically provide for complete equality with German nationals.

Benefits

Social aid includes aid to meet the cost of living, and aid in special exigencies of life. The main difference between these two types is that help to meet the costs of living is mainly in the form of fixed rates, something which is not possible in the case of aid to meet special exigencies of life, and that the latter type provide for a much further reaching protection of existing income than in the case of cost of living aid.

Maintenance Allowances

Maintenance Allowances are intended to cover in particular the need for food, accommodation, clothing, personal hygiene, household effects, heating, and the personal requirements of daily life. The latter include relations to the environment, and participation in cultural life. Maintenance allowances also include some special elements, such as contributions to voluntary health insurance, reasonable provision for old age, a reasonable amount of death benefit, and burial costs.

There is a legal entitlement to maintenance allowances. Outside institutes and homes they are normally in the form of cash payments. Although the level of benefits varies in principle with individual need, for reasons of a uniform assessment of benefit a certain routine has been established. On the basis of need as ascertained from practical experience, current maintenance allowances are paid according to fixed scales. The rates payable to the head of a household are in a fixed proportion to those paid in respect of other members of the household, the rates payable to heads of household are also payable to single persons.

Head of the household	100 %	
Members up to the age of 6	45 — 50 %	of the fixed
Members between 7 and 13	70 — 75 %	rate of the
Members between 14 and 17	85 — 90 %	Head of the
Members aged 18 and over	75 — 80 %	Household

Rent allowances are payable in addition to the fixed rates, to the amount of the actual rent paid, in so far as the rent does not exceed the amount considered reasonable in the particular circumstances of the applicant.

Single payments, for example for the purchase of clothing and footwear, are made to regular recipients of social aid, to meet needs not included in the fixed rates, and to such applicants not in regular receipt of maintenance allowances whose income is not sufficient fully to cover maintenance. Immates of homes normally receive a reasonable amount of pocket money, except in cases in which they are unable to make a proper use of it.

Changes in the Scale of Allowances in Social Aid
As accountancy averages

Year	Single Persons		Heads of Household		Members of Household over 18		18 — 14		14 — 7		under 7 years	
	DM	1957 100 %	DM	1957 100 %	DM	1957 100 %	DM	1957 100 %	DM	1957 100 %	DM	1957 100 %
1957	70	100	63	100	51	100	51	100	45	100	35	100
1960	84	120	75	119	63	124	63	124	56	124	41	117
1965	118	169	118	187	91	178	100	196	84	187	56	160
1968	131	189	131	208	103	202	114	223	94	209	63	180
1969	137	194	137	217	107	210	119	233	98	218	66	189
1970	155	220	155	245	120	233	133	261	110	242	72	206

To these scales of allowances must be added Rent Allowances and an Old Age Allowance of 30 % (up to 30.9.65 = 20 %)

For certain groups of persons additional allowances are payable, corresponding to their needs, for example persons over 65 years of age, persons living alone, unemployable persons, persons bringing up several children, expectant mothers, and employed persons.

In the case of blind and handicapped persons who, as war injured would be entitled to a care and attendance allowance, additional need is officially recognised.

The authorities must endeavour to ensure that the applicant is genuinely seeking work, and that he receives an offer of work. If he refuses work he can reasonably be expected to accept, his claim for social aid lapses. In the event of persistent refusal to co-operate, aid may be reduced to the subsistence minimum, or he may be required to enter a home or an institute by order of the courts.

Scale of Allowances for Maintenance in DM per month

w.e.f.	land	Head of Household single person DM	Members of Household aged			
			under 7 DM	7 – 14 DM	14 – 18 DM	18 and over DM
1.6.70	Baden-Württemberg					
	Stuttgart	162	77	117	142	126
	remaining local authorities	155	74	112	136	120
1.6.70	Bayern (min. rates)	148	67	104	126	111
1.6.70	Berlin	157	73	110	134	125
1.6.70	Bremen	156	75	109	132	126
1.8.70	Hamburg	160	75	112	136	124
1.6.70	Hessen	156	71	110	133	117
1.6.70	Lower Saxony	156	70	109	132	117
1.6.70	Northrhine Westphalie					
	min. rates	156	74	113	137	121
	max. rates	160	76	116	140	124
1.6.70	Rhineland-Palatinate					
	min. rates	144	66	101	123	110
	max. rates	150	70	105	129	114
1.6.70	Saarland	152	73	110	133	118
1.6.70	Schleswig-Holstein	156	70	109	133	125

Since the middle of 1970 the following rates of maintenance allowance may be accepted as the Federal average for a married couple over 65 years of age:

Head of the Household	154.00 DM
Wife	119.00 DM
273.00 DM	
30 % Additional Needs Supplement	81.90 DM
354.90 DM	

In addition, and as a general rule, rent allowances are payable.

Aid in Special Situations in Life

Since, above all by reason of the improved benefits being provided by other forms of social security, the main field of activity of public welfare is increasingly concerned in dealing with cases of social need arising out of exceptional situations in life, the types of aid being granted to deal with such situations have been considerably improved and coordinated under the comprehensive title „Aid in Special Situations in Life". This includes help to establish or secure a means of livelihood, and for vocational training, preventive health measures, help in sickness, help for expectant and nursing mothers, integration help for handicapped persons, for consumptives, for the blind, constant attendance aid, home help, help for endangered persons, aid for old persons.

If help in special situations in life is supplied in a home or similar institute, it also includes the maintenance provided there.

Over and over the types of aid here enumerated, help may be granted in other exigencies, if the expenditure of public money appears to be justified. The purpose of this rule is to enable help to be given in new cases of social need arising in individual cases without the necessity for specific detailed legislative provision.

Aid for Establishing or Securing a Means of Livelihood

Help for establishing or securing a livelihood is, in its aims, primarily of a preventive nature. It can be granted to persons who have no adequate means of livelihood, or in which such means are endangered.

It is considered as a rule only in cases in which the applicant might otherwise be compelled to claim maintenance allowances. It is intended to enable the recipient to establish or to secure for himself a basis of livelihood by his own efforts.

Vocational Training Aid

Vocational Training Aid is granted for a suitable occupation, or other suitable employment. The concept of suitability requires that particular consideration must be given to the aptitude and ability of the trainee, but also, if the circumstances justify it, that training for a vocation of a socially higher status may be approved. If certain aptitude conditions are fulfilled, vocational training aid may be granted for attendance in schools of higher education, up to university standard. Aid is provided primarily in the form of cash or kind, and includes, in addition to fees, maintenance allowances, whereby in the case of trainees no longer of school age an additional allowance of 50 % above the standard rate is granted. Aid is, in general confined to persons who commence their training before their 25th year of age.

Preventive Health Measures

Preventive health measures are sanctioned in the case of persons who, according to medical opinion, are threatened by a specific illness or danger to health. This form of aid includes necessary recuperative treatment as prescribed by the medical practitioners, particularly in the case of children, young persons, elderly persons, and mothers. It also includes precautionary medical examinations for the early detection of illnesses; this is particularly important in the case of cancer.

Sick Aid

Sick aid includes, in conformity with the corresponding regulations of other social service laws, medical and dental treatment, the provision of medicines, dressings, and dentures, hospital treatment, as well as other services necessary for recovery from, and improvement and alleviation of, the effects of an illness. The sick person has a free choice amongst doctors who are prepared to give treatment at the rates laid down by the Local and Land Health Insurance Funds.

Help for Expectant Mothers and in Confinement

Help for expectant mothers, and in confinement, includes medical treatment and aid, the provision of medicines, dressings, and other medical supplies, a lump sum to meet the expenses arising from confinement, attendance, including, attendance and care in the home, or in an institute or maternity home, and a maternity allowance. Benefits are as a rule in line with those provided under social insurance regulations for the dependants of an insured person.

Integration Aid for Handicapped Persons

Intergration aid is granted to people who are physically handicapped, blind, partially sighted, deaf, hard of hearing, or suffering from impediments of speech, or who are threatend by such handicaps, people who are mentally underdeveloped or mentally disordered. Such people have a claim to integration aid. This aid can also be granted to other categories of physically or mentally handicapped persons.

The object of integration aid is to avert a threatened or existent handicap, to eliminate or to alleviate the effects thereof, and so to make possible, or to facilitate, the participation of the handicapped person in the life of the community. Measures primarily adopted include out-patient and hospital treatment, the provision of artificial limbs and orthopaedic and other aids, assistance for educational and vocational training, further training or re-training, assistance for integration into working life, and the safeguarding of such integration.

The claim to integration aid also includes, in addition to a number of other measures, continuous maintenance for the handicapped person, in which connection the greater needs of persons over school age are met by payments at least 50 % higher than standard rates.

A further substantial benefit is granted to the parents of handicapped children of school age. This applies in cases in which the children, by reason of their physical or mental handicap, are unable to take part in normal schooling, and are thus compelled to attend special schools. There are, however, too few special schools to accommodate all handicapped children. In these cases parents are compelled to resort to daily arrangements, or to homes for handicapped children — and this, varying with their income and financial positioon — at their own expense. For attendance in these institutions, payments must be made only to the amount in which home savings in respect of the child or the young person are effected. The same applies in the case of children or young persons suffering, or who have suffered, from tubercolosis, and who for this reason require additional aid for their education.

Integration renders the implementation of varied measures necessary, according to the needs of the individual case. In order that these measures may be available in good time, the administrators of social aid have drawn up an Overall Plan.

Tubercolosis Aid

Tuberculosis aid includes curative treatment, aid for integration into working life, maintenance allowances, special services and preventive aid. Tuberculosis aid occupies a special position, in that its purpose is not only the cure of the consumptive and the safeguarding of the cure, but also the safeguarding of the environment of the sick person against the spread of the disease.

Help for integration into working life includes in particular suitable educational and vocational training, and help in securing suitable employment; such help must be in accord with the physical capacity and the aptitudes of the sick or convalescent person.

Maintenance allowances must take account of the nature and extent of the requirements of the sick or convalescent person, as well as of others resident in his household. So far as allowances at the standard rate are payable, an increased need of 50 % of the rate must be granted. Over and above these allowances, additional allowances for special nourishment are payable, according to individual needs.

Special grants are made in particular for domestic help, or help in small businesses, and in obtaining accommodation. Further, grants or loans may be obtained for the improvement of living accommodation, and grants to the sick person or his dependants towards the expense of visits during hospitalisation.

Aid to the Blind

Aid to the blind is provided from the third year of life onwards, to cover additional expenditure due to the blindness, in so far as no similar benefit is payable under other legal regulations. The amount of aid to the blind payable is based on the current minimum rates for care and attendance payable to war pensioners, to the uniform amount for blind persons over 18 of 319 DM per month, under 18 of 159,50 per month. Aid to the blind may be withheld if the blind person refuses to perform work which he may reasonably be expected to perform, or refuses training, advanced training, or retraining, designed to facilitate his re-integration into working life. Blind persons resident in institutes or homes receive an allowance of 140 DM or 70 DM per month.

Help in the Care of the Sick and Handicapped

Help in care of the sick is granted in respect of persons who, in consequence of sickness or physical handicap, are so helpless that they are unable to manage without care and attendance. It includes accommodation in institutes, and home help. If, in an individual case, home help suffices, the authorities must endeavour to obtain such help from friends or relatives, or from neighbours. A reasonable amount of the resultant expenditure must be refunded; in addition special grants may be made. If circumstances so require help must be granted in the form of the costs of a trained nurse. If permanent and extensive home care and attendance are needed and available, a fixed allowance of at least DM 150 per month may be made. Persons suffering from particularly severe handicaps and in need of care receive a nursing allowance of DM 225 per month.

Home helps

Home helps are provided in cases in which no member of the household is capable of keeping house, and the continued conduct of the household is essential. This help includes the personal care of the members of the household. It can in certain circumstances include the reasonable costs of temporary alternative accommodation for members of the household.

Help for endangered persons

Help for endangered persons is provided in the case of persons over 20 years of age and those over 18 who have achieved majority, who by reason of weakness of character, are not capable of leading an orderly life in the community. It is the aim of this type of aid to induce them to lead an orderly life. Above all, the endeavour is to accustom them to regular work. If all other forms of aid prove ineffective, persons in danger are advised to enter a home. Help is given without regard to available income or assets, though in case of accommodation in an institute the person is required to make a reasonable contribution to the costs.

Aid in old age

Aid in old age is intended, in the case of elderly persons, to help them to overcome the difficulties attendant on old age, and to avert loneliness. Account is taken of the fact that, by reason of the changing age structure of the population, the care of elderly people is assuming growing importance.

Individual aid measures are directed primarily to enabling elderly people to maintain their contacts with their environment. In particular, help is given to enable them to pursue some activity in which they are interested, to obtain suitable accommodation or to retain existing accommodation, to visit events and institutions serving their requirements, and help to enable them to maintain their contacts with friends and relations.

Help for Germans living abroad

Social aid may be granted to German nationals normally resident abroad who are in need of assistance, and if it is justified in individual cases. They may receive maintenance grants, sick grants, and grants for expectant and nursing mothers; other forms of social aid may also be granted. The nature, type, and extent of aid granted, as well as the amount of income and resources taken into consideration, are dependent on the conditions obtaining in the country of residence, with special consideration for the requirements of a German resident there.

Expenditure for Social Aid, according to different Types in mill. DM

Types of Aid	Outside Institutes		In Institutes		Total		Increase or Decrease in %
	1967	1968	1967	1968	1967	1968	
Maintenance Allowance Totals	785,4	793,0	189,8	196,5	975,2	989,5	+ 1,5
Current Allowance	663,6	669,3					
Single Grants	121,8	123,8	.	.	.	.	
Aid in special Exigencies							
— Totals	458,0	472,4	1 117,2	1 209,2	1 575,2	1 681,7	+ 6,8
Aid for the Establishment or							
Securing of Means of Livelihood	1,1	1,2	—	—	1,1	1,2	+ 7,8
Training Grants	16,4	19,9	8,9	9,0	25,3	28,9	+ 14,2
Preventive Health Measures	4,4	4,4	58,8	59,3	63,2	63,7	+ 0,8
Sickness Grants	102,7	110,1	132,2	135,6	234,9	245,8	+ 4,6
Aid for Expecting and							
Nursing Mothers	1,0	0,9	1,9	1,8	2,9	2,7	− 4,2
Integration Aid for Handicapped Persons	61,3	72,9	149,3	165,9	210,6	238,8	+ 13,4
TBC Aid	101,5	94,6	29,8	27,8	131,2	122,4	− 6,8
Aid for the Blind	91,1	88,9	3,7	4,7	94,8	93,7	− 1,2
Nursing Grants	63,4	63,4	714,6	785,6	778,0	849,0	+ 9,1
Home Helps	7,5	8,1	1,7	2,0	9,2	10,1	+ 10,5
Aid for Endangered Persons	0,2	0,2	11,6	12,1	11,8	12,3	+ 4,5
Aid for the Elderly	5,5	6,0	3,9	4,2	9,4	10,2	+ 9,1
Other Types	2,1	1,9	1,0	1,1	3,1	3,0	− 1,7
Totals	1 243,4	1 265,5	1 307,0	1 405,7	2 550,4	2 671,1	+ 4,7

Reckonability of Income and Private Means

Social aid is granted — with few exceptions, such as that for endangered persons — only if the applicant is without income or private means, or if they are inadequate. In this connection a clear distinction is made between maintenance allowances and help in special exigencies.

Income is the net income, that is to say, the amount at the disposal of the applicant to meet actually existing needs. Basic war pensions are not taken into account, either in the case of the beneficiary or his survivors.

In the case of maintenance allowances, the law requires the full reckonability of income before aid is granted. The applicant must use his own income, as must husband or wife not living separated, and the parents of unmarried minors living in the parental household. For instance, if an elderly married couple needs 400 DM per month to meet living costs and rent, and if both receive a total pension of 350 DM per month from some other social security scheme, an amount of 50 DM monthly is payable.

Help in special exigencies is granted if the applicant, or the husband or wife of the applicant not living separated, or, if he is a minor and unmarried, the parents, cannot reasonably be expected to find the money from their income. Whether or not this is the case is determined in the first instance on a level of income which varies in the case of different types of aid. If income is below the fixed level, and in special exigencies, it is granted in full, if it is above, the amount in excess is taken into account to a reasonable amount. In fixing the amount to be regarded as reasonable, the administrators of social aid will consider primarily the nature of the need, its duration, the amount required, and particular commitments. The result can be that income in excess of the fixed limit may either be disregarded or taken fully into account.

Whereas between the matter of income to be taken into account in the case of maintenance allowances and in the case of special exigencies, considerable differences are made, this is not so to the same extent in the matter of private means to be taken into account. The categories of persons on whose private means the grant of social aid is dependent are the same as those whose income is taken into account. From the basic obligation to use any private income or assets considerable exceptions are made in all types of social aid (e.g. earmarked assets, a small piece of land, household effects, a small amount of cash, a housebuilding savings account for the purchase of a small building site).

Refunds

There is an obligation to make a refund in three cases, namely if the recipient, deliberately or as a result of gross negligence, is himself responsible for the conditions leading to the grant of social aid, in the case of a single or short term maintenance grant, if the income subsequently rises to a certain amount, and in the case of inheritance. The claim to a refund is independent of other regulations on the participation of the recipient and other persons in the casts of the aid.

Any person over the age of 18, who deliberately, or as a consequence of gross negligence, is himself responsible for the conditions under which social aid has been granted to him, or to dependents for whose maintenance he is responsible, may be called upon to refund the costs thereof. Insofar as such refund would result in hardship for the person affected, or would jeopardize the aid already granted, it may be remitted.

Refunds may also be demanded from the recipient of maintenance allowances, the spouse, and from those persons whose income is taken into account when the aid is granted, when a single payment or payments for not more than three successive months have been made. The underlying idea here is that a person who, shortly after the grant of short term maintenance allowances, has again come into possession of a reasonable amount of money is not to be regarded as being continuously in need of support, and that he should be obliged to refund to the public the sums advanced to him as a kind of transitional aid. Consequently, the obligation to make a refund holds only if those under such obligation are once again in receipt of a reasonable amount of income.

Heirs of recipients may also be called upon to make a refund, since it is not regarded as reasonable that they should profit at the expense of the public from the inheritance of property, of which the recipient, and the remaining persons whose income had been taken into account, could not reasonably have been expected to dispose. The heir of the recipient, or of the spouse, if he or she dies before the recipient, is required to refund all the costs of social aid in excess of 1.200 DM arising in the five years preceding death. An exception is made in the case of tuberculosis aid. The heir is, of course, responsible only up to the amount of the inheritance. A claim for refund of costs is not made if the estate is worth less than 1.200 DM, or if the heir is related to the recipient and has been living in his household and caring for him, not merely temporarily, in so far as the estate does not exceed 30.000 DM, or if, in the circumstance of the individual case, a claim would occasion undue hardship for the heir.

Organisation

The administration of Social Aid is the responsibility of Local and District social aid authorities. Local authorities are the Kreis free cities and Land Administrative Districts, which latter may, on the basis of Land regulation, entrust certain of their communities or communal associations with the duties involved. District authorities are appointed by the Land. In part, the District authorities in social aid are manicipal self-administering corporations, in part they are governmental authorities. There are at present 22 such District authorities in the Federal Republic.

District Administrations of Social Aid

BADEN-WÜRTTEMBERG
Land Welfare Association Baden
                                    in Karlsruhe
Land Welfare Association Württemberg
                                    in Stuttgart
Land Communal Association of the Land
Hohenzollern   in Sigmaringen

BAVARIA
District Upper-Bavaria — Social Aid
Administration   in Minich
District Lower Bavaria — Social Aid
Administration   in Landshut
District Upper Palatinate — Social
Administration   in Regensburg
District Swabia — Social Aid
Administration   in Augsburg
District Middle Franconia — Social Aid
Administration   in Ansbach
District Lower Franconia
— Social Aid Administration in Würzburg
District Upper Franconia
— Social Aid Administration in Beyreuth

BERLIN
Senator for Social Affairs, Health
and Sport   in Berlin

BREMEN
Land Social Office   in Bremen

HAMBURG
Land Social Office   in Hamburg

HESSE
Land Welfare Association Hesse in Kassel

LOWER SAXONY
Lower Saxony Land Social Office
                                    in Hannover
Land Social Aid Authority   in Brunswick
Land Social Aid Association Oldenburg
                                    in Oldenburg

NORTH RHINE-WESTPHALIA
Land Association Rhineland   in Cologne
Land Association Westphalia — Lippe
                                    in Münster

RHINELAND-PALATINATE
Land Social Office Rhineland-Palatinate
                                    in Mayence

SAARLAND
Minister for Labour and Social Affairs
                                    in Saarbrücken

SCHLESWIG HOLSTEIN
Office for Welfare and Social Aid   in Kiel

The District administrations are competent for certain measures characterised by the fact that they are of more than local public importance, and entail special financial expenditure (hospital treatment for the integration of handicapped persons, tuberculosis treatment, help for the blind). They are also responsible for the grant of aid to Germans living abroad. For other matters the local administrations are responsible.

Under certain circumstances an adjustment of expenditure takes place between different administrations. This is in particular the case when hospitals and similar institutes are situated in the district of one administration and when beneficiaries from other districts are admitted.

Finance

On the basis of the division of responsibility between the Federal Government and the Federal Lands, it is the responsibility of the Lands to decide how the funds to finance social aid are to be raised. The Federal Government bears a share of the expenditure for migrants, for tuberculosis aid, and social aid for Germans living abroad, and social aid for refugees from Hungary.

Expenditure for Social Aid
in mill. DM

Year	Cash Benefit	Treatment in Institutes	Total	1950 = 100 %
1950	693	348	1 040	100
1955	696	552	1 248	120
1960*)	572	628	1 199	115
1965	1 045	1 061	2 106	203
1968	1 266	1 405	2 671	257

*) nine months

Legal aid

For disputes in common law in the field of social aid legislation, the Administrative Courts are competent, since such disputes have not been specifically allocated to other courts by Federal legislation. The rules of procedure of the Administrative Courts are applicable.

Co-operation between Social Aid and Voluntary Welfare Services

A systematic description of social aid would be incomplete without a reference to voluntary welfare services. These include the ideological and humanitarian organisations and associations which have made themselves responsible for providing aid for people in need, and which have established numerous institutes and homes for the purpose.

The Federal Working Community of Voluntary Welfare Services in Bonn

Workers' Welfare	in Bonn
The German Charitable Association	in Freiburg
The German Parity Welfare Association	in Frankfort
The German Red Cross	in Bonn
The Diaconian Mission	in Stuttgart
The Central Welfare Office of the Jews in Germany	in Frankfort

The Administrations of Social Aid make free use of these organisations in carrying out their own work. They have a duty to co-operate with the voluntary services in the interests of those seeking assistance, but, in so doing, to respect the independence of their aims and objects, and the carrying out of their own work. They also provide all reasonable assistance to the voluntary organisations. The public offices may request the voluntary services to give them general support in their work, or may ask them to undertake special tasks, if they agree to do so.

Legislative bases

The Federal Social Aid Law dated 30.6.1961 (BGBl. III-2170-1), in the version of 18.9.1969 (BGBl. I S. 1688)

Special Benefits

Financial Aid for the Blind

In the Federal Republic of Germany there are almost 32.000 blind persons, including about 26.000 civilian blind, and 6.500 war blind. The war blind are cared for by the War Pensions and Related Services. See details in the sector "Provision for War Victims". Under certain conditions the civilian blind have a claim to Financial Aid for the Blind under the Social Aid Law. See the sector "Social Aid". Since the principle of subsidiarity in social aid requires that the income and financial position of a civilian blind person should be taken into account, some Federal Lands have introduced a system whereby, on the basis of Land legislation, funds are made available for financial assistance to the blind without regard to their financial position.

Regulations differ in different Lands, varying according to the persons affected and the benefits payable; in general allowances to the blind are on the same scale as the lowest rate payable for care and attendance in the case of war victims. Implementation of Land legislation is the responsibility of the Land Insurance Institutes.

Compensation for Damages and Loss arising out of Political Persecution

Persons in the Federal Republic of Germany who have been victims of Nazi persecution are compensated to an adequate extent, and according to particular circumstances, on the basis of the Federal Compensation Law of 29.6.1956 (BGBI. III - 251 - 1), last amended by the Law dated 25.6.1969 (BGBI. I.S. 654). In the main, lump sum payments are made, but pensions may also be awarded; these are based on the pensions of comparable public officials. By 1975 these payments, together with those already made, will have amounted to almost 30 milliard DM.

In 1969 a "Foundation for Former Political Prisoners" was established. The Fund of the Foundation, which was financed exclusively by the Federal Government, amounts to 10. mill. DM. Interest accruing and a sum of 500.000 DM annually from the Fund, are to be devoted to the support of persons who, as a consequence of political imprisonment, have suffered particular financial losses. Losses and damages sustained as a consequence of political persecution are compensated in part through social insurance. Improvements are under consideration.

Compensation for Special War Damages and Losses

Late returnees from prison of war internment after the second world war receive, pursuant to the Returnees Law dated 19.6.1950 (BGBI.III—84—1), amended by the Law dated 30.5.1969 (BGBI. I S. 451), and the Prisoners of War Compensation Law of 30.1.1954, in the version of 29.9.1969 (BGBI. I S. 1800), certain loans, grants, and compensation; certain disadvantages arising in the field of social and unemployment insurance are evened out. In 1969 an Incorporated Foundation in Public Law for the benefit of returnees was established. The Federal Government provided a sum of 60. mill DM for the "Returnees Foundation for former Prisoners of War". From the interest on this sum, and from the original Fund, loans may be made to establish or secure a livelihood, to obtain living accommodation, or for other purposes deserving of support, and also grants for the alleviation of undeserved distress. The Fund can also award scientific assignments for research into delayed damage to health arising from detention as a prisoner of war, or from internment. All persons who were imprisoned in connection with the second world war may be considered for assistance.

Expellees and evacuees have a claim to specially favoured treatment in all fields of economic life on the basis of the Federal Expellees Law of 19.5.1953 (BGBI. III - 240 - 1) last amended by the Law of 14.8.1969 (BGBI. I. S. 1153) and the Federal Evacuees Law of 14.7.1953, (BGBI. - III - 241-1), amended by the Law of 14.8.1969 (BGBI. I. S 1153).

Persons who have suffered loss or damage through the Occupation Powers can be compensated on the basis of the Law in Settlement of Occupation Damages of 1.12.1955 (BGBI. III - 624 - 1).

Pursuant to the Reparations Damages Law of 12.2.1969 (BGBI. I S. 105), persons who have suffered reparations, restitution, destruction, or repayment losses, may in the event of inadequate pensions, receive War Losses Pensions on the same basis as those payable under the Equalisation of Burdens Law, and in respect of material war losses.

Financial Security for Soldiers' Dependents

Persons called up for military service, and their dependents, receive payments to cover the cost of living. Such payments are also made to those serving voluntarily. They are not payable if the person is entitled as a regular soldier, a short term regular, an established official, or a judge, or as a manual or non-manual worker in the public service, to continued payment of salary or wage. (Security of Maintenance Law of 26.7.1957, in the version of 31.5.1961 (BGBI. III-53-3), last amended by the Law dated 14.4.1969 (BGBI. I. p. 289). Benefits consist of current cash payments, special services (sick aid, help in obtaining accommodation, refund of contributions, rent allowances, and similar). Expenditure in 1969 amounted to 287 mill. DM.

International Social Security

Introduction

Economic relations between peoples and states are growing ever closer. Reciprocal influence makes itself felt in two ways: As a result of progressive industrialisation, and fashioned on existing models, mostly with particularly favourable social benefits, a process of adaptation of the varying social systems is taking place (now designated as harmonisation). The level of expenditure on social services in international comparison is shown briefly in the Sector "Overall Picture of Present Day Social Security". The migration of workers from one country to another has led to efforts to facilitate such migration by means of bilateral and supra-national agreements, of which details here follow. The social security systems of many countries discriminate against aliens as compared with their own nationals, or against persons resident abroad as compared with those living in their own country. Further, in the case of persons who have been alternately insured, employed, or resident at home and abroad, most countries take into account only the periods of insurance, employment, or residence in the home country in considering whether the conditions for benefit have been satisfied, and in assessing the amounts payable. The elimination of such disadvantages is the most important object of bilateral and supra-national agreements and regulations in the field of social insurance. Such agreements and regulations are based on the conviction that the political and economic coalescence of the different states must lead to an ever increasing exchange of workers over and beyond national boundaries, and that, consequently, no restrictions should be imposed on, in particular, the mobility of workers. The first such agreement had already been concluded by the former German Reich before the First World War. Between the two world wars a whole network of such agreements were concluded in Europe, and this development has continued in a much greater measure in the post-war years.

Interstate Relations

The Federal Republic of Germany has concluded bilateral agreements on social insurance (social health, accident, and pensions insurance) with a great many countries, also on family allowances and unemployment insurance. These agreements are based in general on the following principles:
equal treatment for the different nationalities,
credit for insurance and similar contribution periods under the law of other contracting states in considering the admissibility and maintenance of social insurance claims,
unrestricted payment of pensions to beneficiaries in other contracting states,
mutual aid in social health and accident insurance by the insurance institutes in the other contracting states, the payment of family allowances, including allowances for children resident in other contracting states.
The Federal Republic of Germany is also a partner to a series of multilateral treaties; these are concerned as a general rule with the work of interstate institutes. Amongst these is, in particular, the International Labour Office in Geneva. It has been in existence since 1919 — the German Reich was a member from 1919 to 1935 — and has, since 1946, been a Special Organisation of the United Nations. It has at present 121 members; the Federal Republic has been a member since 12.6.1951. This organisation regards it, inter alia, as its

most important function to improve social security throughout the world through the medium of Conventions and Recommendations. Of the Conventions affecting social security, 13 are, or will shortly be, binding on the Federal Republic. These include the particularly important Convention 102 on Minimum Standards of Social Security dated 28.6.1952 (BGBl. 57 II S. 1321) in force since 21.2.1959. The branch of social security for which the Member State affected accepts responsibility must conform to these minimum standards. The Federal Republic of Germany has, as the first State, accepted the obligations arising from this Convention for all branches of social insurance.

The most recent agreements, which received the sanction of the Federal Parliament in the summer of 1970, are the Convention No. 118 on equal treatment for nationals and aliens in matters of social security, and no. 1228 — Benefits payable in the event of Disablement, Old Age, and to Survivors.

The European Social Charter of 18.10.1961 (BGBl, 64 II 2 1261), in force since 26.2.1965, as a new multilateral Treaty of the Council of Europe, has the object of emphasising important socio—political demands as the commom aim of the 18 Member States of the Council of Europe. The bases of the Charter, which must be accepted as binding by every Signatory State are, inter alia, the right to work, to social security and to protection of the family. A European Social Security Code was ratified by the Federal Parliament in Summer 1970. It lays on all Member States an obligation to continue the development of their systems of social security in such a fashion, particularly in respect of the scope, the conditions, and the amount of benefits, that they conform to certain minimum standards. The two transitional European Agreements on Social Security dated 11.12.1953 (BGBl. 56 II S. 507) in force since 1.9.1956, are to be replaced by a Consolidating Agreement.

Social Security in the European Economic Community

The Federal Republic of Germany, Belgium, France, Italy, the Netherlands and Luxembourg, as members of the European Economic Community, have long been associated in the field of social security by numerous bilateral and multilateral treaties. These treaties are, however, applicable only to certain groups of persons, such as self-employed persons and seamen, or deal only with specific questions, since the majority of their provisions for employed employees and similar categories have been replaced with effect from 1.1.1959 by Ordinances Nos. 3 and 4 of the Council of the European Community (EEC) on the Social Security of Migrant Workers (BGBl. 59 II S. 473). The Ordinance 36/63 EEC (BGBl. 63 II S. 893), and the Ordinance 73/63 EEC of 11.7.1963 have regulated the social security of border crossers, seasonal workers, and others not resident in the countries in which they are employed. Ordinances 3 and 4 are constantly being extended and improved by further Ordinances and Agreements. New relevant treaties may be concluded between the Member States only in so far as they are in conformity with the principles and the spirit of Ordinances 3 and 4.

The Ordinances regulate social insurance (health, accident, and pensions insurance, unemployment insurance and assistance, as well as family allowances. They are applicable to the nationals of the six Member States, as well as to refugees and stateless persons normally resident in the territory of these States; they conform to the customary principles of social insurance agreements. Within the EEC there is an Administrative Commission for the Social Security of Migrant Workers. Its function is to regulate all administrative questions and questions of interpretation arising from the Ordinances, and to promote and consolidate co-operation in the field of social security.

Liaison Offices and Competent Authorities for the Administration of the Ordinances of the European Economic Community.

Liaison Offices
KV Federal Association of Local Health Funds
UV Federal Association of Industrial Injuries Insurance Institutes
ArV Association of German Manual Workers Pensions Insurance Administrations
AnV Federal Insurance Institute for Non-Manual Workers
KnV Federal Miners' Special Scheme Insurance
KG Federal Institute for Labour

Competent Authorities
KV The Sickness Fund of which the beneficiary is a member, or the General Local Sickness Fund, Bad Godesberg
ArV Land Insurance Institute Westphalia for the Netherlands. Land Insurance Institute Rhine Province for Belgium
Land Insurance Institutes Swabia for Italy
Land Insurance Institute Rhineland Palatinate for France and Luxembourg.
AnV Federal Insurance Institute for Non-Manual Workers
KnV Federal Miners Special Scheme Insurance.

There are separate arrangements for the Saarland, for the Seaman's Fund, and for the Federal Railways Insurance Institute.

Payment of Social Benefits Abroad

Social benefits are not generally payable abroad, or only to a limited extent. There are, however, several exceptions to this rule, in particular when there exist between the State in which the beneficiary is resident and the Federal Republic of Germany treaties or other agreements laying down when payments may be made abroad to Germans — and, according to the provisions of the agreements — to all aliens, or only to the nationals of the other contracting party — similar treatment being accorded to refugees. In so far as an agreement provides for equal treatment, without regard to residence at home or abroad, pensions are payable to the nationals of the other contracting party resident in a non-contracting State, at the same rate as those payable to German nationals resident in that State.

Welfare Agreements

Agreements concluded in the field of Social Aid (Welfare) accord, on the basis of reciprocity, the same benefits under social welfare to aliens as to nationals. This applies to agreements with Switzerland and Austria, as well as to the European Welfare Agreement of 11.12.1953, in force since 1.9.1956 (BGB 56 II S.563) stateless aliens receive the same social assistance benefits as German nationals on the basis of the Law on the Legal Position of Stateless Aliens in the Federal Republic of 25.4.1951 (BGB I S.269), amended by the Law of 9.9.1965 (BGB I S. 1273).

If there is no treaty in force between the State of which the beneficiary is a national and the Federal Republic of Germany, and if there is no other form of regulation, interstate legal regulations are applicable when he is resident abroad. They are set out in the sectors "Accident Insurance", "Pensions Insurance", "War Pension and Related Services", and "Social Aid".

**Liaison Offices responsible for the Implementation of
Bi-latieral and Multi-lateral Agreements.**

KV	Federal Association of Local Sick Funds
UV	Federal Association of Industrial Injuries Institutes
AR	LVA Schleswig Holstein for Denmark
	LVA Rhine Palatinate for France
	LVA Württemberg for Greece
	LVA Free and Hanseatic City Hamburg for Great Britain
	LVA Swabia for Italy
	LVA Westphalia for the Netherlands
	LVA Upper Bavaria for Austria
	LVA Baden for Switzerland
	LVA Rhine Province for Spain and the Rhine Shipping Agreement
	LVA Upper Franconia and Middle Franconia for Turkey
	LVA Lower-Bavaria-Upper Palatinate for Yugoslavia
ANV	Federal Insurance Institute for Non-Manual Workers
KNV	Miners' Special Scheme
ArbIV	Federal Institute for Labour

(see Abbreviations in Appendix).

Treaties on War Pensions and Related Services

The treaties concluded in the field of Provision for War Victims solve the problems arising from the service of aliens in the German armed forces during the second world war. The Compensation Treaty concluded with Luxembourg on 11.7.1959 (BGB 60 II S. 2077), in force with effect from 29.9.1961, and the treaty with Belgium on Provision for War Victims of 21.9.1962 (BGB 64 II S. 455), in force with effect from 1.4.1964, provide that each State shall compensate its own war victims and their survivors; the Federal Republic of Germany has paid once and for all compensation sums to these two States.

The treaty concluded with Austria on 7.5.1963 (BGB 64 II S. 220), in force with effect from 1.9.1964, lays down that pensions are payable by the homeland to the war victim or his survivors, whereas curative treatment is provided by the country of residence; costs are regulated between the two countries. The treaty with Spain dated 29.5.1962 (BGB 65 II S. 273), in force with effect from 1.6.1965, accords to Spanish war victims and their survivors a claim to a basic pension pursuant to German law; curative treatment is provided by the country of residence.

Legislative Bases

The following list contains only the main agreements on social security to which the Federal Republic of Germany is a party, in so far as they concern social insurance and unemployment insurance.

Bilateral Agreements

Belgium
General Agreement on Social Security dated 7.12.1957 (BGBl. 63 II S. 404), in force with effect from 1.1.1959.
Special Agreement on Unemployment Insurance dated 7.12.1957 (BGBl. 64 II S. 170), in force with effect from 1.9.1964.

Denmark
Agreement on Unemployment Insurance dated 1.8.1959 (BGBl. 60 II S. 2109) in force with effect from 1.3.1961.
Agreement on Social Insurance dated 14.8.1953 (BGBl. 54 II S. 753), in force with effect from 1.11.1954.

Finnland
Agreement on Accident Insurance dated 18.6.1927 (BGBl. 28 II S. 20), in force with effect from 4.4.1928.

France
General Agreement on Social Security dated 10.7.1950 (BGBl. 51 II S. 177), in force with effect from 1.1.1951.

Greece
Agreement on Social Security dated 25.4.1961 (BGBl. 63 II S. 678), in force with effect from 1.11.1963.
Agreement on Unemployment Insurance dated 31.5.1961 (BGBl. 62 II S. 1109), in force with effect from 1.8.1963.

Great Britain and Northern Ireland
Agreement on Social Security dated 20.4.1960 (BGBl. 61 II S. 241), in force with effect from 1.8.1961.
Agreement on Unemployment Insurance dated 29.4.1960 (BGBl. 61 II S. 585), in force with effect from 1.9.1961.

Italy
Agreement on Unemployment Insurance dated 5.5.1953 (BGBl. 54 II S. 485), in force with effect from 1.12.1954.
Agreement on Social Insurance dated 5.5.1953 (BGBl. 56 II S. 1), in force with effect from 1.4.1956.

Yugoslavia
Agreement on Unemployment Insurance dated 12.10.1968 (BGBl. 69 II S. 1473), in force with effect from 1.11.1969.
Agreement on Social Security dated 12.10.1968 (BGBl. 69 II S. 1437), in force with effect from 1.9.1969.

Luxembourg
Compensation Treaty (applies to reparation payments, provisions for war victims, and social insurance), dated 11.7.1959 (BGBl. 60 II S. 2077, in force with effect from 29.9.1961.

Netherlands
Agreement on Unemployment Insurance dated 29.10.1954 (BGBl. 55 II S. 909), in force with effect from 1.4.1956.
Agreement on Social Insurance dated 29.3.1951 (BGBl. 51 II S. 221), in force with effect from 1.11.1951.

Norway
Agreement on the Reciprocal Award of Social Services dated 2./6.9.1965 (BGBl. 66 II S. 301), in force with effect from 6.9.1965.

Austria
(First) Agreement on Unemployment Insurance dated 15.5.1951 (BGBl. 52 II S. 612), in force with effect from 1.1.1953.
Second Agreement on Unemployment Insurance dated 31.10.1953 (BGBl. 55 S. 609), in force with effect from 1.11.1955
Agreement on Social Security dated 22.12.1966 (BGBl. 69 II S. 1233), in force with effect from 1.11.1969, with a Supplementary Agreement dated 10.4.1969 (BGBl. 69 II S. 1260), in force with effect from 1.11.1969.

Portugal
Agreement on Social Security dated 6.11.1964 (BGBl. 68 II S. 473), in force with effect from 1.1.1969.

Switzerland
Agreement on the Unemployment Insurance of Border Crossers dated 4.2.1928 (RGBl. 28 II S. 311), in force with effect from 4.6.1928.
Agreement on Social Security dated 25.2.1964 (BGBl. 65 II S. 1293), in force with effect from 1.5.1966.

Spains
Agreement on Social Security dated 29.10.1959 (BGBl. 61 II S. 598), in force with effect from 1.10.1961.
Agreement on Unemployment Insurance dated 20.4.1966 (BGBl. 67 II S. 1945), in force with effect from 1.12.1967.

Turkey
Agreement on Social Security dated 30.4.1964 (BGBl. 65 II S. 1169), in force with effect from 1.11.1965.

United States of America
Friendship, Trading and Mercantile Marine Treaty dated 29.10.1954 (BGBI. 56 II S. 487), in force with effect from 14.7.1956.

Multilateral Agreements
Belgium, Federal Republic of Germany, France, The Netherlands, Switzerland.
Revised Agreement on the Social Security of Rhine Boatmen dated 13.2.1961 (BGBI. 69 II S. 1357, 1412), in force with effect from 1.2.1970.

Self Government of Social Insurance Institutes

Introduction

Social services for recipients are provided by public administrations which, in some cases, also collect the relevant contributions. These administrations are segregated, in part or entirely, from State and local administrations; they are special administrations; for the larger part they are even independent corporations and institutes in public law, over which the State exercises (only) limited supervision. In order to mitigate any differances which may arise between the administrations and the persons affected, and to maintain good relations between them, there are in nearly all social service fields honorary representatives of the insured person, or of the beneficiaries, who work together in varying degrees with the administrations. The greatest influence in this field is exercised in the self-governing bodies in social insurance administration, in which the following types are operative:

Pensions Insurance of Manual and Non-manual Workers, and Miners' Special Scheme	Self-governing
Pensions Insurance for the Free Professions	Self-governing, with especially far-reaching powers in regard to the Statutes (autonomy)
Health Insurance	Self-governing
Industrial Injuries Insurance	Self-governing
Federal Institute for Labour	Self-governing, with State participation
War Pensions and Related Services	Advisory Committees
Equalisation of Burdens	Adjustment Committees

In the case of Social Aid, the elected representatives of local authorities participate, in part directly, in part indirectly. Pensions insurance for farmers, equalisation of family burdens, the payment of rent allowances, and assistance measures for refugees are entrusted to administrations in other branches.

The following paragraphs deal only with self-government in social insurance administrations, and in the Federal Institute for Labour.

Self Government in Social Insurance Administrations

The Imperial Proclamation of 1881, Bismarck's then government programme for social policy, already announced that the insurance of the workers was to be "established in close relation with the real forces in national life . . . ." in the form of corporations, and associations under "State auspices, and with the support of the State". On the basis of this policy the Funds were administered by an Executive Committee and a Representatives Assembly, comprised in part only of workers or employers (e.g. in accident insurance), partly by both jointly, varying with the source and distribution of the contributions. The Executive Committees in Pensions Insurance were staffed by public officials.

In 1934 the self-administration of the funds was replaced by a single responsible official (Leader), assisted by an Advisory Committee. In 1951/52 the present system was established, which resembles the pre-1934 system in many respects. New regulations issued in 1967 were designed to provide an improved basis for the 1968 elections to the self-governing bodies, whilst utilising past experience.

Objects and Functions

By means of the system of self-government, workers and employers, those directly affected, play their part in the policies adopted by the Funds, and in the performance of their legal obligations. They elect their own representatives. These then comprise the government of the Insurance Funds, i.e. those bodies which determine their objects, and are responsible for them. They lay down the Statutes, organise the administrations, elect the executive management, and, within the framework of relevant legislation and of the Statutes, they also lay down procedure. That is their responsibility. The offices are honorary. The conduct of day to day business is in the hands of the executive management.

Elections

Groups of persons affected by social insurance: the insured persons, the employers, the pensioners, and — exceptionally — self-insured persons in agricultural accident insurance, elect the members of the Representatives' Assemblies at 6 yearly intervals; under the Miners' Special Scheme Insurance stewards (or elders) are elected, who then elect their own Representatives' Assembly. Elections are free and secret; they are, however, greatly simplified by the fact that the different groups, e.g. the trade unions, which are entitled to submit lists of nominees, as a rule reach agreement amongst themselves on the lists to be submitted, thereby rendering elections unnecessary, since the nominees are then regarded as elected. Elections were held in 1953, 1958, 1962, and 1968. In 1968 elections were held only in 52 of the 2.100 Funds. In these 52 cases about 28.9 mill. insured persons were entitled to vote — about 5.6 mill. did so.

Administrative Bodies

The administrative bodies — the organs — of self-government are the Representatives Assembly and the Executive Committee. They exist in every Fund, and, generally speaking, consist of equal numbers of workers' and employers' representatives, with the following exception: Under the Miners' Special Scheme the bodies are comprised as to two thirds of representatives of the insured persons and as to one third of employers' representatives. In the case of the Agricultural Injuries Insurance Institutes, self-employed persons not employing labour have one third representation. In the case of Health Insurance Funds inside individual enterprises, — Works Funds — and in the case of the Federal Railways Insurance Institute, the employer is represented by one member only, who, however, has the same number of votes as the representatives of the insured persons. In the case of the Substitution Funds (Ersatzkassen — corresponding largely to Friendly Societies : Translator), the insured persons are autonomous.

Executive Committee

Pursuant to the law, the Statutes fix the number of the members of the Executive Committee in accordance with the size of the Fund. The Committee represents the Fund in law, and in general; it has the status of a legal representative.

The Executive Committee lays down the guide lines for the work of the Fund, makes urgent decisions, and is responsible for their proper implementation. The chairman has the duty to query any resolutions adopted by the Representatives Assembly and the Executive Committee which do not comply with the law, or with the Statutes, by entering an objection with the Supervisory Authority.

Representatives Assembly

The Representatives Assembly must comprise a maximum of 60 members. For the composition of its personnel, the same rules are applicable as in the case of the election of the Executive Committee. The Representatives Assembly resolves on the Statutes, and elects the Executive Committee. It also draws up the budget of the Fund, approves the report and accounts, sanctions additional benefits, and fixes the rate of contributions, in so far as this is not done by law.

Management

The members of the Executive Committee and the Representatives Assembly fulfill their office in the governing bodies of the Social Insurance Funds in addition to their normal occupations; the office is honorary, expenses only being payable. The conduct of the day to day business, nowever, calls for a full time management — the business management — at the head of the administration; it consists as a rule of a manager and his deputy. In the case of the Land Insurance Institutes and the Federal Institute for Non-Manual Workers, a management triumvirate conducts the business. The managers are ex-officio advisory members of the Executive Committee.

Self Government of the Federal Institute for Labour

The self-government of the Federal Institute for Labour deviates in many respects from the law governing social insurance. Its governing bodies are the Executive Committee (9 representatives), and the Administrative Council (39 representatives) of the Federal Institute for Labour, and the Administrative Committees in the Regional Offices and the Employment Exchanges. They comprise equal numbers of representatives of workers, employers, and public authorities. These representatives are not elected directly by the insured persons, but are nominated by designated bodies. In the case of the workers' representatives, the right of nomination lies with the trade unions, of the employers with their associations. The representatives of the public authorities in the administrative committees are proposed by local authorities, and nominated by their supervisory authorities; in the case of the Executive Committee and the Administrative Council a certain right of nomination is vested in the Federal Government, the Federal Council, and the National Municipal Associations.

Legislative bases

Self-Administration Law of 22.2.1951, in the version of 28.8.1967, last amended by the Law of 28.7.1969 (BGBl. I S. 974). Labour Promotion Law of 25.6.1969 (BGBl. I S. 582), last amended by the Law of 22.12.1969 (BGBl. I S. 2360).

Social Jurisdiction

Introduction

The Federal Republic of Germany is a democratic and social Federal State under the rule of law (Art. 20, Basic Law). Should any person's rights be infringed by a public authority he may appeal to the courts (Art. 19, Basic Law), in the case of disputes affecting statutory social services to the Social Courts, and, in some instances, to the Administrative Courts. In the case of social insurance, legal disputes on entitlement to benefits were, from 1884 to 1911, decided by Arbitration Offices; from 1912 to 1953 they were decided by the Insurance Authorities Insurance Offices, the Higher Insurance Offices, in some Lands by the Land Insurance Offices, and by the Reichs Insurance Office in a three instance procedure. The Reichs Insurance Office ceased to function in 1945. After the first world war, Pensions Courts were established, whose rulings could be reconsidered by the Reichs Pension Court until 1945. Because of the absence of a Federal Court, and because of the separation of the Social Courts from the administrative authorities as required by the Basic Law, Social Jurisdiction was established in 1954. It is a special form of social jurisdiction, segregated from administrative jurisdiction.

The Functions of Social Jurisdiction

The Social Courts adjudicate on statutory disputes affecting Health Insurance, Accident Insurance, Pensions Insurance of manual and non-manual workers, the Miners' Special Scheme, self-employed craftsmen's insurance, the law as affecting insurance schemes' doctors, farmers' pensions, unemployment insurance, and all other matters affecting the Federal Institute for Labour, war pensions and related services, continued payment of wages during sickness, the Federal Children's Allowances Law, the Prisoners' Aid Law, the Soldiers' Pensions Law, as well as the health services pursuant to the Federal Compensation Law. Disputes affecting War Victims' Welfare are dealt with by the General Administrative Courts, which are also competent for disputes affecting the Equalisation of Burdens Law, public social aid, rent allowances, and for certain Pensions Funds of the free professions.

The Office of Judge

Professional judges must have the qualifications for the exercise of their office as required by generally valid regulations for all judges; they are appointed as judges of the first and second instance pursuant to Land laws. The professional judges in the Federal Social Court are appointed by the Federal President on the joint nomination of the Federal Minister of Labour and Social Order and the Judges Selection Committee. Honorary assessors assist the professional judges at all stages; they are appointed for a period of office of 4 years by the Land and Federal Governments, on the nomination of the entitled organisations (workers' and employers' organisations, war victims' associations) in consultation with certain Federal and Land authorities. The participation of these honorary judges in jurisdiction is intended to promote and strengthen the links between jurisprudence and social reality.

The Social Courts give their rulings in Chambers, with a professional judge as Chairman and two social (lay) judges. In the second and third instances, rulings are given by Senates comprising 3 professional judges and two Land or Federal Social judges. The Great Senate of the Federal Social Court reaches decisions on questions of fundamental importance, or when necessary to ensure uniformity of jurisdiction, or the further build up of case law, or in the event that one Senate desires to give a different ruling from another Senate on a specific point of law. The Great Senate operates with the President of the Federal Social Court as chairman, the Presidents of the Senates involved, 6 professional judges, and the Federal Social judges; Chambers of experts, and expert Senates competent for particular fields, are attached to the Courts.

The Process of Law

Legal protection is granted on application to the courts. In the majority of cases the complainant begs for judgement against the defendant, requiring him to cancel the ruling complained of, and to sanction an insurance or other benefit. The point at issue may also be a plea for the cancellation or amendment of some administrative act, further, in certain cases, the confirmation of the existence of a certain legal position, of competence to rule, or for a ruling that some administrative act is null and void.

Administrative measures undertaken at their own discretion by a public authority, or an Insurance Fund, may be the subject of court action designed to ascertain whether the limits of such discretion have been exceeded and an improper use made thereof. The Procedure in Social Courts is largely the same as that in the General Administrative Courts. The courts officially consider the points at issue, and the case is conducted officially. The participants may conduct their own case before the Social Courts and the Land Social Courts, or may be represented by an authorised agent, including a solicitor.

Number of complaints in 1000s

Year	No. of cases	New cases	Disposed	Remaining
1955	405	224	301	328
1960	261	205	228	238
1965	175	159	170	164
1968	168	162	165	166
1969	166	154	158	162

The case must be opened if a complaint has been entered against a ruling of a Health Insurance Fund, of the Miners Special Scheme, of an office of the Federal Institute for Labour, or of an administrative authority of War Pensions and Related Services. In the case of disputes affecting contributions to Accident Insurance, and in the Pensions Insurance of manual and non-manual workers, further, in disputes in common law on the basis of the Law on Continued Payment of Wages during Sickness, a preliminary hearing takes place. This preliminary hearing is not a part of the process of law, but it gives the administrative authorities an opportunity to amend their ruling, and thus to relieve the pressure on the Social Courts.

As a rule the Social Court reaches its decision in the form of a judgement. Appeal against such judgement is permissible, to the Land Social Court, unless it has been specifically precluded. Under certain circumstances appeal is still possible, for instance, if the Social Court approves of an appeal because of the fundamental importance of the point of law at issue. In the Court of Appeal the subject matter and the legal inplications are considered and adjudged anew.

Appeal against the judgement of a Land Social Court to the Federal Social Court is permissible, if the Court so rules. The Court is compelled to give its sanction if it has given a ruling of fundamental legal importance, or its ruling deviates from one given by the Federal Social Court. It is always permissible if a complaint of incorrect procedure is entered, or if, in its judgement of the causal connection of an impairment of health with an industrial injury or disease, or an injury within the meaning of the Federal Pensions Law, the law has not been complied with. The Federal Social Court is restricted to a review of points of law.

Parties before the Federal Social Court must be represented by a duly accredited person. An exception is made in the case of public authorities and corporations in public law. Duly accredited persons are solicitors and attorneys, and representatives of trade unions and War Victims Associations. In order to secure proper representation before the Federal Social Court a complainant may claim assistance as a poor person, in which case a solicitor or duly accredited person is appointed.

In order to reduce the prolonged periods entailed in court procedure — complaints take in 41 % of the cases, appeals in 53 % of the cases, revisions in 30 % of the cases, more than a year — a law designed to expedite procedure and to relieve the pressure on the Federal Social Court is in course of drafting.

Number of Appeals
in 1000s

Year	No.	New cases	Disposed of	Remaining
1955	79	45	32	92
1960	68	25	40	53
1965	31	17	22	26
1968	21	18	18	21
1969	21	17	18	20

*) first 6 months

Number of Revisions
in 1000s

Year	No.	New cases	Disposed of	Remaining
1955	0,9	2,3	1,6	1,6
1960	2,3	2,7	2,7	2,4
1965	2,4	2,7	2,8	2,3
1968	2,1	2,4	2,4	2,1
1969	2,1	2,2	2,4	1,9

Finance

Cases heard before the Social Courts are in principle free of charge. Only corporations and institutes in public law are required to pay a fee in respect of each dispute in which they are engaged. This fee amounts in the case of the Social Courts to 100 DM, the Land Social Courts to 150 DM, and the Federal Social Court to 200 DM; in certain cases lower fees are payable. The personnel and administrative costs of social jurisdiction are borne by the Lands. The Federal Social Court is financed by the Federal budget.

Organisation

The Federal Social Court, as one of the Supreme Federal Courts, with its 12 Senates, has its seat in Kassel; it is subject to the overall supervision of the Federal Minister of Labour and Social Order. In every Land in the Federal Republic of Germany there is a Land Social Court, that is to say that 11 Land Social Courts with some 100 Senates, and 49 Social Courts, are subject to the supervision of the supreme labour authorities in the Federal Lands, or, more recently in some Lands that of the Land Ministerof Justice. Some 3.500 persons are engaged in social jurisdiction, including over 950 professional judges. In addition there are more than 10.000 honorary judges (Social Courts, Land Social Courts, Federal Social Court).

Federal Social Court in Kassel

LSG Baden Württemberg	in Stuttgart	LSG Lower Saxony	in Celle
SG Freiburg		SG Aurich	
SG Heilbronn		SG Brunswick	
SG Karlsruhe		SG Hannover	
SG Constance		SG Hildesheim	
SG Mannheim		SG Lüneburg	
SG Reutlingen		SG Oldenburg	
SG Stuttgart		SG Osnabrück	
SG Ulm		SG Stade	
Bavarian LSG	in Munich	LSG North Rhine Westphalia	in Essen
SG Augsburg		SG Aachen	
SG Bayreuth		SG Detmold	
SG Landshut		SG Dortmund	
SG Munich		SG Düsseldorf	
SG Nürnberg		SG Duisburg	
SG Regensburg		SG Gelsenkirchen	
SG Würzburg		SG Cologne	
		SG Münster	
LSG Berlin	in Berlin		
SG Berlin		LSG Rhineland Palatinate	in Mayence
		SG Coblenz	
LSG Bremen	in Bremen	SG Speyer	
SG Bremen		SG Treves	
LSG Hamburg	in Hamburg	LSG for the Saarland	in Saarbrücken
SG Hamburg		SG for the Saarland	in Saarbrücken
		LSG Schleswig-Holstein	in Schleswig
Hessen LSG	in Darmstadt	SG Itzehoe	
SG Darmstadt		SG Kiel	
SG Frankfort		SG Lübeck	
SG Fulda		SG Schleswig	
SG Giessen			
SG Kassel			
SG Marburg		LSG = Land Social Court	
SG Wiesbaden		SG = Social Court.	

Legislative bases

Social Courts Law dated 3.9.1953 (BGBl. III - 330 - 1), last amended by the Law dated 27.7.1969 (BGBl. I S. 946).

Advisory and Information Offices

Introduction

As can be seen from the extent and content of the preceding review, social security has now grown into a widely diversified branch of law, the exact knowledge of which cannot, as a rule, be expected from the persons affected by it. In this matter, of such vital importance to them, they require advice and guidance. The legislator was, from the beginnings of social security, concerned to ensure that the relevant administrations should take steps to inform the populace of their rights and obligations, and that public offices should be established to give the necessary information and guidance.

The Insurance Offices

Attached to every local administration of the Land Districts and the larger cities in the Federal territory there is, as a general rule, an Insurance Office, whose business it is to advise and assist the populace in matters of social insurance. In some Federal Lands the Insurance Offices have been given additional functions, alternatively the functions of the Insurance Office as an information and advice office are performed by some other department, or by an office with a different title. For instance, in the Province of Württemberg, the function is performed by the "Local Authorities for Manual and Non-Manual Workers Insurance" attached to the office of the local Mayor, in the Saarland by the municipal administrations, in Berlin by the Information Office of the Senator for Labour, Health, and Social Affairs, which has been entrusted with the task of advising and assisting insured persons and pensioners, and in Hamburg by the Social Security Departments of the District and Local Offices.

The heavy pressure falling on the Insurance Offices can be evidenced by the example of a city with about 630.000 inhabitants. In 1969 information to insured persons and to employers was supplied in 192.000 cases, 13.000 applications for pensions were received, and 118.000 insurance cards were exchanged.

In the majority of cases the Insurance Cards under Manual and Non-Manual Workers Insurance are issued and exchanged by the approximately 550 Insurance Offices. For some years past the pensions administrations have been issuing insurance code numbers; applications for issue are received by the local Insurance Offices. Applications for pensions and for rehabilitation measures are also received and are given a preliminary examination in such a manner that, so far as possible, all the documents necessary for reaching a decision can be forwarded to the Fund together with the application.

Pensions Insurance

General information on the rights and obligations of the insured population and of pensioners is provided by the managements of the Pensions Insurance Funds. They issue, free of charge, leaflets and periodicals, and more recently they have been producing films. In the Pensions Insurance of Manual Workers, the Land Insurance Institutes have established information offices within their own offices. In addition, Sick Fund Stewards are employed, who, over and above their control functions, are available to give information, in particular to voluntarily insured persons. In many communities, including the smaller ones, they conduct "Advice and Guidance Days". The Federal Insurance Institute for Non-Manual Workers, which, as the Central Fund for Non-Manual Workers' Pensions Insurance, has its seat in Berlin, maintains Information and Advice Bureaux in 14 large cities in the Federal territory (Bremen, Kassel Nürnberg, Düsseldorf, Cologne, Oberhausen, Frankfort, Mannheim, Saarbrücken, Hamburg, Munich, Hanover, Münster, Stuttgart), and has also established about 100 Control and Information Offices. For the purpose of the Non-Manual Workers Insurance, more than 1.400 Insurance Stewards are engaged in an honorary capacity. Under the Miners' Special Scheme Pensions Insurance more than 1.300 Stewards safeguard the interests of the insured persons. They act as honorary intermediaries between the insured persons and the Scheme.

Information and Advice Bureaux of the Federal Insurance Institute for Non-Manual Workers.

28 Bremen Am Wall 50—54 Tel.:314074	3 Hannover Georgswall 12 Tel.:26765	8 Munich Karlsplatz 4 Tel.:557745
4 Düsseldorf Klosterstr. 79 Tel.:353416	35 Kassel 1 Kölnische Str. 9 - 11 Tel.:16305	44 Münster· Alter Steinweg 34 Tel.:40148
6 Frankfort/Main Zeil 17/19 Tel.:284667 / 284785	5 Cologne Hohenzollernring 84 Tel.:219891	85 Nürnberg Dennerstr. 4 Tel.:267342
2 Hamburg 36 Große Theaterstr. 32 Tel.: 340455	68 Mannheim P7, 16—17 Auf den Planken, Tel.: 27987	42 Oberhausen Markstr. 163—165 Tel.: 22463/27860
66 Saarbrücken Großherzog-Friedrich- Str. 16—18 Tel.: 24733	7 Stuttgart 1 Werastr. 89 Tel.: 436385	

Pensions Insurance of Farmers

The Agricultural Pensions Funds and their Association have a duty to keep their members and their pensioners fully informed on matters of social security within their scope, and on their rights and obligations. The municipalities are expected to render assistance in this matter. The Land Agricultural Chambers and the Rural Agricultural Offices are also fully informed in questions of agricultural old age aid.

Health Insurance

The Sick Funds keep their members informed on matters of social insurance within their scope. The very large number and the ready availability of the Local Sick Fund Offices render it unnecessary to establish special information offices, particularly since the Funds frequently have sub-offices, and offices for the issue of sick certificates. The Funds employ inspectors, who are often requested to give information and guidance by employers in the enterprises inspected. The Funds also issue and exchange the Insurance Cards of Manual and Non-Manual Workers, in the course of which they also give relevant information.

Industrial Injuries Insurance

The administrations of Industrial Injuries Insurance remain in close contact with their enterprises. Their technical inspectors have the duty of supervising the observance of accident prevention regulations, and of advising the enterprises on safety precautions. They do not maintain any special Advice Bureau.

Labour Administration

In addition to providing information and advice on the placing and vocational guidance of school leavers, the Employment Exchanges give advice on the facilities for occupational promotion contained in the various relevant programmes, and on the selection of suitable relevant courses of instruction. Such advice is also given in the evening hours, in order to give employed persons adequate opportunity of informing themselves on the chances of vocational promotion, or of improved performance, open to them.

Equalisation of Burdens

Applications for payments and services from the Equalisation of Burdens Fund may be made to local authorities, whose business it is to ensure that the applications are well founded, and that all necessary information is supplied. Some Land Equalisation of Burdens Offices maintain special advisory offices to deal with applicants from the different countries of origin. They examine the applications of the expellees for the purpose of assessing the losses incurred, and give information and advice. These offices also maintain information offices for the benefit of former residents in Eastern Germany and the Eastern Sector of Berlin in matters affecting the ascertainment, or the production of proof, of losses sustained.

Social Aid

The administration of social aid is under an obligation, in the framework of personal assistance, to give advice and help in matters of social aid, and in all other social matters, in so far as some other authority or person is not competent for this purpose. If voluntary welfare services and institutions undertake to give advice and aid in defined matters, the applicant should first be referred to them.

Other Facilities for obtaining Advice and Guidance

The provision of advice and guidance in malters affecting social security, and representation in the Social Courts, is also undertaken by the trade unions and by independent associations of workers with social and/or occupational policy aims and objects, as well as by employers' associations and war victims associations; these are — in addition to solicitors — authorised to plead in the Social bounts, the Land Social bourts, and the Federal Social bourt. During the last few years, and in ever increasing measure, private pensions advisers have been admitted in legal processes by the bourts, About ISO such advisers are employed at any one time, full time or peut time.